Chinese Utopianism

Chinese Utopianism

A Comparative Study of Reformist Thought
with Japan and Russia, 1898–1997

Shiping Hua

Woodrow Wilson Center Press
Washington, D.C.

Stanford University Press
Stanford, California

EDITORIAL OFFICES

Woodrow Wilson Center Press
One Woodrow Wilson Plaza
1300 Pennsylvania Avenue, N.W.
Washington, D.C. 20004-3027
Telephone 202-691-4029
www.wilsoncenter.org

ORDER FROM

Stanford University Press
Chicago Distribution Center
11030 South Langley Avenue
Chicago, Ill. 60628
Telephone 1-800-621-2736
www.sup.org

2 4 6 8 9 7 5 3 1

Library of Congress Cataloging-in-Publication Data

Hua, Shiping, 1956–
   Chinese utopianism : a comparative study of reformist thought with Japan and Russia,
1898–1997 / by Shiping Hua.
      p.   cm.
   Includes bibliographical references and index.
   ISBN 978-0-8047-6161-1 (cloth : alk. paper)
   1. Utopias—China—History—20th century. 2. Communism—China. 3. China—Economic
policy. 4. Social change—China—History—20th century. 5. Japan—History—Meiji period,
1868–1912. 6. Social change—Japan—History—20th century. 7. Communism—Soviet Union.
8. Soviet Union—Economic policy. 9. Social change—Soviet Union—History. I. Title.
   HX806.H813   2008
   335′.020951—dc22

                                                                    2008032237

For Jia, Helen, James, and Eric

Contents

Preface

At the turn of the twenty-first century, many thinkers recalled the twentieth century as an age of extremes in which humankind had faced both its greatest hopes and greatest disappointments. Raymond Firth, a British anthropologist, wrote that the world saw "the change from a relatively rational and scientific view of things to a non-rational and less scientific one." Yehudi Menuhin, a British musician, remarked, "I would say that it raised the greatest hopes ever conceived by humanity, and destroyed all illusions and ideals."[1]

Although many countries, including Japan and Russia, shared in this chaos, China seemed to have experienced more of it. Attempts at drastic social and cultural transformation were interrupted when China was torn by two civil wars from 1927 to 1949 and occupied by Japan during World War II. During the late Qing period, many Chinese intellectuals followed the steps of Kang Youwei (1858–1927) with the ambition of building a future world based on *datong,* or grand harmony. This contrasts with the Meiji period (1868) when the Japanese ruling elites adopted realizable and moderate platforms.

Similar contrasts can be found in the communist experiences of the Soviet Union and China. Communist systems are characterized by one-party rule in politics and central planning and public ownership of the means of production in the economy. Their leaders are periodically compelled to make system adjustments to ameliorate the effects of poor planning, official abuse of power, and people's lack of economic incentives. The Soviet New Economic Policy (NEP) in 1921–1929 and the Thaw in 1953–1964 were such adjustments. In a slightly different way, the Chinese Great Leap Forward in 1958–1960 and the Cultural Revolution in 1966–1976 were also such adjustments. However, while Soviet adjustments moved "to the right" in the sense of temporarily retreating from communist ideals, Chinese adjustments moved "to the left" in the sense of radicalizing these same ideals.

Deng's reforms (1978–1997) and Gorbachev's reforms (1985–1991) were prompted by similar structural problems of the communist system. Nevertheless, the two leaders adopted different strategies, with very different results. Gorbachev's reform went in the same direction of the NEP and the Thaw by retreating from communist ideals. Deng's reform, with a focus on economics, was heavily influenced by Chinese political culture. Most noticeably, many Chinese intellectuals' dream was still datong.

Reflecting on these radical events in the twentieth century, some Chinese scholars describe the numerous Chinese attempts at creating a utopia in the last century as "cultural radicalism" (*wen hua jijin zhuyi*). Characteristics include the voluntarist attempt to change society in disregard of existing conditions, populist tendencies to rely on the masses for social change, worship of violence at the expense of democratic procedures, an emphasis on organizations to mobilize society, concentration of power in the hands of a few leaders, and finally emphasis on ideology for mass mobilization.[2]

Other Chinese scholars use the term "utopianism" to describe the same phenomena. Their books have addressed such subjects as the People's Commune,[3] Chinese utopian thought from ancient times through the Qing dynasty,[4] China's utopian attempts in the twentieth century,[5] the historical roots of Chinese utopianism,[6] utopianism in a global perspective,[7] China's datong tradition,[8] and China's image in formulating Western utopian thought.[9]

Significant studies about Chinese utopianism in English-language publications have covered such issues as voluntarism in Mao's thought,[10] the Chinese Communist Party's experience of utopianism,[11] the datong syndrome among communist and noncommunist Chinese intellectuals,[12] the utopian factor in Kang Youwei's thought,[13] and comparing utopian thought in the East and the West.[14]

Joining the flow of these studies, this book examines Chinese utopianism using social science methods. Adopting a contrast-oriented, comparative-case method, I will analyze Chinese utopianism by comparing various "reforms" that China, Japan, and the former Soviet Union experienced in the twentieth century. The sources are mostly original writings of leading intellectuals.

This study principally attempts to shed light on the following questions:

- Given that all cultures have utopias, what characteristics of Chinese utopianism distinguish it from those of Japan and the former Soviet Union?

- How did Chinese utopianism affect the country's socioeconomic and political developments in the last century?
- What are the characteristics of reforms undertaken to implement transition from authoritarian-traditional society to modern society in non-Western societies such as China and Japan?
- What are the characteristics of reform in communist countries such as China and the former USSR?

The central argument of this project is that the various reforms were implemented as responses by ruling elites to structural problems, but the directions that the reforms took were heavily influenced by cultural traditions, especially by the various understandings of human hope for the future, or of utopianism. The time frame of this study is from 1898, the year of the Late Qing Reform, to 1997, when Deng Xiaoping died.

Acknowledgments

The first draft of this book was completed when I was an Asian Policy Studies Fellow of the Woodrow Wilson International Center for Scholars and the George Washington University during the 2004–2005 academic year. I would like to thank Robert Hathaway, director of the Asia Program, and Gang Lin, program associate of the Asia Program, at the Wilson Center; and Mike Mochizuki, director of the Sigur Center for Asian Studies at the Elliott School of International Affairs, George Washington University, for their most valuable support. The Department of Political Science and the McConnell Center for Political Leadership at the University of Louisville also provided support.

Yasuku Sensui, my colleague at Eckerd College, and Igor Danchenko, my graduate assistant at the University of Louisville, helped me enormously with the Japanese and Russian sources. Many scholars have read the manuscript in part or in whole, or shared their thoughts with me on the book, including Roger Ames, Lowell Dittmer, Ed Friedman, Gao Hong, Tomila Lankina, Guoli Liu, Vojtech Mastny, Peter Moody, Andrew Nathan, William Parsons, Blair Ruble, James Sadkovich, and Brantly Womack. The early draft of the book was also read by my students in a graduate seminar, "Clash of Civilizations," that I taught at the Department of Political Science, University of Louisville, in the fall of 2005. My students commented extensively on the draft.

I am also grateful to the two anonymous reviewers for their helpful comments on the early draft of the manuscript. While their comments were extremely helpful to me in revising the manuscript, I alone am responsible for all errors.

The early drafts of comparative studies about the Meiji Restoration versus the Late Qing Reform and the Gorbachev Reform versus the Deng Reform appeared in two separate research articles in *East Asia: An International Quarterly* (vol. 21, no. 3, Fall 2004) and *Problems of Post-Communism* (vol. 53, no. 3, May/June 2006). I am republishing the two comparative studies here with the permission of the two journals. *The Wilson Quarterly* (Autumn 2005) published the central ideas of this book in the form of a short essay, "A Perfect World," excerpts of which appeared in *The New York Times* on November 6, 2005.

Chinese Utopianism

Chapter 1

Theory and Method

Culture may not be able to explain why any one alternative was chosen over another, but it may explain why certain alternatives were never considered at all.

—David Elkins and Richard E.B. Simeon[1]

Comparative studies increase the 'visibility' of one structure by contrasting it with another.

—Reinhard Bendix[2]

Political Culture Theory

The central argument of this study is that cultural determinants heavily influenced the directions of a series of reforms in Japan, Soviet Russia, and Maoist China, although the reforms were prompted by structural problems of their respective societies. In this section, we will briefly examine the terms "structure," "centralization," "reform," "political culture," and "ideology," since they are connected with the central idea of this book.

What is "structure"? Structure, as studied by social scientists, can be divided into two kinds: (1) categorical structure, that is, the distribution of individuals across various social, economic, and political categories, such as ethnicity, income, education, and party affiliations; and (2) institutional structure, such as formal or informal organizations or institutions.[3] This study uses the latter.

A key structural problem of this study is "centralization" versus "decentralization." When premodern societies were ushered into the modern world,

1

the tendency was to centralize, such as the cases for China and Japan in the nineteenth century. These societies needed to concentrate their national resources on resisting Western intrusions on the one hand, while modernizing their countries on the other. However, the various reforms or systems adjustments of communist countries tended to decentralize power, because the orthodox Marxist system was already over-centralized, thus creating problems of inefficiency, corruption of officials, and a lack of incentives for workers.[4]

For Karl Marx, centralization and decentralization played different roles in the communist movement. In the early stage, centralization was necessary for the proletariat, and all communist and former communist countries did this in the early stages of their experiments. Marx wrote,

> The first step in the revolution by the working class is to raise the proletariat to the position of ruling class, to win the battle of democracy. The proletariat will use its political supremacy to wrest, by degrees, all capital from the bourgeoisie, to centralize all instruments of production in the hands of the State, i.e., of the proletariat organized as the ruling class.[5]

According to Marx, as the communist transformation matures, centralization of power will give way to decentralization.[6]

> What at first may seem like a clear demand for governmental centralization turns out to refer to centralization in the hands of a class—or, rather, what had been a class—that was expected to constitute the great majority of the population or of a vast association of the whole nation [a concept of centralization that is at best quite vague and may even be self-contradictory, as it may imply decentralization]. The government of persons is replaced by the administration of things, and by the direction of the process of production. The state is not abolished, it withers away.[7]

In the view of Marx, the maturation of the communist movement would lead to his definition of an ideal society, which was similar to the Paris Commune (1871), a highly decentralized political system.[8] In the Paris Commune, workers were able to form self-governing bodies to protect themselves from possible abuses from the central government.

What is "reform"? Reform in this context is a process in which at least one of the following has changed: (1) the dominance of the official ideology, (2) the dominant position of state and quasi-state ownership, and (3) the preponderance of bureaucratic coordination.[9] For example, the Late Qing

Reform and the Meiji Restoration changed the respective societies in fundamental ways, as did the Deng and Gorbachev reforms.

The New Economic Policy (NEP) and the Thaw did not radically change Soviet society although the leaders of both events, Nikolai Bukharin (1888–1938) and Nikita Khrushchev (1894–1971), respectively, were referred to as "reformers."[10] But bureaucratic coordination during these time periods changed a great deal. Similarly, during the Great Leap Forward (GLF) and the Cultural Revolution (CR), the official ideology and ownership of the means of production were not greatly changed, but bureaucratic coordination changed profoundly. These four events are not habitually referred to as "reforms" largely because the old structure, including centralization, was subsequently restored. Thus, temporary decentralization of power was a characteristic of all of these four reforms within the communist system.

What is "political culture?" Political culture comprises a set of subjective orientations to politics held by people in a particular society. It has cognitive, affective, and evaluative components, and is the result of childhood socialization, education, media exposure, and adult experiences with governmental, social, and economic performance. It also affects political and governmental structure and performance.[11]

The impact of political culture on politics and economics has been widely noted.[12] Examples include the effect of Protestantism on capitalism according to Max Weber's study[13] and the role of Confucianism in so-called Asian-style democracy.[14]

But political culture's impact on society is often subtle, not straightforward. People in any kind of cultural environment tend to take for granted a particular course of action. In the words of Gabriel Almond, "That they choose from a restricted set will, for most of them, remain below the threshold of consciousness, because they seldom encounter individuals who take for granted quite different assumptions."[15]

According to David Elkins and Richard E.B. Simeon, "Culture may not be able to explain why any one alternative was chosen over another, but it may explain why certain alternatives were never considered at all."[16] In general, we may not know exactly where China is headed in its social transformation, but it is probably easier to predict that, in the foreseeable future, China will not be like the United States.

Given that over 90 percent of its population belongs to the Han ethnic group, China is relatively homogenous. Thus, it is relatively easy to identify China's so-called "national character."[17] In addition, cultural changes occur more slowly than institutional and economic changes (unless big traumatic events occur, such as the Cultural Revolution, which may change people overnight) and Chinese culture has proved to be especially resilient. Western religious leaders were more successful in bringing Western technology to China than in bringing their Christian beliefs.[18]

Political culture includes ideology,[19] which is the focus of this study. Ideologies fall into two broad domains: knowledge and politics. According to Giovanni Sartori, "In the first case 'ideology' is contrasted with 'truth,' science, and valid knowledge in general; whereas in the second case we are not concerned with the truth-value, but with the functional value, so to speak, of ideology."[20] Ideologies are essentially action-related systems of ideas. They typically contain a program and a strategy for their realization, that is, their operational code. Their essential purpose is to unite (integrate) organizations that are built around them.[21]

The role played by ideology is also extremely important in China's modern history. In the words of Brantly Womack,

> One essential aspect of China's modernization process which is likely to remain important for the foreseeable future is the role of ideological politics. Ideology almost necessarily plays a larger role in the modernization process of later starters because the presence of targets, models and threats from advanced countries invites prescriptive, transformative politics.[22]

Confucianism, the official ideology for pre-modern China, and Marxism, the official ideology of the Chinese Communist Party,[23] often serves as the starting points for students of China studies.

"Culture" and "structure" influence each other. Scholars have taken three positions on the relationship between "culture" and "structure": Those who emphasize the discontinuity of history stress the role played by structure, while those who emphasize the continuity of history stress the role played by culture. A third option, however, is to find the mechanism and dynamics of the interaction between structure and culture.[24] The current study has adopted the third option: This author believes that structure and culture influence each other and that cultural values persist.

Contrast-Oriented Comparative Case Study

This section addresses the following questions: (1) What reforms are compared in this study? (2) Why are they compared? (3) How are they compared?

This study identifies four major Chinese reforms that can be placed in three categories during the twentieth century: (1) the Late Qing Reform in

1898 that emerged from the authoritarian-traditional society, (2) the Great Leap Forward (GLF) (1958–1960) and the Cultural Revolution (CR) (1966–1976) that occurred within the communist system, and (3) the Deng Reform (1978–1997) that led China out of the communist system.

Chinese utopianism is studied through an analysis of these reforms assuming that the Chinese national character reveals itself more clearly during social upheavals than during periods of stability. Although Chinese utopianism also demonstrated itself in other important events, such as the Taiping Rebellion (1851–1864) and the Chinese Communist Party's Yenan Years (1936–1949), the focus on these four reforms will allow a more systematic approach through which the thesis is tested in multiple time periods. The reforms selected for this study are the most important ones for China in the twentieth century, and it is hoped that the order and logic imposed by choosing them will create a suitable, but narrow, range of options for interpretation.[25]

With the belief that knowledge is by definition comparative, this study compares these Chinese reforms with their counterparts in Japan, the other major East Asian country, and in the former Soviet Union, the other major communist country. In the words of Theda Skocpol and Margaret Sommers, comparative studies "increase the 'visibility' of one structure by contrasting it with another."[26]

The current project joins other fruitful studies that compare the communist experiences of Russia and China,[27] the rural reforms of China and Vietnam,[28] and the transition from state socialism of China and Hungary.[29] These studies will also compensate for the relative lack of comparative studies involving China. For example, *The China Quarterly,* a leading journal in the field of China studies, has not published even one that compares China and Soviet Russia, or China and Japan, in the last two decades. Apparently, this absence reflected the notion of Chinese exceptionalism held by many scholars in the field.[30] Michel C. Oksenberg, however, predicts that there will be more comparative studies in the China field in the near future.[31]

How are the cases in this study compared? This study has adopted the contrast-oriented comparative case study model, which is historically interpretative and causally analytic.[32] The various reforms are the cases that are analyzed through the method developed by Skocpol and Sommers.[33]

The Chinese Late Qing Reform (1898) is comparable with the Japanese Meiji Restoration (1868), because these reforms occurred at the conjunction of tradition and modernity in the two countries. Looking at the Late Qing Reform and the Meiji Restoration from the vantage points of various perspectives, this study joins those by Benjamin Schwartz, who tries to explain the different outcomes of the two reforms,[34] Li Qingting, who focuses on the differences of these reforms in general,[35] and John Schrecker, who compares the Chinese *Ching-I* and the Japanese *hirazamurai* during that period.[36]

The four reforms within the communist system, that is, the NEP, Thaw, GLF, and CR, are arguably the most important deviations from the orthodox Marxist model of one-party rule in politics, central planning, and public ownership of the means of production in the two communist countries prior to the reforms of Gorbachev and Deng. Other historical periods that represent other kinds of change are still largely within the orthodox Marxist model, such as War Communism,[37] Stalin's First Five-Year Plan, and China's First Five-Year Plan.

The two Soviet-communist deviant cases of NEP and the Thaw provide a parallel comparison. NEP and the Thaw were the only major deviations from the orthodox Marxist model before Gorbachev's reforms. David Nordlander noted that besides Nikolai Bukharin, the leader of NEP, the only other reformer in Soviet history before Gorbachev was Nikita Khrushchev, who initiated the Thaw.[38]

The two Chinese-communist deviant cases of the GLF and the CR provide another parallel comparison, as noted by leading scholars in the field. Roderick MacFarquhar noted that Mao deviated from the orthodox Marxist model three times: the Hundred Flowers, the GLF, and the CR.[39] In the current study, the Hundred Flowers is considered part of the GLF, because, as a movement largely confined to the intellectuals, it was limited in scope. Stuart Schram also noted that the GLF and the CR were of similar ideological orientation.[40]

Nevertheless, the NEP–Thaw as a parallel pair retreating from communist ideals contrasts with GLF–CR, a parallel pair radicalizing communist ideals.

The Deng reform is comparable to the Gorbachev reform in the sense that these are the reforms that actually led the two major communist countries out of the orthodox model. This study adds a new perspective to existing studies that compare the two: Yan Sun compares the two reforms in terms of official discourse and corruption;[41] Minxin Pei compares the private sector and the media;[42] Yasheng Huang compares the two reforms from the perspective of information and bureaucracy;[43] and Steven Solnick compares the hierarchies in the USSR and China, including the two reform periods, from an institutional perspective.[44]

The Chinese reforms share similarities with each other, yet they differ significantly from their counterparts in Japan and the former Soviet Union.

The Late Qing Reform and the two reforms within communism, the GLF and CR, inherited the Chinese tradition of datong in terms of worldview.[45] They were also populist in terms of ideological orientation, antirationalist in epistemology, and monistic in their way of thinking.[46] The Deng Reform was in the same direction as the previous ones in the sense that it inherited the datong worldview and monistic understanding of the universe.

In contrast, Japanese Meiji political culture was noted for its pragmatism and nonuniversal claims, while NEP and the Thaw were temporary retreats from the orthodox Marxist model of central planning, public ownership of the means of production, and political authoritarianism. Gorbachev's reforms were in the same direction as the first two Russian reforms of the NEP and the Thaw in terms of retreating from communist ideals. The difference was that this time, the Soviet retreat from communist ideals was not temporary, but long term.[47]

While acknowledging the usefulness of the comparative method, this study realizes that it is not a panacea.[48] In addition, if it is hard to compare two cases, it is even harder to compare multiple ones. So in the current study, each of the four comparative case studies can stand on its own, although they are intimately related to one another. For instance, the comparative study of the Late Qing Reform and the Meiji Restoration can stand on its own, as can the one that compares the Deng Reform and the Gorbachev Reform.

In addition, although this study focuses on the differences in the reform process in contrast to similarities of structural backgrounds, similarities in the reform process can also be identified.[49] For instance, both the communist reforms in the former Soviet Union and Maoist China share the common structural trait of decentralization.

Political Discourse

This study focuses on the political discourse of the reforms by analyzing the rhetoric of the political strategies and philosophical underpinnings. Political discourse is defined as the use of language to communicate ideas, values, and facts. Language serves more social functions than to simply communicate information. It is to "scaffold the performance of social activities and to scaffold human affiliation within cultures and social groups and institutions. Language-in-use is everywhere and always 'political.'"[50]

The discourse by leading intellectuals analyzed in this study is all "official," with the exception of that by Fukuzawa Yukichi (1835–1901) during the Meiji Restoration. Official discourse is very important in the political process. In commenting on Margaret Thatcher's domestic policies, Vivien A. Schmidt writes that it can create an interactive consensus for change in advocating reform and negotiating its implementation. Although there is nothing inevitable about discourse, "it can exert a causal influence on policy change, serving to overcome entrenched interests and institutional obstacles to change by altering perceptions of interest and showing the way to new institutional paths."[51] For instance, Thatcher's success in reforming the country's welfare system owed partly to her discourse aimed at persuading the British people that individuals had the right to be unequal.

Compared with the case in Great Britain—a liberal democracy that values pluralism—official discourse plays an even more important role in totalitarian countries such as the former Soviet Union. Carl J. Friedrich and Zbigniew K. Bzrezinski refuted the view that "the key leadership groups [in totalitarian societies] are said not to take the ideology seriously, but to manipulate it, to change it arbitrarily to suit their shifting policy lines."[52] Governments in totalitarian countries use official discourse to create consensus among the population for maintenance of the existing system.

China was not only a communist country under Mao, but also a country in which political discourse historically was considered essential to political life. In the words of Confucius: "*ming bu zheng, ce yan bu shun; yan bu shun, ce shi bu cheng.*" (The name has to be right. Otherwise, the discourse won't be right. If the discourse is not right, things cannot be done.)[53] Official discourse traditionally was carried in the statements of scholar-officials who were supposed to represent the conscience of society and therefore speak on behalf of society. Kang Youwei (1858–1927), a leader of the Late Qing Reform, was such an intellectual.

In both China and the former Soviet Union, the official discourse was often carried in the statements of establishment intellectuals. The most important ones sometimes served in the Politburo, such as Mikhail Suslov (1902–1982), who served in pre-Gorbachev regimes, Alexander Yakovlev (1923–2005) under Gorbachev, Chen Boda (1904–1989) under Mao, and Hu Qiaomu (1912–1992) under Deng. Unlike the situation in liberal democracies, the official discourse in communist countries is controlled by a few key leaders, and there is typically only one ideology czar in the Politburo.[54] An analysis of their remarks can serve as a useful tool in decoding the political ideology of the respective regimes under study.[55]

Methodologically, the analysis of political discourse complements empiricism in China studies, which became prominent during the post-Mao era. Empiricism can lead to a focus on increasingly smaller units of analysis and, as Harry Harding complained, "may have resulted in the loss of a cumulative, syncretic, and macro perspective on a rapidly changing China." Harding said that increased specificity ought not to come at the cost of novel interpretation and the ability to generalize.[56]

Thomas Metzger, too, argued that the "specter of Spenglerian *Gisteswissenschaft* has intimidated us too much, and the exaggerated positivistic demand for behavioral specifics has diverted attention away from the meaning and context of ideas."[57] For Gloria Davies, "Western scholarship, in which Anglophone Chinese studies predominate, has confined itself, in the main, to providing empirical surveys of the Chinese 'scene.'"[58]

Anthony J. Kane noted the shortage of work on contemporary Chinese philosophy.[59] Li Junru, vice president of the Chinese Communist Party (CCP) Central Party School, criticized the Western Sinologists' tendency to rely heavily on empirical methods. He said that sometimes party documents often presented a better picture of Chinese politics than empirical research.[60]

The current research joins other fruitful discourse studies in the China field such as that by Neil Renwick and Qing Cao, who studied discourse on Chinese nationalism;[61] Shu-Yun Ma, who studied Chinese discourse on civil society;[62] He Ping, who studied the Chinese discourse on modernity;[63] and W.L. Chong, who wrote on the political discourse of the Cultural Revolution.[64]

Chapter 2

Utopianism: Japan, Russia, and China

The earliest description of life in Japan, which was recorded in the Chinese Kingdom of Wei (221–65 BCE), was noted for optimism of the present, with no nostalgia for an ideal past or in longings for a glorious life after death. They must have felt that just as growing seasons of the year alternate with cold seasons of little growth, birth and death precede and follow the departure of a soul.

—Delmer M. Brown[1]

Pure waiting for the return of happiness has been much less frequent in China, and the waiting for salvation through the sudden transformation of the world into a new paradise, through a comet never seen before and appearing in a blinding light, has been even rarer. This is probably one of the decisive differences between China and Russia which in many respects, is both a geographic and a spiritual neighbor today and whose philosophies throughout history were suffused with messianic ideas.

—Wolfgang Bauer[2]

The word "utopia" was first used in 1516 by the English writer Sir Thomas More (1478–1535) in his book, written in Latin, entitled *Utopia.* The book pictures a paradise where common social evils such as crime, poverty, inequality, and injustice are eliminated. But as the word "utopia" suggests, this is a place that does not exist. "U," the Latin prefix from the Greek word *ou,* denotes a general negative. *Topos* is the Greek word for "place." More created the word also to suggest the two Greek neologisms of *eutopia,* which means "good place," and *outopia,* which means "no place."[3]

Utopias are academically defined as a unique way of reflecting on politics. It seeks the perfect, best, or happiest form of society, untrammeled by commitments to existing institutions.[4] Since utopias comprise the best societies, they do not progress. Utopias often presume that human nature is good, and therefore conflicts among members simply do not exist. Although the specific contents of utopias are hard to generalize, since they are inspired by various kinds of human hope, most utopias seem to favor egalitarianism and the benevolently dictatorial implementation of the utopian ideal.[5]

Utopian thought under certain circumstances can become a very powerful tool for social change, since it is driven by people's dissatisfaction with life, either with imperfect human nature or with imperfect social institutions. In fact, many things that were considered utopian a century ago are actually reality now. In the view of Karl Mannheim, "We should not regard as utopian every state of mind which is incongruous with and transcends the immediate situation (and in this sense, 'departs from reality')."[6]

In modern times, science of various forms has been used to formulate utopias. Francis Bacon held in his *New Atlantis* that once science and technology were put into proper place, an ideal human society would come about.[7] In *Walden Two,* B.F. Skinner asserted that if human behavior were conditioned through psychological experiments, conflicts would disappear.[8]

Marxism, the theory that guides the communist efforts of the former Soviet Union and China, was presented as "science." According to its proponents, it was opposed to utopianism. Karl Marx (1818–1883) tried to distinguish his theory from those of utopian thinkers who intended to build a better society based on human goodwill, such as Saint Simon (1691–1709), Charles Fourier (1772–1837), and Robert Owen (1771–1858).[9] For Marx, communism is a movement toward a better society and not an ideal state to which reality must adjust itself.[10] V.I. Lenin (1870–1924), who led the world's first successful communist revolution in Russia in 1918, also opposed utopianism. Lenin wrote, "The less freedom there is in a country, the scantier the manifestations of open class struggle, and the lower the educational level of the masses, the more easily political utopias usually arise and the longer they persist."[11] But Marxist "science" was often interpreted in such a way as to justify various kinds of social engineering that were themselves utopian in communist countries like the former Soviet Union and Maoist China.[12]

In this book, I use the terms "utopia" or "utopianism" in a generic way. The book is not an intellectual exercise about the various forms of utopias that have been described since Thomas More. Instead, I study humanity's need for hope that, central to utopias, has been in existence since the beginning of human history. One example is Plato's *The Republic,* which was written almost 2,000 years before the birth of Thomas More.[13] The method of using the concept of "utopia" to describe the general notion of hope has also been adopted by other social scientists.[14]

Some parts of this book are dense. This is because, writes Wolfgang Bauer, the happiness of the individual as well as that of a community is indescribable. "It is invisible like the air we breathe and yet recognized only at a distance where it takes on color. If happiness is to be described faithfully, it always appears either so close as to blind the eye or, more frequently, so distant as to allow only faint, shadowy contours to be perceived."[15] This challenge becomes even more severe if we attempt to describe human happiness in cross-cultural terms.

In the following three sections of this chapter, with each being devoted to the studies of Japan, Russia, and China, respectively, Japanese hope lies in the natural, that is, life as it is; Russian hope lies in the supernatural, such as a savior; and Chinese hope lies in human endeavors to change the world.

Japan

Japanese tradition combines Confucianism borrowed from the Chinese and indigenous culture.[16] Living under the shadow of the powerful and prosperous China for centuries, Japan incorporated Confucianism into its political system during the Taika Reform (645 CE). Confucianism was influential during the Tokugawa period (1603–1868), the dynasty at the end of which the Meiji Restoration occurred. During this period, Japan experienced stability and prosperity with a rapid increase in population from 18 million to 30 million and an increase in land under cultivation.[17] The dominant stream of Tokugawa Confucianism drew on the neo-Confucian thought of Song (960–1279 CE) in China.[18] Confucianism became so integrated in Japanese culture that a seventeenth-century Japanese scholar, Yamaga Soko, claimed that it was Japan, not China, that embodied Confucianism, as Confucian principles were actually revealed to Japan's sage-emperors.[19] Confucianism is discussed further later in this chapter.

In spite of the influence of Confucianism, Japanese culture was distinctly unique.[20] This situation became even more obvious toward the end of the

Tokugawa era when Confucianism lost influence, because of China's decline of power after the Opium War in 1840. Neo-Confucianism, which gave central importance to ethics, was attacked.[21] According to Kamo Mabushi (1697–1769), a Japanese philosopher during the Tokugawa period, the Chinese emphasis on morality marked by benevolence, honesty, and knowledge went against the thrust of nature. The four seasons in nature, for example, do not follow Confucian order in the sense that they go in cycles by following the logic of nature, not a human-imposed order.[22] In the view of Motoori Norinaga (1730–1801), another scholar during the Tokugawa period, the Chinese worship of antique morality such as goodwill, integrity, propriety and modesty, love of parents, respect for kin, loyalty to the ruler, and faith in humans goes against the pure heart. For Motoori, the Confucian doctrine only brought about unhappiness, because happiness was naturalness and depended on abandoning teachings and doctrines.[23]

Some Japanese intellectuals argued that the emperor's authority was independent of his virtue, or the lack thereof,[24] unlike Chinese Confucianism where the emperor should be the benevolent father figure with a high degree of morality. Some writers during this period started to refer to Japan, not China, as the central Asian country with its own unique national character.[25]

What, then, is the Japanese indigenous notion of hope? The earliest description of life in Japan, which was recorded in the Chinese kingdom of Wei (221–65 BCE), carries an optimistic tone toward life. Unlike the Confucian datong and Russian pessimism, Japanese indigenous culture had no nostalgia for an ideal past nor longings for a glorious life after death.[26]

In the words of Delmer M. Brown, "They must have felt that just as growing seasons of the year alternate with cold seasons of little growth, birth and death precede and follow the departure of a soul."[27] For the Japanese, the world is not something that humans can impose their logic on. Instead, humans must adapt themselves to it.[28]

This optimism has impacted on multiple dimensions of Japanese society, such as social transformation, human relations in general, the current political system, and the Japanese attitude toward religions. The attitude of accepting life as it is has made social transformations easier for Japanese people. In premodern times, the Japanese found it easy to borrow from China, because the Chinese way at that time was considered to be the way of the universe. The Taika Reform in 645 CE, when Japan incorporated China's political system into its own, was a success. So was the 1868 Meiji Restoration, which was largely a Westernization process ushering Japan into modernization. This time, the Japanese leaders assumed that the way of the universe was Western. Of course, this contrasts with the failed Late Qing Reform in 1898 when the Chinese ruling elites found it hard to willingly accept Western systems and values. Even the democratization of Japan after World War II has been successful.

This optimism has also impacted the Japanese understanding of human relations. In contrast with the Western tradition that sees human conflicts as inevitable, and the Chinese tradition that stresses the need for continued self-cultivation through education, for the Japanese, the spirit of the human personality is fundamentally pure and true.[29] In the view of Tuetuo Janita, "[it] is this ideal self, or cultural spirit that affirms the deep value the Japanese place on humanness that persuades men to create and act critically on behalf of others."[30] This is best seen in the relationship of *giri,* a sense of obligation that one feels or ought to feel in response to a pure blessing bestowed by another. This reciprocation is understood as being pure and without selfish intent and springs from one's spiritual self.

Against this cultural background, Japan has not developed the Western-style checks and balances in its political system or the Chinese righteous attitude that may lead to authoritarianism. The current Japanese parliamentary system is not characterized by the separation of powers. The American political system was based on the assumption that humans often fail morally, and therefore the primary function of a political system is to prevent the abuse of power by the leaders and to prevent the majority from imposing their will on the minority. In contrast, the Chinese not only want themselves to be moral, but expect other people to follow the same standards of morality.[31] The alternating occurrences of authoritarianism and populism in modern times were based on the moral trust of the leaders and the masses, respectively.

Japanese optimism is also reflected in their highly inclusive attitude toward religion, which is conducive to a pluralistic society. Quite often, beliefs from different religions can be found in the same individual: an individual will get married in a Christian church, relate to other people with Confucian principles, worship nature in the spirit of Shintoism, and treat animals in accordance with the Buddhist beliefs.[32] In a departure from religious fundamentalism in which the faithful kill each other over different interpretations of the same religion, such as the conflicts between Christian groups during the Reformation or Shiites and Sunnis within Islam, the Japanese are not known for killing each other over religious beliefs.

Russia

The Russian tradition has roots in Western Europe and the Byzantine Empire with the former being more influential in Russian formal intellectual thought[33] and the latter dominant in popular culture.[34] Nevertheless, both share a pessimistic view toward life: Hope lies in the "other" world. This pessimism contrasts with Japanese hopefulness.

Utopianism in the Western intellectual tradition follows three major paths exemplified by Plato's *The Republic*,[35] St. Augustine's *The City of God*,[36] and Thomas More's *Utopia*.[37] Plato's perfect society addressed social problems created by imperfect human nature through the division of labor. In this polity, people performed different duties according to the qualities they embodied: The philosopher who represented wisdom would rule, the warrior who represented courage would guard, and the artisan who represented human physical needs would labor.[38] The utopian spirit of *The Republic* was so obvious that the Chinese translation of the book title is "imagined country" (*li xiang guo*).

With the decline of the Roman Empire, Plato's utopia was gradually forgotten. In its place appeared a different kind of utopia. In *The City of God*, written in 413–426 CE, paradise is in heaven, detached even further from human society than Plato's utopia.[39] The author, Augustine, born in Algeria in 354 CE, was a pagan converted to the Roman Catholic Church. His interpretation of human hope was consistent with the Judeo-Christian tradition that optimism is otherworldly.[40] Augustine divided man's existence into two parts—The City of God, which was the ideal place, and the City of Earth, which was full of evil. It was not possible to have happiness in this life. Paradise, created by God, belonged to the other world.[41]

Another millennium passed before the third major work on utopia emerged in the West, Thomas More's *Utopia*.[42] More's utopia was revolutionary in the sense that it brought the Christian notion of hope to the real world. Human hope, although remote, was secularized.[43] In More's *Utopia*, officials were elected, although the leader of Utopia served for life. Social order was achieved through benevolence, not the rule of law. There were, however, slaves, some of whom were former criminals. There was no prostitution. All members in Utopia had to do manual labor. They ate in public dining halls and received free medical treatment, since private property and the market did not exist. Members of the Utopia wore the same clothes, except for differences between genders. Utopia traded and had peaceful relations with foreign countries.[44]

Like Western intellectual thought, the Byzantine tradition, embodied in the Russian Orthodox Church via Constantinople (c.a. 988 CE), is also pessimistic about life. In Byzantine theology, the future coming of a messiah is a characteristic feature, and Russian religious communities often enthusiastically expect and prepare for the savior. Russian philosophies throughout history were suffused with messianic ideas. That attitude, by the way, is essentially foreign to the Chinese, for whom, according to Wolfgang Bauer,

> pure waiting for the return of happiness has been much less frequent, and the waiting for salvation through the sudden transformation of the world into a new paradise, through a comet never seen before and appearing in a blinding light, has been even rarer.[45]

Russian pessimism, rooted in both Western intellectual and Byzantine traditions, discouraged utopian attempts to transform nature and society. This attitude of moderation is in accordance with the spirit of modern liberal democracy, whereby people tend to adopt the mental habits of businessmen. "Their attitude takes a serious, calculating, and positive turn," writes Alexis de Tocqueville. "They tend to willingly veer away from the ideal to pursue some obvious and available goal, which seems to them to be the natural and essential object of their desires."[46]

Tocqueville continues that it is the concept of equality in a liberal democracy that discourages utopian thinking. Unlike aristocratic societies, where properties tend to stay in certain families and classes for multiple generations, wealth is gained and lost with higher frequency in a liberal democracy, so nothing is absolute, and nothing is worth fighting for with too much passion. In addition, people in an environment of equality take naturally to pluralistic thinking, recognizing that any drastic social change will be favored by some and opposed by others. Thus, utopian attempts for drastic social change are unlikely to win sufficient support in a liberal democracy.[47]

Although Russian pessimism generally discouraged utopianism,[48] under certain circumstances, utopian actions could and did in fact occur, as was the case with the Marxist experiments in Soviet Russia in the twentieth century. As political culture theory holds, there is nothing absolute about cultural determinants. Western utopian pursuits in the twentieth century were connected with industrialization and the emergence of modern "nation-states" that offered powerful means for action.[49] But the Russian tradition of pessimism may explain why Soviet Russia tended to retreat from communist ideals in its reforms such as the New Economic Policy, the Thaw, and the Gorbachev reform.

China

Chinese hopefulness has three major sources: the Confucian datong, the Taoist "small kingdoms with limited population," and the peasant-rebellion type of egalitarianism, such as that of Zhang Lu,[50] with datong being the most important. All three sources of Chinese hope are opposed to selfish gain. Compared with the Japanese indigenous optimistic stance that accepts life as it is and the Russian tradition that places human aspirations for happiness in the other world, Chinese hopefulness, as represented by Confucian datong, lies in human endeavors to change the world.

Accordingly, when scholars describe Western utopias, they tend to refer to a "no place"; when they describe Chinese utopias, they tend to refer to a "better place."[51] For instance, Thomas Metzger uses the terms "utopianism" and "optimism" interchangeably to describe the Chinese experience.[52] Wolfgang Bauer refers to the same phenomenon as people's pursuit of "happiness."[53]

Because of the differences embodied in Chinese hopefulness compared with the Western counterpart, the word "utopia" does not have an equivalent in the Chinese language. Thus, a three-character word, *wu tuo bang,* was created that mimics the sound of the Western word "utopia."[54] Not surprisingly, in a departure from the negative connotations associated with the term "utopianism" in the Western context,[55] Chinese scholars have praised Chinese-style utopianism, saying that it was precisely this "utopian spirit" that has enabled the country's civilization to flourish for over three thousand years.[56]

Confucian Datong

Confucian hopefulness is characterized by an emphasis on the collective good rather than selfish gain, a stress on morality rather than rationality, and an emphasis on the pragmatic transformation of this world. Confucius (551–479 BCE) is not a religious figure like Jesus Christ in Christianity. Confucianism was the dominant Chinese official ideology in premodern times and was never considered a religion but rather a code of ethics. Confucianism takes the existence of the universe for granted. It also lacks a theory of creation or stories of supernatural events, such as Moses parting the Red Sea to lead the Jews out of Egypt.

The hope of Confucius is datong, or Grand Harmony. It is a real human community that is supposed to have existed long before Confucius, during the Yao (around 2350 BCE) and Shun (around 2250 BCE) periods.[57] Most scholars believe that the concept of datong is by Confucius,[58] although the authorship of it was disputed not only in ancient times,[59] but also in modern times,[60] and not only among Chinese scholars,[61] but also among Westerners.[62] Some Chinese scholars argue that datong is a product of various Confucian thinkers, not of Confucius himself.[63]

It is also unclear whether such a paradise actually existed, as Confucius insisted. Some scholars believe that the paradise described in datong was simply a reflection of the author's desire for a bright future. This imagination was driven by the horrible situations that the author witnessed when the warring states during the period attacked each other frequently,[64] because utopian thought is more widespread during social turmoil. Nevertheless, it is beyond doubt that datong is a major source of Chinese sense of hope. Here is a detailed description of datong:

> When the Great Way was in practice, then the Empire was held in common. They chose people of talent and ability whose words were sincere, and they cultivated harmony. Thus people did not only love their own parents, not only nurture their own children. The elderly were cared for till the end of their life, the able-bodied pursued their careers, while the young were nurtured in growing up. Provisions were made to care for widows, orphans, childless men, and the disabled. Men had their part to play (work), while women had their home (marriage). Possessions were used, but not hoarded for selfish reasons. Work was encouraged, but not for selfish advantage. In this way selfish schemes did not arise. Robbers, thieves, rebels, and traitors had no place, and thus outer doors were not closed. This is called the Great Unity of Harmony (Datong).[65]

At the center of Confucian hope in human life is the emphasis on the collective good as opposed to selfish gain, as revealed in the description of datong. Confucius adds, "[W]ith equality, one does not need to worry about poverty."[66]

With this tradition, it is not a surprise that modern communism stressing the collective good found an eager audience in China. In 1925, four years after the founding of the Chinese Communist Party (CCP), Guo Moro published a fictional work entitled "Marx Enters the Confucian Temple." In the story, Confucius and Karl Marx have a conversation about the hopes of humankind. For Marx, humanity's hope is communism; for Confucius, it is datong. However, by the end of the book, the two have agreed that communism and datong are the same.[67]

The idea of communism had so much appeal among the Chinese that even the anarchists of the late Qing and the early republic were all anarchists of communism, not of individualism.[68] Both Marxists and anarchists wanted to abolish the state. For Marxists, although the eventual goal of communism was to abolish the state, the means through which this goal was realized was often through strengthening the state's power not weakening it. For anarchists, however, the state was evil per se.[69] Because of this linkage between communism and anarchism, many Chinese communists were former anarchists.[70]

Related to the concept of the collective good, morality is also emphasized in the Confucian idea of hope for the future. For Mencius, the second most important sage in Confucianism, who summarized the ideas of the great philosopher, "[A]ll that matters is that there should be benevolence and rightness. What is the point of mentioning the word 'profit'?"[71] Mencius comments,

> A man who cares only about food and drink is despised by others because he takes care of the parts of smaller importance to the detriment of the parts of greater importance. He who is guided by the interests of the parts of his person that are of greater importance is a great man; he who is guided by the interests of the parts of his person that are of smaller importance is a small man. . . .[72] [T]he sole concern of learning is to go after this strayed heart [i.e., "save this soul"].[73]

With its strong emphasis on morality, Confucian thought can be irrational,[74] which contrasts with the teachings of Plato.[75] For the Chinese, what distinguished humans from animals was ethics; for Plato, the touchstone for human nature is rationality.[76]

Irrationality in Chinese social philosophy has had an enormous impact on the country's social transformation in modern times. Thomas Metzger wrote that the neo-Confucian thought developed by Zhu Xi and Wang Yangming during the Song Dynasty (960–1279 CE) encouraged the belief that radical social transformation was possible.[77] For the Chinese philosophers

Li Zehou and Liu Zaifu, China's revolutionary enthusiasm in the twentieth century was connected to the irrational way of thinking in Confucianism.[78]

Besides emphasizing the collective good and morality, Confucian hopefulness is also found to be highly pragmatic. This quality is embodied in the duality of the Confucian sense of hope that although the eventual goal is datong, the immediate goal is xiaokang, or lesser prosperity.[79] Xiaokang refers to the rule of Yu (2205–2198 BCE), Tang in the Shang Dynasty (1700–1027 BCE), and Kings Wen and Wu in the Zhou Dynasty (1027–221 BCE).[80] Noticeably, the list does not include such evil rulers as Jie of the Xia Dynasty (2100–1600 BCE) or Zou of the Shang Dynasty (1700–1027 BCE). Although xiaokang is not as good as datong, it comprises the better years of normal times. The following is a description of xiaokang:

> Now the Great Way has become hidden and the world is the possession of private families. Each regards as parents only his own parents, as sons only his own sons; goods and labor are employed for selfish ends. Hereditary offices and titles are granted by ritual law while walls and moats must provide security. Ritual and rightness are used to regulate the relationship between ruler and subject, to ensure affection between father and son, peace between brothers and harmony between husband and wife, to set up social institutions, organize the farms and villages, honor the brave and wise, and bring merit to the individual. Therefore intrigue and plotting come about and men take up arms. Emperor Yu, Kings Tang, Wen, Wu, Cheng, and the Duke of Zhou achieved eminence for this reason: that all six rulers were constantly attentive to ritual, made manifest their rightness, and acted in complete faith. They exposed error, made humanity their law and humility their practice, showing the people wherein they should constantly abide. If there were any who did not abide by these principles, they were dismissed from their positions and regarded by the multitude as dangerous. This is the period of Lesser Prosperity.[81]

Xiaokang differs from datong in many ways. While datong supports the public ownership of land, xiaokang advocates private ownership; while one works for society in datong, one works for self in xiaokang; while there is simple human differentiation only in terms of gender and age in datong, there is a whole range of hierarchical human relationships in xiaokang; while the focus in datong is on communities as a whole, xiaokang supports families; while people have a high degree of morality in datong, they have low moral standards in xiaokang; and while bandits and wars are nonexistent in datong, they are all too common in xiaokang.

Xiaokang's lower expectations of life make it highly realizable. It often serves as the first step in the eventual realization of datong. In fact, this two-step division of Confucian hope for the future ultimately served as a useful social transformation strategy. For instance, the post-Mao leadership used the same language for their reform programs: In order to achieve the eventual goal of communism, that is, datong, China needed to first have xiaokang, meaning the raising of the standard of living for the Chinese people by focusing on economic development.

Taoist Small Kingdoms with Limited Population

Although Confucianism was the dominant form of governance in premodern times, Taoism also influenced Chinese politics. Occasionally, rulers adopted Taoist strategies for governing, such as the so-called *Wen Jing zhi zhi* (the governance of Emperors Wen and Jing in the Han Dynasty (206 BCE–220 CE). Taoism was developed by Lao Tzu, who lived at the end of the Spring–Autumn Period (771–221 BCE) in Chu, near present-day Hubei Province. As with the case of datong, the Taoist utopia also drew on a real human community that was supposed to have existed in primitive times. In addition, Lao Tzu's yearning for this earlier paradise was also in response to the deplorable situation during the Spring–Autumn period (770–476 BCE) when warring states caused untold suffering.

Taoist hope largely came from the following language found in the *Tao Te Ching,* the teaching of Lao Tzu:

Small country, few people—hundreds of devices, but none are used. People ponder . . . death and don't travel far. They have carriages and boats, but no one goes on board; weapons and armor, but no one brandishes them. They use knotted cords for counting. Sweet their food, beautiful their clothes, peaceful their homes, delightful their customs. Neighboring countries are so close. You can hear their chickens and dogs. But people grow old and die without needing to come and go.[82] The more prohibitions and rules, the poorer people become. The sharper people's weapons, the more they riot. The more skilled their techniques, the more grotesque their works. The more elaborate the laws, the more they commit crimes.[83] Heaven and Earth are not kind, the ten thousand things are straw dogs to them; the Sages are not kind, people are straw dogs to them.[84] Great trouble comes from being selfish.[85]

Obviously, Lao Tzu's response to the existing horrors in society was very different from that of Confucius. Lao Tzu felt that since social evils were due to the fact that society had become too sophisticated—such as the advance in productivity, the increased power of the state, and the increased intelligence of people—human society had to return to primitive times. In the Taoist utopia, the elected ruler must labor, since everybody was equal. The administrative style was *wu wei,* a hands-off system. In this society, members were all related by blood.[86]

The literary expression of the Taoist utopia was found in Tao Yuanming's (365–427 CE) book, *Tao Hua Yuan Ji* (Peach Blossom Shangri-la).[87] Tao's utopia is a place of isolation. Although this community is small, people do not interact. There is no hierarchy, no monarch, no ministers, no government, and no taxes. People work hard voluntarily.[88] In this egalitarian society, people collectively cultivate the publicly owned land. Neither exploitation nor luxury exists.[89]

Although both the Confucian datong and the Taoist hope for the future are of this world and opposed to selfish gain, the two utopias differ in many ways. While Confucian sense of hope strives for Grand Harmony, the Taoist hopefulness aims at a "small kingdom with limited population." While the Confucian hope advocates human endeavor to change the world, the Taoist one is satisfied with "the natural." While Confucian hopefulness has the key value of "benevolence," Taoism believes that "benevolence" is against the natural order of the universe.

In a sense, the complementary philosophical traditions of Confucianism and Taoism in China[90] parallel those of Japan where the imported Confucianism and the indigenous Shintoism complement each other. While the Confucian hope is to change the world for the better, the hopes of Taoism and Shintoism both endorse "the natural." But Confucianism was dominant in China in premodern times, while Shintoism was more popular in Japan toward the end of the Tokugawa era, when the Meiji Restoration occurred.

Zhang Lu's Peasant Rebellion

In addition to Confucian datong and the Taoist "small kingdom of limited population," a third major path of Chinese utopianism is represented by Zhang Lu, who led a peasant rebellion during the Eastern Han Dynasty

(25–220 CE).[91] Peasant rebellions were much more widespread throughout China's history as compared to other countries. For instance, in the nineteenth and twentieth centuries, the peasants in India and in China suffered under similar conditions. But India did not have as many large-scale peasant revolts as did China, a situation that suggests causes other than socioeconomic ones.[92]

The collapse of several major Chinese dynasties such as Qin (221–206 BCE) and Ming (1368–1644 CE) was caused by large-scale peasant rebellions that often involved hundreds of thousands of people. However, Western Europe did not record its first peasant rebellion until the seventh century, and it was fairly small in comparison to China's. The British Watt Taylor rebellion did not occur until the thirteenth century, and there were only 30,000 to 40,000 people involved. The largest revolt in Western Europe history was the German peasant rebellion in 1524–1526, but the number was less than 200,000.[93]

The frequent occurrences of large peasant rebellions were partly due to the Confucian "Mandate of Heaven": On the one hand, the ruler did not have to ask the ruled for consent to rule. On the other, the ruled had the right to revolt in case the ruler did not rule benevolently. For Mencius, "Heaven sees with the eyes of its people. Heaven hears with the ears of its people."[94] People are the most important, society comes second, and the monarch comes last.[95]

In 191 CE, Zhang Lu became the leader of a faction of the Yellow Turban Rebellion, which triggered a civil war that brought down the Han Dynasty. For the next three decades, Zhang Lu launched an experiment in central China that had far-reaching impacts on the country: He abolished officialdom and combined the political state with religion.[96] Tai Ping Jing, the teaching of Zhang's government, included the following principles: (1) The religion of Zhang's regime taught that since all properties are created by heaven, they should belong to the public. Market prices were controlled by the state. (2) Everyone had to perform manual labor. No work meant no material gains. (3) "Benevolence" was important. The talented should help the unskilled; the strong must help the weak. A welfare system was created. (4) Criminals were not executed. Redemption was important.[97]

The Taiping Rebellion's (1850–1864 CE) "land system of the heavenly dynasty" (*tianchao tianmu zhidu*) was another good example of a peasant utopia.[98] Karl Marx called the Taiping Rebellion "China's socialism."[99] It had the following principles: (1) The land was to be distributed equally to everybody in the kingdom. (2) The government performed a combination of functions such as administration, organizing religious practice, and finance. (3) Government officials were elected. (4) Exploitation, oppression, and conflict did not exist. People would love each other in this kingdom.[100]

In the view of China specialist Kung-Chuan Hsiao, the Zhang Lu–style egalitarian society was similar to the Confucian datong heritage in terms of ideological orientation.[101] The difference is that while the Confucian datong was often reserved for the remote future, peasant rebellions demanded total egalitarianism in the present.

Chapter 3

Modernizing Reforms: Japan and China

The reformers [of the Late Qing Reform] have carried out radical reforms in all departments of the government. This has left the whole world in shock. Compared with the rapid reform of this "young China," the speed of the Meiji Restoration was no comparison.

—*Zi Lin Xin Bao*[1]

In contrast to the fact that most of China's leading intellectuals tended to endorse the Rousseauian version of democracy of equality, most of the Japanese intellectuals during the Meiji era found appealing the writings of John Stuart Mill (1806–1873) and Herbert Spencer (1820–1903) who provide intellectual support to modern libertarian ideologies.

—Douglas Howland[2]

What made the Meiji Restoration (1868–1912) a spectacular success? What made the Late Qing Reform (Hundred Days Reform) (1898) a failure? Interpretations vary—some are from a constructionist perspective while others are deconstructionist. Constructionists have argued that the success of the Meiji Restoration was due to such factors as the deeds of heroic figures (*shishis*) or to the efforts of small groups of lower-ranking former elites.[3] Similarly, the failure of the Late Qing Reform was attributed to the entrenched power of the conservative Empress Dowager Cixi's faction or the naiveté of the reformers.[4] Obviously, these interpretations are not very sophisticated.

Therefore, some scholars have adopted a deconstructionist position by pointing out the limitations of the various constructionist approaches. For the Meiji Restoration, success was attributed to a variety of factors with no single factor being more important than others, including, for instance, the modernization program that had already been underway in the Tokugawa regime (1615–1868), domestic popular uprisings, or the international environment at that time when the Civil War in the United States had recently ended and France and Britain were preoccupied with China, thereby having no opportunities to interfere in Japanese domestic politics.[5] The spontaneity of the Meiji Restoration has also been noted by scholars. They believed that the Meiji Restoration was not an outcome of a good design from above, since the Meiji leaders were surprised at every major turn of events. All vested interests, including, among others, Western envoys, *bukufu* and *daimyo* (local landowners and nobles), popular revivalists, and imperial loyalists, had different agendas. The Meiji Restoration was a highly volatile process with no dominant social forces being in control.[6]

For the Late Qing Reform, deconstructionist scholars refuted common beliefs such as the Empress Dowager Cixi's (1838–1908) opposition to reform, Emperor Guangxu's (1871–1908) initiative for the reform, and Kang Youwei's (1858–1927) role in the reform. In addition, although the proposals for reforms to the throne might have been radical, as many scholars believed, the policies as actually carried out by the Qing court were not.[7] This deconstructionist approach has pinned down the limitations of other interpretations without offering clear answers to the diverse outcomes of the reforms. Above all, in an effort to discredit prevailing interpretations, some deconstructionist scholars occasionally carried their arguments too far. For instance, the allegation that Kang was not knowledgeable about the West was not substantiated by empirical evidence.[8]

Such complex events as the Meiji Restoration and the Late Qing Reform must have been caused by a multitude of factors. Thus, diverse interpretations of the two events should receive credit. In addition to the interpretations presented, timing also had an impact on the outcomes of the two reforms. The Meiji Restoration occurred after the Opium War (1840) in which the Chinese were defeated by the Western powers. The war demonstrated to the Japanese that the spears and swords of the Asians were no match for the weaponry of the Westerners. Therefore, the leaders of the Meiji Restoration adopted moderate measures, a strategy that led to the success of the reform.

Although it is always useful to add another factor, the current study intends to go a step further by looking at complex social reforms from a different methodological perspective. Instead of selectively collecting historical data that can prove or disprove a given hypothesis, this study has adopted a contrast-oriented, comparative case study approach. In the current study, the most obvious likeness between the Meiji Restoration and the Late Qing Reform is the fact that both Japan and China were premodern East Asian societies that were forced into facing challenges from the West. The most obvious disparity is that the political cultures of the two countries were drastically different. These cultural differences were reflected in the political strategies adopted by the elites of the two countries during respective time periods. Although the cultural factor in the reforms has been noted by some scholars,[9] no systematic attempt has been made to address the issue.

In order to understand the strategies and philosophical underpinnings during the two reforms, I will analyze the writings of two intellectual leaders, Fukuzawa Yukichi (1835–1901) and Kang Youwei. These writings cover decades leading up to through the peak years of the Meiji Restoration and the Late Qing Reform, which were 1868 and 1898, respectively. Fukuzawa was Japan's undisputed leading intellectual figure in the Meiji period.[10]

Few historical transformations match in scope or drama than that of Japan during the second half of the nineteenth century. Rarer still are instances when one can point to a single figure and say, here is the man who more than any other provided the intellectual impetus for the change. Fukuzawa Yukichi was such a man.[11]

Fukuzawa was so popular at that time that his *An Encouragement of Learning* sold 3.4 million copies.[12] In 1901, fifteen thousand mourners attended his funeral.[13] In order to enlighten the common people, Fukuzawa not only translated many Western works, an act that was dangerous at the time, but also invented a new prose style that was close to the vernacular.

Fukuzawa's intellectual counterpart in China was Kang Youwei, who led the Late Qing Reform in 1898. Kang was born into a wealthy scholar-official family in Nanhai, Guangdong Province. He attracted national attention by sending seven appeals to the emperor from 1885 to 1898, advising the Qing ruler on how to resist foreign invaders and how to modernize China,[14] Kang was eventually appointed as one of the secretaries in the Grand Council, or Zongli Yamen. In that capacity, he was able to discuss issues with and memorialize the emperor, thereby making him the undisputed leader of the reform.

Structure: Historical Background of the Meiji Restoration and the Late Qing Reform

The Meiji Restoration and the Late Qing Reform were responses to external intrusions, that is, the U.S. invasion of Japan in 1853 and the First Sino-Japanese War (1894–1895). In the case of Japan, the Tokugawa regime had closed its door to all but a few Dutch and Chinese traders for two centuries before 1853 because Japanese rulers feared that Japan's existing relations with Europeans gave Japanese dissidents the possibility of alliance with a military force outside the regime's control, and the country would also be open to the "corruption" of Christianity. Japanese isolation was ended on July 8, 1853, when four black ships, led by USS *Powhatan* and commanded by Commodore Matthew Perry, arrived at Edo (Tokyo) Bay. The Americans demanded trade and the use of Japanese ports to replenish coal and supplies for their whaling fleet.

Overwhelmed by American military power, and heeding the lesson of the Chinese who had been defeated by the British in the 1840 Opium War, the Japanese agreed to sign a treaty on March 31, 1854, after weeks of talks. The treaty included the opening of the Shimoda and Hakodate ports, providing support to American ships wrecked on the Japanese coast and protection for shipwrecked persons, and permission for American ships to buy supplies, coal, water, and other provisions in Japanese ports.

The Japanese yielding to the Americans was relatively easy because the country's political structure at the time of the invasion was ill-suited to resist outside incursions. Japan's central government had no effective political control over the country during the Tokugawa period.[15] The Japanese emperor typically was a figurehead. Although the *shogun,* or general, nominally had absolute power, no dictator emerged after 1650. Those who were in charge at the central government level were *bafuku,* a group of senior statesmen. Although the *bakufu* were responsible for national defense, they had access only to financial resources derived from their own landholdings.[16] At the local level, *daimyos* (lords) who controlled "domains," or prefectures, had considerable autonomy.[17] At the beginning of the Meiji era, the government had access to resources from only a quarter of Japan's productive capacity.[18] Because of this, the cash-poor government ordered that temple bells be melted down to make guns.[19]

The fragmented nature of Japanese society was also reflected by the fact that Japan at that time did not have an official ideology that would unite the people. Unlike China, Japan had to create an official ideology from scratch.

This lack of an official ideology continued for two decades after the beginning of the Meiji Restoration in 1868. Localities as well as departments of the government each had their own ideologies.[20] The Japanese experience was similar to the challenges faced by many Africans before World War II—in most areas of Africa, there had been no such a thing called "nation" or "country." Instead, African societies were organized in villages and tribes.

Similarly, China's opening to the outside world was also involuntary. The success of the Meiji Restoration gave Japanese elites more confidence in following the Western way, including colonialism. Korea was the natural first step for Japan's expansion. The Yi Dynasty of Korea at that time sought to preserve its traditions, including seclusion and a tributary relationship with China, which attempted to protect its principal vassal. However, the Qing regime lost again to outsiders in the First Sino–Japanese War (1894–1895) over the control of Korea following its defeat in the 1840 Opium War.

The defeated Chinese were compelled to sign the Treaty of Shimonoseki in April 1895. Although Korea was still nominally recognized as a sovereign state, it became a Japanese protectorate; China ceded Taiwan, the Liaodong Peninsula, and the Pescadores to Japan; China paid a war indemnity of 200 million taels of silver to Japan; and China opened four more treaty ports to external trade. The war shook the foundation of the Qing Dynasty more than the Opium War because, unlike Great Britain, Japan was traditionally viewed by the Chinese as inferior. China's defeats were not surprising, because the country's traditional political structure was ill-suited to meet the challenges of a modern Great Britain and a reformed Japan.

Traditionally, China had a virtual all-encompassing social structure that was maintained by a common written language, Confucian ideology, and a bureaucracy staffed by people who had successfully taken the uniform civil service examinations. Although this all-encompassing structure was more effective in social control than that in many other premodern societies, faced with incursions from the Western powers, the system under Qing was unable to defend China. The government's ability to mobilize the population, including the taxation capacity of the central government, was very limited.[21] For instance, the Qing government's revenue in 1894, just before the First Sino–Japanese War, was only 88,909,000 taels of silver. This sum of money was inadequate to meet the government's expenditures under normal circumstances, much less during a period of military buildup and conflict.[22]

When domestic upheavals occurred in conjunction with foreign threats, the Qing government felt even more pressured. During the Taiping Rebellion (1853–1864), the central government encouraged officials to return to their hometowns to organize local militias in order to put down the uprisings. Both Zeng Guofan's (1811–1872) *xiang*[23] army and Li Hongzhang's (1823–1901) *huai*[24] army were of such origins. In 1900, the desperate Empress Dowager Cixi tried to use the "boxers" to resist foreign invaders.[25]

Political Strategies

The Meiji Restoration began on January 3, 1868, after certain domains defeated the shogun forces. Rebel leaders took control of Kyoto court, and in the name of the emperor announced the resumption of direct imperial rule. In four decades after the start of the Meiji Restoration, Japan had largely accomplished its social transformation—the old elites of the *samurai,* or warriors, and the *daimyos,* or lords, were deprived of their privileges and a new constitution was adopted in 1889.

The Late Qing Reform began on June 11, 1898, when Emperor Guangxu made the announcement of Ding Guo Shi Zhao, the imperial edict of strengthening the country. In the course of 103 days, Kang and his followers submitted approximately two hundred recommendations to the emperor who, in turn, made about one hundred imperial edicts to the country based on those recommendations. These imperial edicts covered a wide range of issues in politics, economics, military, culture, and education.[26] The reforms ended on September 21, 1898, when the Empress Dowager Cixi staged a coup, put the Emperor Guangxu under house arrest, and persecuted the reformers. On September 26, the Empress Dowager revoked all the important policy innovations that the emperor had announced during the Hundred Days Reform.

The purpose of the two reforms was to build more effective social systems by following the example of Western countries. Therefore, to centralize power so that the resources of their respective countries could be used in more effective ways was a shared strategy by the leaders in both reforms. The Japanese and the Chinese departed with each other, however, on the pace and the path of the reforms, as well as whether to treat the reforms as the end or as a means to a loftier goal.

For these nation-building efforts, both Fukuzawa and Kang recognized the necessity of borrowing from the West. In Fukuzawa's words, "[I]f we look at present conditions, it seems that the deficiencies are all on our side, and the talents all on theirs (the West)."[27] Similarly, Kang's commitment to learning from the West was beyond doubt. He purchased 3,000 out of the

12,000 titles of translated books published by a major press, Shanghai Jiangnan Zhizaoju Yishuju, in the course of thirty years,[28] and Kang read all the books about the West that he could find.[29]

In Japan, the centralization of power occurred immediately after the start of the Meiji Restoration. In 1869, lords of the most powerful domains, including Satsuma, Choshu, and Tosa, surrendered their registers to the court, with other lords following suit. These actions were taken to end the decentralized political structure of the Tokugawa regime. The process of centralization was also reflected in the land tax reform of 1873, which stabilized government revenues by basing taxes on the value of the land rather than on fluctuating agricultural yields.[30] The Meiji government increased national and local taxes three times during the 1897–1912 period.[31]

Similarly, in China, Kang's strategy was "a bold call to strip the whole court and bureaucracy of power and concentrate it all in the hands of the emperor and his reform advisers. For all practical purposes, it was a declaration of war on the entire Qing official establishment." Accordingly, Emperor Guangxu's goal during the Late Qing Reform was nothing short of "a drastic recasting of the whole political structure of the empire."[32]

The purpose of these centralization efforts was to strengthen their respective countries. For Fukuzawa, "our motive need not be mutual struggle between brothers, but intellectual competition with the West."[33] For Kang, "the weak are to be controlled by the strong; the strong will control the weak."[34] Commenting on China's ceding of Taiwan to Japan in his appeal to the emperor, Kang said, "this act was to the harm of China, to the pleasure of Japan, and to the joys of other [W]estern powers."[35] Kang's views were shared by most leading Chinese intellectuals of this period. In a document issued by the influential organization Qiang Xue Hui (Strengthening China Society), it was said that those who were not wise (like camels) and those who did not work together (like tigers) were doomed to fail. To be strong, one had to learn, and had to work with others, *xue ze qiang; qun ze qiang.*[36]

However, Fukuzawa and Kang departed from each other on the following issues: the pace of the reforms, the path of the reforms, and whether to treat the reforms as the end or the means to a loftier goal.

For Fukuzawa, Japanese reform had to occur at a gradual pace. The Meiji Restoration largely followed this pattern. Although the Japanese were willing to depart from the past, they also recognized the difficulty of rapid social change. Fukuzawa had no sympathy with demands for the rapid creation of a popularly elected parliament. He emphasized that "[t]he times and places must be considered when discussing the merits and demerits of things." He believed that extreme views tended only to cancel one another out.[37]

Fukuzawa's moderate viewpoints were representative of mainstream Japanese intellectual thought at that time. Most intellectuals realized that the Japanese people's enlightenment level was low because of their lack of education and exposure to the West. Therefore, raising their political consciousness was the most important objective.[38]

Most people in the Japanese government also shared this moderate view, although they and the intellectuals normally did not work closely with each other as was the case in China. One of the officials put it this way: "Even if we cause the people to run, we shall not overtake the West in less than a few decades." Government leaders reiterated that the customs and feelings of the people were insufficiently developed to allow for popular sovereignty.[39]

The Chinese strategy on the pace of reforms was the opposite: more reluctance to reform at the beginning and more haste when the reforms were set in motion. The Tongzhi Restoration (1862–1874), which intended to go back to China's past, resulted in slow changes. Even when many Chinese leaders genuinely wanted to reform the system, they often used the pretext of restoring genuine Confucianism of the past.

Kang reinterpreted Confucian classics to advocate new politics, that is, *tuo gu, gai zhi*. For instance, he alleged that elections had actually existed in Chinese history. Elections in the Han Dynasty (206 BCE–220 CE)[40] were a feat Kang attributed to Confucius.[41] He also praised Confucius for his advocating the *chan rang* system, that is, giving up the throne voluntarily.[42] Kang alleged that Otto von Bismarck (1815–1898), the Prussian chancellor who united Germany in 1871, held the highest regard for Confucius.[43] Kang also alleged that centuries in the past, public opinion in Japan was also able to reach the top.[44] His allegations about Japanese public opinion were far-fetched, because it was generally believed that in premodern times, Japanese national politics had little to do with commoners.

Kang's position was a departure from the Japanese intellectual elites, including Fukuzawa, who, although he used the myth of "Japan's past glory" for national mobilization by increasing the power of the emperor, did not use Japan's past to justify the present in any intellectually sophisticated way. In addition, Fukuzawa's critique of Japan's Confucian past was straightforward.

One result of the inertia by China's leaders was the slow pace of social transformation. When an American visited a typical Chinese school in 1890s, he found hardly any mention about the West. This contrasted with his experience in Japan two decades earlier, when he was very impressed by the Western subject matter in the Japanese curriculum.[45] The Japanese receptive attitude toward the West was also demonstrated by the popularity of Fukuzawa's books and the fact that Chinese geographer Wei Yuan's *Haiguo tuzhi,* an introduction to the West, went through many editions in Japan following the Opium War (1840).[46]

The Chinese were not only unwilling to change at the beginning, but also impatient once the reforms were set in motion. For Kang, "slow reform is not as good as rapid reform; little change is not as good as wholesale change."[47] A zealous Guangxu wanted "to get as many projects started and as quickly as the publication of edicts would permit."[48] As radical as Kang was in comparison with the Japanese Meiji leaders, he was widely considered to be a "conservative" among other Chinese reformers at the time.[49]

The radical nature of the Late Qing Reform in comparison with the Meiji Restoration was widely noted. According to an analysis published by the then-influential newspaper, *Zi Lin Xi Bao,*

> The reformers have carried out radical reforms in all departments of the government. This has left the whole world in shock. Compared with the rapid reform of this "young China," the pace of the Meiji Restoration was no comparison.[50]

Even in contemporary times, Chinese extremism has been noted by the Japanese. Mariko Hayashi, a popular Japanese essayist said, "Chinese people are very aggressive and too energetic. Once they start things, they can't stop. Everything they do is extreme."[51]

The path of the Meiji Restoration and the Late Qing Reform also differed. Although both Japan and China needed to introduce Western technology, to adopt elements of the Western political system, and to transform the political consciousness of their peoples, the order of their priorities was completely opposed. For leading Japanese intellectuals, the first step was to change the political consciousness of the Japanese people, followed by changing the political structure of the country, and then they would worry about other things. This reflected a more gradual approach. As summarized by Fukuzawa,

> We should first reform men's minds, then turn to government decrees, and only in the end go out to external things. It may be more difficult to follow this order, but it is a thread which has no truly insurmountable ob-

stacles. We can reverse the order and seem to have easy going, but this latter course will lead to a dead end.[52]

In contrast, following China's defeat in the Opium War against the British in 1840, the dominant thought among elites was "Chinese learning for essence, Western learning for mundane matters," as put forward by Zhang Zhidong (1837–1909), a governor in the Qing Dynasty. This meant that only Western technology should be adopted. Neither change in China's political system, nor change in the official ideology of Confucianism was necessary.[53] It took another humiliating defeat at the hands of the Japanese in 1894 before the Chinese ruling elites decided to support political reform. After the failure of the Late Qing Reform, the Chinese finally realized the necessity of changing the people's consciousness. Ultimately, the "New Cultural Movement" (*xin wenhua yundong*) took place in the 1920s and 1930s.

Significantly, the priority order of the Chinese enlightenment during the late Qing period, that is, technology first, political reform second, and culture third, was repeated in the late 1970s and 1980s for the Deng Xiaoping (1904–1997) reforms. After the Cultural Revolution, the Dengist reformers first focused on introducing Western technology without changing China's political system. This strategy did not work well because of bureaucratic inefficiency. Then came the discourse of political reform in the early 1980s. When the Chinese bureaucracy proved difficult to reform, the transformation of people's consciousness was put on the agenda in the mid- and late 1980s, that is, the so-called "Culture Fever" (*wenhua re*).[54]

Chinese and Japanese intellectual leaders were also different in terms of their overall vision of respective reforms. For instance, viewing Westernization as the end in itself, Fukuzawa wanted to establish a constitutional monarchy only. His frequent use of the term "advanced civilization" meant that he equated Westernization with modernization. Although Fukuzawa did not exclude the possibility of a global utopia, he considered it a remote possibility at best, something that might happen several thousand years in the future.[55] Fukuzawa considered Europe and North America civilized, and China and Asia semicivilized, while Africa and Australia were uncivilized. He wrote,

What I mean when I say that we should take European civilization as our goal is that we should turn to Europe in order to make the spirit of civilization ours, and thus I am in complete accord with their opinion.[56]

Although Fukuzawa acknowledged Western society's problems on an abstract level,[57] he did not criticize it in a comprehensive way. Fukuzawa also recommended that Japan should distance itself from the rest of Asia.[58] In support of this, Fukuzawa disapproved resistance against Western products, believing that such resistance would weaken Japan.[59]

In contrast, Kang had two platforms in his reforms—to establish a constitutional monarchy first and then to realize datong. Kang was not only specific about what this utopia looked like, but he also predicted that the utopia would come about in 100 to 150 years.[60] Kang divided the development of world civilization into three stages: *ju luan shi* (uncivilized), *sheng ping shi* (process leading to datong), and *tai ping shi* (datong). Kang said to his friend, Liang Qichao (1873–1929), in 1894,

> [C]urrently we are in the first stage of *ju luan shi,* and therefore we can only talk about reaching the second stage of *sheng ping shi.* It is not to our advantage to talk about the third stage of Datong now.[61]

The steps taken by Kang during the reforms were mostly aimed at establishing a constitutional monarchy, such as eliminating the civil service exams, training modern troops, and streamlining the court bureaucracy.[62]

The problem is that these stages are hard to separate. Although Kang realized that his goals had to move on two levels—the lower-level one of the immediate reform and the higher-level one of datong[63]—his idealistic goal of datong probably had colored his reform goals. This situation is similar to the difficulty in separating datong from xiaokang in Chinese tradition: Although most premodern Chinese rulers strived for xiaokang, instead of datong, China still had more grand human projects than other societies in premodern times.

The dilemma of separating the stages of social development occurred again in Chinese history after the Late Qing Reform. In his attempt to modernize China, Mao Zedong (1893–1976) also had two campaigns: the "new democracy" (*xin minzhu zhuyi geming*) and the "socialist revolution" (*shehui zhuyi geming*).[64] Actually, the wrong assessment of the demarcation between the two was crucial for Mao to begin the ill-conceived collectivization in 1957. In his book *On Ten Great Relationships* written in 1956, it was clear that Mao viewed the socialist revolution, to which the collectivization and people's communes belonged, as something in the remote future.[65] Nonetheless, by 1957, Mao felt that the time was ripe for the next stage, the socialist revolution.

Philosophical Underpinnings

The fact that Japan and China adopted very different strategies during their respective reforms was connected with the different political cultures of the two countries. The traditional Japanese notion of accepting life as it is, as discussed in Chapter 2, probably explains why the Meiji leaders adopted moderate strategies with limited goals, while the Chinese traditional belief that striving will lead to a better life for the group may explain the impatience and greater ambition of the late Qing reformers.

This section is focused on philosophical differences between Kang and Fukuzawa on the issues of universalism versus particularism, monism versus pluralism, high moral standards versus moral relativism, and populism versus elitism. Such different philosophical underpinnings may explain why the Chinese treated the reforms only as a means to reach the eventual goal of datong, while the Japanese Meiji leaders treated the reform as the end in itself. The two were also distinct in terms of focus on abstract philosophical issues or empirical knowledge of applications.

Kang's universalistic spirit was clearly demonstrated in his well-known *Datongshu,* or the book of datong.[66] The title of the book suggests that Kang drew his ideas from the Confucian concept of datong. When Kang wrote the first draft of *Datongshu* in 1884–1885, he also completed his essay, "Li Yun Annotated." "Li Yun" is the section in the Confucian classic, *The Analects,* that describes the concept of datong.

Confucianism, especially the concept of datong, is universalistic.[67] In the spirit of datong, Kang advocated the abolishment of the state in politics, private property in economics, and families in the social structure. This is because, according to Kang, all evils in society come from the differences among countries, classes, races/ethnicities, genders, families, and wealth levels.[68] The utopian spirit in *Datongshu* is so obvious that a Western translator intended to translate the title of the book *Datongshu,* into "utopia."[69] Kang remarked:

> Now to have states, families, and selves is to allow each individual maintain a sphere of selfishness. This infracts utterly the Universal Principle (*Gong Li*) and impedes progress. . . . [S]elfishness itself should be banished, so that goods and services would not be used for private ends. . . . The only (true way) is sharing the world in common by all (*tian xia wei gong*). . . . To share in common is to treat each and every one alike. There should be no distinction between high and low, no discrepancy between

rich and poor, no segregation of human races, no inequality between sexes. . . . All should be educated and supported with the common property; none should depend on private possessions . . .[70]

A yearning for datong was characteristic of the late Qing intellectuals. To be sure, not every Chinese intellectual and political leader at that time agreed with Kang. For instance, Tan Sitong (1865–1898) was more radical in his political reform, and Sun Yet-sun was known as a "revolutionary," not a "reformer."[71] However, both Tan and Sun accepted Kang's philosophy of datong, in spite of their political differences. When the Zhongxi Xuexiao (East West School) was established by Sun in 1897, Kang suggested that the name of the school be changed to the Datong School. Sun agreed.

The intellectual scene in Japan during this period looked very different from that in China. First, the intellectual fabric of Japanese society in the late nineteenth century was pluralistic.[72] In addition, Fukuzawa's pragmatically oriented theories with the aim of saving Japan from Western incursions had no universalistic claims, unlike Kang's two-stage agenda.

Datong is characterized by not only universalism in world outlook, but also monism in ways of thinking. The monistic understanding of the universe assumes that truth has a single source, as does power. Monism was reflected in traditional Chinese social structure in the sense that power and the sacred derived from the same source. According to Fukuzawa, Confucius was always able to provide teachings for the powerful. In China, power and the sacrosanct were integrated.[73] "[T]he people looking up to one completely autocratic ruler and with single-minded devotion were slaves to the idea that the most sacrosanct and the most powerful were embodied in the same person."[74] In Kang's view, pluralistic competition, which clashed with monism and smacked of Darwinism, was contrary to the ways of humans in nature, who are born good.[75]

This monistic consciousness led to the desire of some Chinese intellectuals during the May Fourth Movement (1919) to eliminate tradition altogether.[76] Monism assumed that if Confucianism were to be accepted, as was the case in premodern times, it needed to be accepted in totality; if it had to be negated in modern times, it had to be negated in totality as well.

However, the Japanese believed that powerful and sacred people should always be separate. According to Fukuzawa, by the Kamakura period (1192–1333), political power was exercised by military households. The most sacred people were not necessarily the most powerful, and the most powerful were not necessarily the most sacred. Although these two concepts were obviously distinct, people could endorse them simultaneously. Once they did so, they could not help adding a third: the principle of reason. With the principle of reason added to the idea of reverence for imperial dignity and the idea of military rule, none of the three concepts was able to dominate. And since no single concept predominated, a spirit of freedom existed in the Japanese tradition.[77]

For Fukuzawa, this pluralistic tradition could be applied to modern times in the sense that

> civilization involves the coexistence of many philosophical perspectives. . . .[78] For example, Shinto and Buddhist positions are always at odds, yet if you listen to what each proclaims, both of them will sound plausible.[79]

This pluralistic view could also be applied to politics. Fukuzawa cited the example of "reformers" and "conservatives" in order to show that in spite of their different perspectives, both could make sound arguments.[80] Fukuzawa "extend[ed] this notion to future civilizations as well. For example, Shinto, Confucianism, Buddhism, and Christianity are frequently esteemed not only as institutions of the past but also as formative factors in present-day civilization."[81]

Japan's pluralistic tradition may have made the Japanese absorption of Western ideas during the Meiji period much easier,[82] because both the Japanese and Christian traditions are nonmonistic. For instance, matter and spirit are believed to be distinct in Christianity.[83]

Kang and Fukuzawa diverged from each other not only in terms of their positions on universalism and monism, but also on morality. Kang's viewpoint about human nature was in accordance with the Confucian notion that human nature is good.[84] In accordance with Mencius's remark that "benevolence overcomes cruelty just as water overcomes fire,"[85] Kang wrote, "[h]owever, if we cannot free the way of man from selfishness of having the family and private enterprise, and yet we desire to do away with competition, how can it be done?"[86]

Late Qing intellectuals as a whole were quite "preoccupied with the problem of how to create a world based on *ren,* or benevolence, which is the highest Confucian virtue. This preoccupation was basic to the vision of democracy that developed in China at the turn of the twentieth century. It was a vision according to which democratization would take selfishness out of history."[87]

In contrast, Fukuzawa criticized the Chinese tolerance of injustices performed by other ethnic groups against them, such as that by the Mongols and Manchu. He said that the Chinese were oppressed by other ethnicities and nations, but they still wanted "benevolent government." Japan should not learn from China.[88]

Fukuzawa believed that civilization required not only morality, but also intelligence,[89] a position similar to that of Plato, who insisted that wisdom and morality cannot be separated.[90] Fukuzawa's viewpoint was shared by most members of the Mei Roku Sha Society, who insisted that Japan should deny the Confucian moral tendency that stresses spiritual civilization over material civilization. This mindset was shared by most Japanese intellectuals during the Meiji era.[91]

Japanese moral relativism is reflected in the remarks by more recent leaders as well, such as Japan's post–World War II Prime Minister Shigeru Yoshida (1878–1967). He said that Japan should not trade with "beggar" countries in Southeast Asia. He also believed that the Korean War in which Chinese and American troops killed one another was "a gift from God" for Japan, because the war brought lucrative contracts for the Japanese industry.[92]

On the issue of morality, Lu Xun, the most influential Chinese literary critic in the first half of the twentieth century, was contrasted with Kita Ikki (1883–1937), the Japanese radical intellectual during the late Meiji period: Lu Xun's passion was to hate self (China), whereas Kita Ikki's passion was to hate others (Westerners).[93] *The True Story of Ar Q,* a major piece of Lu Xun's literary *oeuvre,* was representative of his cultural critique style. Ar Q, a comic-tragic character who was noted for his self-deception, was a personification of the average Chinese person. This self-loathing attitude in Chinese political culture continued through the 1980s. The TV documentary, *Yellow River Elegy (He shang),* is a typical example. For Kita Ikki, however, the Japanese should not have mercy on those who wish to conquer Japan.[94]

Kang and Fukuzawa also had varying ideas on the issue of populism versus elitism. Compared with Japan, premodern China had more equality, the root of populism. The social hierarchy in premodern Japan was more rigid than China.[95] Kang noted that China's aristocracy was abolished after the Qin (221–206 BCE) and Han (206 BCE–220 CE) dynasties, and believed that this was good for China's political modernization.[96] Most of China's leading intellectuals in the late Qing and early republican period endorsed this populist tradition.[97]

Fukuzawa believed, however, that the common people should not play a key role in their country's modernization. For him, the fundamental difference between the Chinese tradition and the Japanese tradition was that

> the Confucianists accept the overthrow of evil rulers by Tang (about seventeenth century B.C.) and Wu (about eleventh century B.C.) as correct, and the (Japanese) scholars of National Learning stress the unbroken lineage of the Japanese emperor.[98]

It was noted that Fukuzawa's "spirit of the times" as the moving force of history did not refer to the acts of the masses or the lower classes, as they possessed insufficient knowledge.[99] Although Fukuzawa took the position of the dissident, he criticized the "stupidity" of the common people. He argued that "foolish subjects"—who had prevented Japan from becoming modernized—should be punished.[100] During the Meiji period, the Japanese were noted for the saying, *kanson mimpi,* or "government praised, people despised."[101]

Fukuzawa also did not support the radical popular rights movement. He believed that such moves would be counterproductive in the sense that the government would feel itself obligated to resort to more despotic measures.[102] For Fukuzawa, there were three attitudes toward a despotic government: to compromise principle by yielding to it, with the result of no change; to rise up in rebellion, resulting in a despotic government replacing the previous one; and to live under tyrannical government while adhering to one's principles even at the cost of martyrdom. Fukuzawa advocated the third option.[103]

Japanese elitism versus Chinese populism was also reflected in different attitudes toward the two sources of modern democracy: that of Jean-Jacques Rousseau (1712–1778), characterized by equality, and that of John Stuart Mill (1806–1873) and Herbert Spencer (1820–1903), characterized by liberty. Most Japanese intellectuals during the Meiji era found Spencer's and Mill's writings more appealing than Rousseau's.[104] In contrast, most of the late Qing Chinese intellectuals tended toward Rousseau, instead of Mill and Spencer. Liang Qichao was one of the few who leaned toward the Millsian vision of democracy. But the more he leaned toward it, the more he lost influence.[105]

The Chinese had a particularly difficult time in accepting individualism and liberalism.[106] Liang Qichao (1873–1927) summarized Kang's philosophy by labeling it as socialism.[107] Sun Yet-sun also defined his philosophy, the so-called "Three Principles of the People," as socialism and communism.[108] He believed that the "Soviet," the form of government created by Vladimir Lenin in Russia, was the datong of Confucius.[109]

Differences in strategies and philosophies between the two reforms also had an impact on the academic temperaments of the two societies' intellectual communities. While Kang focused on abstract philosophical understandings of the universe, Fukuzawa stressed areas of knowledge that had pragmatic applications such as natural science disciplines. While Kang worried about concrete political issues of the reforms, as well as abstract issues such as the ultimate goal of humankind, Fukuzawa focused his attention mostly on concrete issues.

Fukuzawa said that

[l]earning in the broad sense can be divided into immaterial and material aspects. The former includes such subjects as ethics, theology and metaphysics; the latter, such subjects as astronomy, geography, physics and chemistry.

He insisted that the latter, which had been previously neglected, should receive more attention.[110] Fukuzawa popularized not only science and technology, but also relatively trivial matters such as personal demeanor[111] and how to make public speeches.[112]

Fukuzawa's predilections reflected the general attitude of the Japanese intellectuals of that time. For instance, the Mei Roku Sha Society, in which Fukuzawa was a leader, stressed moderation in politics and positivism in the philosophy of science.[113] During the Meiji period, utilitarianism and positivism were popular in Japan.[114] Positivism in modern times provided intellectual support to liberals, because it was not monistic.[115]

Kang's academic orientation was different. His works included philosophical treatises, such as *Datongshu;* policy advice, such as his appeals to the emperor; and an analysis of classical works, such as *Kong Zi Gaizhi Kao* (Study of the Confucian Reform). Natural sciences and such everyday matters such as how to make public speeches and appropriate personal demeanor received little attention from Kang.

In sum, the Meiji Restoration and the Late Qing Reform were prompted by similar structural problems, that is, the social structures of premodern Japan and premodern China were unable to meet the challenges posed by the Western incursions in particular and modernization in general. But the strategies taken by the leaders of these two countries were different. The cultural factor had an impact on the two countries' leaders, who ultimately adopted different strategies.

Chapter 4

Reforms within Communism: The Soviet Union

[A]side from Bukharin, who never held leadership in either the party or state, Khrushchev was the only significant reformer in Soviet history [before Gorbachev].

—David Nordlander[1]

Gorbachev was merely following in the footsteps of a greater man. . . . [H]is reforms would have been impossible without changes [that] brought in the glorious decade which preceded the stagnation period. . . . [I]n the final analysis, Gorbachev himself was a product of the Khrushchev Thaw.

—Sergei Roy[2]

Numerous studies are available on the Soviet reforms of the New Economic Policy (NEP) (1921–1928), the Thaw (1953–1964),[3] and the Gorbachev Reform (1985–1991). The logic of the Soviet reforms in particular[4] and the Russian reforms in general[5] have also been analyzed. However, to date studies that systematically compare the NEP and the Thaw do not exist, although their common traits have been widely noted. The current study attempts to fill this lacuna.

Alfred G. Meyer argued that "the conflicts over the NEP were the theme to which more recent debates [during the Khrushchev era] were variations. In the same sense, important elements of [the Khrushchev era] reform communism appeared in the work of Bukharin."[6] Stephen F. Cohen held that, aside from the Thaw, the NEP was the only significant reform before the Gorbachev Reform in Soviet history: "Soviet reformers [during the Khrushchev era] have revived many NEP economic ideas."[7] Fyodor Burlatsky pointed out that "Khrushchev represented a tendency within the party expressed by such dissimilar figures as Dzerzhinsky, Bukharin, Rykov, Rudzuntak and Kirov, who had advocated the development of the NEP and democratization."[8]

The traits of the Soviet reforms have even extended beyond the borders of the former Soviet Union. Meyer noted that "there are significant parallels between, say, Soviet Russia in the 1920s and Eastern Europe in the 1950s. Similar questions came into focus; similar attitudes and philosophies contended with each other; similar positions were taken; similar experiments made."[9]

The lack of systematic study of the logic of the Soviet reforms has resulted in the misunderstanding of not only the reformist leaders, but also the reforms themselves. For example, Bukharin is widely recognized as the main advocate for the NEP, although he enthusiastically endorsed War Communism during the Russian Civil War, which was the opposite of the NEP.[10] Khrushchev was acclaimed as a "great reformer,"[11] although immediately after Stalin's death, he initially acted as an obstacle to Georgy Malenkov's reforms.[12]

To add to the confusion, political leaders tended not to pay attention to the logic behind the reforms. For instance, the leaders of the Thaw hardly made any reference to the NEP.[13] Without realizing the similarities between the NEP and the Thaw, Khrushchev was condemning Bukharin, the NEP leader, as late as 1957.[14] It was not until he retired from the political arena that Khrushchev expressed the desire to rehabilitate Bukharin.[15] In his 580-page autobiography, Khrushchev did not mention Bukharin or the NEP.[16]

Following the general thesis of this book, this chapter argues that the NEP and the Thaw are structural responses to the problems of state socialism, which include low efficiency for government and low incentives for people. "State socialism," supposedly built on the theories of Karl Marx, was known in the West by its more common name, "communism."

The first section of this chapter holds that the NEP was a direct response to the failure of War Communism, while the Thaw was a direct response to the failure of Stalin's policies. The structural issues to be discussed include central planning, development priority, market, ownership of the means of production, and political control. In the second section, I discuss the fact that strategies adopted by reformers of the NEP and the Thaw are in the direction of retreating from communist ideals. The commonality of the two reforms suggests that it is possible to identify patterns of the reforms, because they are systemic adjustments to state socialism, which, as a system, also has patterns. Similar structural issues as discussed in the first section will be addressed again in the second section. In the third section, I discuss the reformers' theoretical justifications of the two reforms. Because ideology plays such an important role in the building and maintenance of state socialism, the reform strategies often go hand in hand with certain philosophical underpinnings and theoretical justifications. Key philosophical and theoretical issues to be addressed include the ontological issue of "social development stages," the methodological issue of "dialectics," and the "role of the state."

In the case of the NEP, I analyze the works of Nikolai Ivanovich Bukharin (1888–1938), a principal theoretician during the reform, as well as Vladimir Ilyich Lenin (1870–1924), the leader of the October Revolution. Bukharin became the editor of *Pravda,* the mouthpiece of the Bolsheviks in 1917, and joined the Politburo, the highest governing body of the party, in 1924. In 1928, Joseph Stalin (1879–1953) revoked the NEP policies and, in the following year, expelled Bukharin from the Politburo. Bukharin was executed in 1938 on trumped-up charges of attempting to overthrow the Soviet state.

For the Thaw, I analyze the works of Mikhail Suslov (1902–1982), Nikita Khrushchev (1894–1971), and Fyodor M. Burlatsky. Suslov was elected to the Secretariat of the Central Party Committee of the Communist Party of the Soviet Union (CPSU) in 1947, and was placed in charge of ideology. He was elected to the Presidium in 1952, but lost his position briefly after Stalin's death. Suslov was transferred to work in the department that deals with other communist parties throughout the world. In 1955, he entered the Presidium again, a position he held until his death in 1982. On the surface, Suslov, the Soviet ideology czar from 1955 to 1982, was the chief theoretician for the Thaw. But Suslov served under leaders of drastically different ideologies such as Joseph Stalin (1879–1953), Khrushchev, and Leonid Brezhnev (1906–1982).[17] Therefore, I analyze a collection of the writings and speeches by Suslov, Khrushchev, and Fyodor M. Burlatsky, one of Khrushchev's close advisers. Khrushchev was First Party Secretary of the CPSU from 1953, when Stalin died, to 1964, when he was removed from power.

Structure: Historical Background of the New Economic Policy (1921–1929) and the Thaw (1953–1964)

The historical backgrounds against which the NEP (1921–1929) and the Thaw (1953–1964) emerged were War Communism (1918–1921) and Stalinist rule (1928–1953), respectively.[18] Lenin established the basic structure of state socialism during War Communism, the policy adopted by the Bolsheviks during the Russian Civil War (1918–1921) that was fought between the newly established Bolshevik regime and the loosely allied anti-Bolshevik forces, or "whites." Scholars believe that as a model of social system rather than a series of historical contingencies,[19] War Communism was the Bolsheviks' first attempt at total control of society.[20]

Stalin made state socialism more comprehensive in 1936 when, with a new constitution, he claimed that socialism had been realized.[21] This followed the end of the NEP in 1928 when Stalin consolidated his power and returned to many policies adopted during the period of War Communism.[22] This system did not change much from 1936 to 1953 when Stalin died. The system, which was disrupted during World War II, was subsequently restored by Stalin after the war.[23] In the words of Natalia Pliskevitch, "the 1930s, 1940s and the first half of the 1950s were the classic period of the Soviet economic system."[24]

Both War Communism and the Stalinist regime share most of the ingredients of state socialism: central planning, an emphasis on heavy industry, the tendency against market forces, public ownership of the means of production, and one-party rule. For War Communism, central planning began immediately following the Bolshevik Revolution in October 1917. The Bolshevik government took control of all industries in Russia,[25] and by 1920, the framework for a planned centralized economy had been established.[26] In 1921, a cabinet-level office was created for central planning under the name of the State Planning Commission, also known as Gosplan.

For the Stalinist regime, central planning was applied at a larger scale at the start of the first Five-Year-Plan (FYP) in 1928 than that of War Communism. Gosplan put together proposals for the FYP based on guidelines established by the Politburo. It then coordinated production quotas with each of the ministries that controlled enterprises nationwide. The five-year term was chosen because the Russians believed that the cycle of good and poor harvests was five years. They also believed that it took five years to build and commission major new industrial enterprises.[27] In the later years of Stalin's regime, centralization was intensified. In 1950, the number of collective farms nationwide was reduced from 250,000 to 100,000, because smaller farms were merged into larger ones. The rationale at the time was that smaller collective farms were not as efficient as their larger counterparts.[28] All major decisions were made through the ministries.[29]

In terms of development priority, the Stalinist regime emphasized heavy industry that built infrastructure but neglected light industry and agriculture.[30] This was presumably done for the purpose of rapid industrialization. For instance, during the first FYP period (1928–1933), 85 percent of investments went to heavy industry.[31]

War Communism and Stalinist rule both opposed market forces. War Communism introduced a state monopoly of the grain trade and established the surplus-appropriation system, under which all surplus produced by the peasantry was to be acquired by the state at fixed prices in order to accumulate stores of grain for provisioning the army and the workers.[32] On August 30, 1918, money was eliminated as a means of exchange between state institutions.[33] On April 30, 1920, the year when the Russian Civil War ended, the government decreed that wages would be paid in goods instead of cash,[34] direct appropriation of foodstuffs without compensation to farmers, rations for workers, and a ban on trade.[35]

Similarly, according to Khrushchev, "[t]he principle of material incentives for workers in increasing the output of farm products was grossly violated" (i.e., the original objective of raising agricultural output as a means to compensate industrial workers was ignored).[36] In 1951, the regime intensified efforts to suppress private enterprise by proposing to reduce the size of privately held garden plots,[37] which members of the collective farms cultivated in their spare time for additional income.

Public ownership of the means of production also characterizes both War Communism and the Stalinist era. Policies opposed to private ownership began immediately following the Bolsheviks' seizure of power in 1917. In the words of Lenin,

> on the first day of the dictatorship of the proletariat, for instance, on October 26,[38] 1917, the private ownership of land was abolished without compensation for the big landowners—the big landowners were expropriated. Within the space of a few months, practically all the big capitalists, owners of mills and factories, joint-stock companies, banks, railways, and so forth, were also expropriated without compensation.[39]

Throughout the period of War Communism, 82 percent of land previously held by large-scale landowners was confiscated away by the peasants with the support of the Communist Party.[40] Nationalization of all large-scale industry was passed on June 28, 1918. By the end of 1918, a thousand large businesses had been nationalized. On November 29, 1920, nationalization was decreed for those employing more than five workers. By the end of

1920, 37,000 enterprises were nationalized.[41] In 1921, nationalized indus-tries employed 80 percent of the labor force in the cities.[42]

Similarly, public and collective ownership of the means of production continued through the Stalinist period. Most enterprises were owned and run by the state. Before the government imposed collectivization, only about 4 percent of the peasantry were collectivized. By 1936, 90 percent of peasants had been collectivized. The remainder worked on farms run by the state.[43] During the collectivization period, five to seven million rich peas-ants, or *kulaks,* had their farms and personal possessions confiscated.[44]

Tight political control by the party was another major characteristic of War Communism and the Stalinist era. Throughout the period of War Com-munism, economic policies were backed by oppressive politics. Universal labor service for all classes, including the bourgeoisie, was applied by force. The party was implementing the principle, "He who does not work, shall not eat."[45] For the male population, labor conscription was compulsory—all men from eighteen to forty-six years of age were forced to work and peo-ple with technical skills up to age sixty-five were also forced to work. Those who were engaged in commerce were subject to execution and prison.[46]

In the Stalinist era, the one-party monopoly was consolidated, and the opposition was further silenced through terror. For instance, of the 1,966 delegates to the Seventeenth Party Congress held in 1934, a total of 1,108 were arrested.[47] From 1937 to 1938, a total of 98 of 139 members and can-didates in the Central Committee of the Seventeenth Party Congress were arrested and shot. Rigid control of the Party continued throughout the Stal-inist era, as evidenced at the Nineteenth Party Congress in 1952.[48]

Both War Communism and Stalinist rule produced negative conse-quences, which prompted the NEP and the Thaw. Under War Communism, labor productivity dropped by about 22 percent between 1913 and 1919,[49] partly because forced labor was inefficient. Sometimes it took thirty men to do a job that four to five accomplished before the Civil War.[50] In agricul-ture, peasants lost incentives to work because everything they produced was taken away by the government.[51] As a result of these policies and the war, the standard of living plummeted. Half a loaf of bread cost a million rubles. Out of the fourteen to eighteen million who died, only 900,000 were killed at the front. The rest died of starvation and disease.[52]

Similarly, the Stalinist regime also generated numerous problems inher-ent in state socialism: the lack of efficiency because of a highly centralized economic structure, the loss of individual incentives that led to low pro-ductivity, and the people's resentment of oppressive politics. Khrushchev confessed, "It is painful to think that I, a worker, had lived in far better conditions under capitalism than the workers enjoyed under Soviet power."[53] Khrushchev also complained about low agricultural productivity. For instance, livestock numbers, except for hogs, were lower in 1953 than 1928, before collectivization.[54] As a result, Russians deeply resented Stalin's oppressive policies.[55] Indeed, as Fyodor Burlatsky remarked, "[T]he political pendulum had swung so far in the direction of an authoritarian regime and total control that it must inevitably have gathered enormous momentum to swing in the opposite direction."[56]

Political Strategies

The NEP was launched in March 1921 at the Tenth Party Congress and, by early 1922, its basic framework was complete.[57] In 1924, the reform suffered setbacks due to generalized resentment by workers toward the newly emergent uneven income distribution and Bolshevik officials' dissatisfaction for their loss of prestige.[58] From 1925 to 1928, the theoretical debate intensified with the central issue being whether to treat the NEP as a temporary retreat, as Lenin had originally intended, or as a development model, as Bukharin wanted. Although the NEP was successful[59]—for instance, by 1926–1927, state-run industries had reached prewar output levels,[60] in 1928, Stalin revoked NEP policies and started the first FYP.

The Thaw began immediately following Stalin's death in 1953 and went through roughly three stages. The first stage, which set the Thaw in motion, took place from 1953 to 1956, when Khrushchev condemned Stalin at the Twentieth Party Congress. The second stage was from 1956 to 1961, when the Twenty-Second Congress convened and effected a maturation of the economic reforms and the start of political reforms. The third stage was from 1961 to 1964 during which the reformers tried to turn the Thaw into a model of development but the conservatives eventually overwhelmed the reformers and ousted Khrushchev.

As systemic adjustments to state socialism rather than random historical contingencies, the NEP and the Thaw shared certain characteristics. Both reflected decentralization versus central planning, emphasized material incentives versus the communist anti-individualist attitude in values, stressed consumer goods versus the concentration on heavy industry in development priorities, and both placed an emphasis on relaxation of the political atmosphere versus tight controls.

On decentralization of power, the NEP gave specialists in factories more autonomy vis-à-vis party supervision.[61] The NEP also allowed small enterprises of ten to twenty workers to be owned and managed by private individuals or collectives, although major industries, including banking, railways, mines, and large enterprises remained under the control of the central government. Small nationalized enterprises could be leased and managed by the private sector. By September 1, 1922, of a total 7,100 enterprises, employing 68,000 workers, had been leased to cooperatives or to former owners.[62] For leaders who promoted this policy, in the long run, privately run enterprises would eventually turn into the socialist system, because collectively run enterprises were more efficient in market competition.[63]

During the Thaw, decentralization was applied comprehensively to the bureaucracy, agriculture, and industry. In 1957, more than one hundred Councils of the National Economy were established to replace most of the central economic ministries. The main exception to this move was ministries involved in defense production.[64] Parallel to decentralization was bureaucratic downsizing. In the first four years after Stalin's death, the bureaucracy was considerably reduced in size.[65] The number of ministries dropped from seventy to thirty-four; the number of deputy prime ministers from twelve to four; and the number of decrees promulgated by the central government fell from about seventy to forty a year.[66]

In agriculture, Khrushchev decentralized the power of the government in 1958 by abolishing the Machine and Tractor Stations (MTS), which had been a cornerstone of Soviet agriculture since 1927. MTS plowed the fields, harvested the crops, and provided organizational and technical support to farmers in collectives. Both the director and deputy director were state employees. Because of its inefficiency, an attempt was made to abolish the MTS in 1952, but Stalin fought back, charging that such an action would be "taking a retrograde step and attempting to turn back the wheel of history."[67]

In industry, about 11,000 enterprises were transferred from central to lower-level government control from 1953 to 1957. In May 1955, many major planning and financial decisions were transferred from Moscow to republic-level government entities. Factories administered by twelve central government ministries were placed under the leadership of republic governments in May 1956.[68] According to Khrushchev,

[S]hifting the center of gravity of industrial management to the areas in which industry is located will make it possible to manage the economy in a more concrete and practical manner, to give even greater scope to the initiative of the masses and to increase the role and responsibility of the local agencies. Questions pertaining to the work of industry and construction will no longer be decided by the ministries and chief administration but directly on the spot, in the economic regions.[69]

Besides decentralization, another strategy of both the NEP and the Thaw was that incentives were given more attention. The Bolsheviks announced at the Tenth Party Congress in 1921 that under the NEP the substitution of in-kind taxation for the surplus-appropriation system and the policy that produce over and above the amount of the tax was to be at the disposal of the peasants, who could sell these surpluses.[70] While average peasants paid 10 percent as a tax to the state, the poor were exempt.[71] The government also granted the peasants' request to produce crops of their own choosing, although land was still owned by the state. In the words of Bukharin, "How will we be able to draw [the peasant] into our socialist organization? We will provide him with material incentives as a small property-owner."[72] According to Lenin, "under [the] NEP we made a concession to the peasant as a merchant and to the principle of private trade."[73]

Similarly, favorable tax policies toward the peasants were also adopted during the Thaw period. Peasants were allowed greater freedom in the disposition of their small garden plots. Although Georgy Malenkov, who became the leader of the Soviet Union immediately following Stalin's death in 1953, was forced to resign in February 1955, the government did not blame him for his agricultural taxation policy. This was a signal to the peasants that the concessions made by the government with regard to incentives would continue.[74] Khrushchev was given credit for emphasizing incentives by the scholar Seigei Roy: "[T]he first words that Khrushchev uttered for all to hear on taking the helm of the state were about 'material incentives'—words that sounded like ideological heresy, words that were anathema to Stalinism."[75] Khrushchev gave himself credit for this as well:

> We changed [i.e., raised] procurement prices for potatoes and vegetables. Later we went on to abolish the system of forced deliveries whereby peasants had to turn over to the state a certain portion of the meat, eggs, and other goods they produced on their private plots.[76]

Related to the issue of incentives, both the NEP and the Thaw switched the development priority from heavy industry to light industry, a departure from the state socialism model that tended to favor heavy industry at the expense of light industry. During the NEP period, the so-called Left faction within the Party, represented by Leon Trotsky (1879–1940), called for accelerated industrialization by squeezing the peasants as much as possible, putting an end to the NEP, moving toward a planned economy,[77] and favoring heavy industry.[78] The Right faction, represented by Bukharin, favored light industry, agriculture, and consumer goods.[79] The NEP followed the Right faction's path.

During the Thaw, Malenkov announced in the autumn of 1953 a similar policy that consumer products would be given more attention, instead of focusing almost exclusively on heavy industry.[80] This policy continued under Khrushchev, as revealed in his report to the Twenty-Second Party Congress:

> In 1929–40, in industry, the average annual rates of acceleration in the production of means of production exceeded the rates of accretion in the production of articles of consumption by nearly seventy percent, whereas in 1961–1980, the gap between them will be approximately twenty percent.[81]

In addition to the policies of decentralization, incentives, and the development priority switch from heavy industry to light industry, as discussed previously, another strategy used by the NEP and the Thaw was that the authorities allowed a certain amount of political relaxation. Although the NEP was largely an economic reform, politics and economics could not be separated. For Burlatsky, a former adviser to Khrushchev, a basic ingredient of the NEP was democracy, particularly in the workplace.[82] Under the state socialist system, the workers' participation in workplace management often serves as an effective check on the party's monopoly of power in industry.

In addition, apolitical art and literature were tolerated. During the 1921–1923 period, the cultural atmosphere was particularly lively and pluralistic.[83] This practice contradicted communist ideology, which holds that the arts and literature represent class interests; the so-called "apolitical" arts and literature actually represent bourgeoisie.

Political changes during the Thaw were even more profound. In 1955, after eliminating his political competition, Khrushchev complained,

> For three years, we proved to be unable to break with the past and find the courage and resoluteness to raise the curtain and see what had been hidden behind it—the arrests, the trials, the lawlessness, the shootings

and all the other things that had been taking place in our country under Stalin's dictatorship.[84]

Consequently, there was indeed a more relaxed political atmosphere in the Soviet society. In the words of Russian scholar V. Zhuravlyov,

> Liberalization of the administrative-criminal policy radically changed Soviet society, relieving it of its more somber overtones and imparting to it a relatively civilized aspect. Having denounced the "personality cult," Stalin's heir "remembered" that the man in the street had a personality too. For the first time after many years of Stalin's repressions, the individual was made the center of administrative and security policies.[85]

Lavrentij Beriya (1899–1953), a longtime security chief under Stalin, proposed that all political prisoners be freed immediately after Stalin's death.[86] Accordingly, seven to eight million prisoners were released and another five to six million people who had been imprisoned on trumped-up charges were posthumously rehabilitated during the period of 1956–1957.[87]

In response to this relaxed atmosphere, the so-called "decadent lifestyle" such as dancing and rock-and-roll also became prevalent in Soviet society.[88] Intellectuals in unofficial circles also tried to revive the supposedly ideologically neutral empiricism.[89] This was a departure from orthodox Marxism, which asserted that scientific endeavors were not neutral.[90] For those Marxists, Marxism as a science was the weapon of the proletariat.[91]

To further liberalize Soviet society, at the Twenty-First Party Congress, Khrushchev called for a diminished role of formal state institutions and transferring certain functions such as those carried out by ministries to trade unions, women's organizations, and other nongovernmental organizations.[92] He also tried to limit the tenure of party functionaries by setting office term limits.[93] He complained about the fact that the Party Congress delegates were all hand picked, not elected: "But unfortunately, this practice, strictly speaking, remains today. The elections to the Twentieth Congress took place in this way. This is a very distorted form of democracy. These methods are incorrect and intolerable."[94]

Toward the end of the Thaw, theoreticians at the top even started to consider adopting policies that were similar to those in Western liberal democracies. For instance, in preparing for the draft of a new Soviet constitution in 1964, Burlatsky wrote a memorandum that included such principles as rule of law, a jury system, and separation of powers. Multiple candidates would stand for elections for seats in the Soviets, and the head of state would also be elected directly by the people. Important decisions would be made by the organs of state power, not by the Party. According to Burlatsky, "On the whole, Khrushchev approved of our proposals." Khrushchev said jokingly, "[T]here are lads here who propose to remove me from the post of chairman of the Council of Ministers. Well, we'll have to think about that and see if they are right."[95]

However, the political relaxation that paralleled economic reform was often a byproduct, and not a desirable result, since most Soviet leaders actually intended that the state socialist system be sustained rather than transformed. Thus, this relaxation was eventually limited. Leaders such as Bukharin made it clear that the economic retreat did not mean that there would be a political one.[96] Lenin said in 1922,

> [F]or a year we have been retreating. In the name of the party we must now call a halt. The purpose pursued by the retreat has been achieved. This period is drawing, or has drawn, to a close. Now, our purpose is different—to regroup our forces.[97]

The temporary nature of the NEP was also demonstrated by the fact that Lenin's writings in his later years did not deviate from his earlier views in the sense that "[n]o critique of War Communism or deepening of NEP can be extracted from these writings."[98]

Similarly, for the Thaw, the ideological foundation of state socialism was not to be challenged. For Khrushchev, "[t]here will be no peaceful coexistence in ideology."[99] The Central Party Committee condemned certain educational institutions that took advantage of the relaxed political atmosphere during the Thaw to stress academics, instead of communist indoctrination.[100]

Khrushchev also ensured that the media was firmly under the party's control. On May 13, 1957, he charged that

> [t]hese comrades have begun to forget that the press is our chief ideological weapon. It is called up to rout the enemies of the working class, the enemies of the working people. . . . There is a sharp conflict in the world today between two ideologies, the socialist and the bourgeois, and in this conflict there can be no neutrals.[101]

In response to the charge that under Soviet rule, individual freedom was in jeopardy, an official theoretician retorted that in capitalist society, the factory owners had the freedom to exploit the workers and the working class was not free. In addition, freedom was not absolute in any society. Criminals and those who were mentally ill should not be granted freedom.[102]

However, the Soviet leaders' concerns for deviant tendencies were as much ideological as political. In his retirement, Khrushchev said that he regretted that Boris Pasternak's *Doctor Zhivago* was banned, and revealed that the real reason for censoring Ehrenburg's *The Thaw* was that,

> We were scared—really scared. We were afraid that the Thaw might unleash a flood, which we wouldn't be able to control and which could drown us. How could it drown us? It could have overflowed the banks of the Soviet riverbed and formed a tidal wave which would have washed away all the barriers and retaining walls of our society.[103]

Thus, some scholars attributed the failure of the Soviet reforms to the leaders' lack of firm commitment. In the words of American scholar and government official Zbigniew Brzezinski, the leaders of the reform movement adopted these reforms

> usually only in response to social-economic pressures or political unrest, rarely actually initiating them. In the event of occasional reform drives, the usual pattern was one of temporary burst of initiative, followed by lengthier relapses into conservative passivity.[104]

Philosophical Underpinnings

The leaders of both the NEP and the Thaw justified their reformist strategies by reinterpreting Marxist philosophy grounded in the so-called historical materialism and dialectical materialism. The theoretical debates for both reforms centered on the interrelated Marxist concepts of "stage of social development," "dialectics," and "the role of the state."

This reinterpretation of historical materialism was essential, because the theory explains the very purpose of communism as an ideology.[105] In the words of Bukharin, "For the theory of historical materialism has a definite place, it is not political economy, nor is it history; it is the general theory of society and the laws of its evolution, i.e., sociology."[106] According to historical materialism, the evolution of society, independent of human will, was divided into "stages" that were driven by the interaction between the productive forces and relations of production.[107] These stages began with the hunter-gatherer mode of production, followed by slave, feudal, capitalist, (state) socialist, and communist modes.[108] Each stage could be further divided. For instance, state socialism could be divided into primary and mature stages.[109]

Defending the position that these stages could not be skipped over, Bukharin argued that "[n]o new structure can be born before it has become an objective necessity."[110] This determinist interpretation of historical materialism would by necessity lead to evolutionary politics.[111] A "determinist" such as Bukharin[112] tried to justify the capitalist-oriented NEP reform policies by arguing that War Communism was an error committed by the party, because it attempted to skip the stage of a fully developed capitalist society.[113] For Bukharin, Russia needed to develop capitalism first and then move to the next stage of state socialism as historical materialism dictated. By skipping the stage of capitalism, War Communism was doomed to failure because backward Russia at the beginning of the twentieth century was not developed enough to enter into the stage of state socialism. Therefore, the NEP was needed to make up the missing lessons of capitalist development by reversing state socialism toward quasi-capitalism.

At the time of the Thaw, those opposed to reform also used the stage theory to argue that Soviet society was not as "advanced" as the reformers believed; thus the reformers had committed the error of being "voluntaristic and subjectivist."[114] In the view of Suslov, reformers such as Khrushchev mistakenly assumed that the Soviet Union in the early 1960s had passed the stage of state socialism and had almost entered the next stage of communist society. He said, "Marx and Lenin teach us that communism does not appear suddenly, but comes into existence, matures, develops, passes in its development through definite stages or phases."[115]

However, the theoreticians during the Thaw period were not as sophisticated as Lenin and Bukharin. For instance, Suslov justified abolishing the MTS by resorting to the Marxist law of the correspondence between productive forces and relations of production, which was grounded in historical materialism.[116] However, according to Marxist doctrine, the farms owned by collectives belonged to primary-stage socialism, while the MTS, owned by the state, belonged to mature-stage socialism. In other words, by abolishing MTS, the Soviet Union was falling from mature- to primary-stage socialism. Thus, history regressed, a situation that contradicted historical materialism. Therefore, Suslov recognized the "practical" value of reorganizing the MTS, not its "theoretical" value.[117] The "theoretical difficulties" of the reform policies were acknowledged by Suslov himself.[118]

The second Marxist concept adopted during the NEP and the Thaw to justify reformist policies was the so-called "dialectics," which meant different things to different people.[119] Lenin used "dialectics" to argue that there was nothing that distinguished "the contingent" and "the necessary" in an absolute way.[120] Unlike Bukharin, who insisted that Russia needed by necessity to enter into capitalism and then move to socialism,[121] Lenin had the flexibility to justify a variety of political and economic strategies during the NEP without having to worry too much about whether Russian society was in a socialist or capitalist stage, or whether the authorities adopted the reform policies as a matter of contingency or as a matter of principle.[122]

Although Bukharin disagreed with Lenin as to what "dialectics" meant, he was also able to justify reform policies by reinterpreting them. For Bukharin, the so-called postulate of equilibrium seemed to equal Marxist "dialectics."[123] Equilibrium is supposed to be a general method to understand human society.[124] It exists between productive forces and relations of production, between industry and agriculture, between light industry and heavy industry, and between politics and economics.[125]

Justifying the reformist policies to encourage material incentives, Bukharin argued that although in principle production was more important than consumption, under certain circumstances, consumption should be given priority, because if consumption was too low, and consequently the peasants had no money to purchase industrial products, production would suffer. Therefore, it was necessary for the government to institute favorable policies for the peasants to increase their purchasing power.[126]

Bukharin's method of equilibrium was also used to justify the switch from heavy industry to light industry in terms of development priorities. He argued that it was incorrect to emphasize heavy industry at the expense of light industry. Although heavy industry was the foundation of the country's economy, light industry's turnover was a lot faster, and these funds could be used to aid the further development of heavy industry.[127]

During the Thaw, theoretical debates were not innovative, in contrast to those surrounding the NEP. During the Thaw, leaders either did not take theories seriously, like Khrushchev, or treated theories as dogma, like Suslov. Khrushchev often adopted a pragmatic approach toward Marxism to justify whatever strategies he adopted. Khrushchev argued on May 13, 1957, "The theory of Marxism-Leninism is not a dogma, but a guide to practical revolutionary action."[128] As an example, Khrushchev used common sense instead of "dialectics" to justify his policy to encourage incentives:

Pretending to be theoreticians, these sorry scholars [Stalinists] cannot understand the important Marxist truth that people must first of all eat, drink, have homes and clothe themselves before they are in a position to engage in politics, science and art.[129]

Conservatives such as Suslov disagreed with Khrushchev by saying that Marxism-Leninism could only be enriched, not created.[130] But Suslov's theories were not innovative. For the most part, his remarks were simply reiterations of Soviet textbooks, especially *The History of the Communist Party of the Soviet Union (Bolsheviks),*[131] which was the "Bible" of the Stalinist regime.

Khrushchev sometimes clashed with Suslov who charged that Khrushchev had corrupted Marxism-Leninism.[132] Regarding Emmanuil Kazakevich's book, *The Blue Notebook,* Khrushchev wanted to publish it; Suslov was the only one against it. Similarly, in response to Khrushchev who wanted to publish Alexander Solzhenitsyn's book, *One Day in the Life of Ivan Denisovich,* Suslov said, "How will the people perceive this? How will the people understand?"[133]

The lack of theoretical sophistication by the post-Stalin leaders was partly due to the fact that Khrushchev's generation, who were mostly peasants cum workers, was different from Lenin's, many of whom were sophisticated intellectuals. This situation had an impact on Soviet politics even during the Stalinist era. Stalin defeated the opposition during the NEP not only because of his political skills at the top but also because the new recruits into the Party during the Russian Civil War, who were mostly workers and peasants, stood by Stalin, rather than the intellectuals like Trotsky, Kamenev, Zinovyev, or Bukharin. As the son of a peasant, Khrushchev said later that he himself did not understand the debate between the Left, such as Trotsky, who was opposed to further reforms and the Right, such as Bukharin, who advocated deepening reforms. The theoretical debates were too complicated for Khrushchev and others of his generation. But Khrushchev actively fought Bukharin's opposition based on class interests rather than an intellectual understanding of the issues.[134]

The irony of the Thaw is that although theory building during the entire Khrushchev era was poor, the regime put a heavy emphasis on the ideological indoctrination of the population. For Khrushchev,

the molding of the new man is influenced not only by the educational work of the party, the Soviet state, the trade unions and the Young Communist League, but by the entire pattern of society's life. . . . All economic, social, political, and legal levers must be used to develop people's Communist consciousness.[135]

In addition to the Marxist concepts of "social development stage," and "dialectics," a third one that was used to justify reformist policies was "the role of the state," which was grounded in historical materialism. For Bukharin, capitalism in the twentieth century was different from that of Adam Smith's (1723–1790) lifetime, with one key distinction being the role played by the state. Instead of being an impartial "judge" for free market competition, as was the case in Adam Smith's time, the state had taken on greater responsibilities in the early twentieth century, such as the organization of the economy. Therefore, the state in contemporary times represented the interests of the dominant class.[136]

Bukharin argued that as long as the state power was in the hands of the Communist Party, a certain amount of capitalism would not hurt the interest of the proletariat, because the communists could use the state power to protect their interests against the exploitation of the bourgeoisie.[137] He said that "under the state power of the proletariat and upon proletarian nationalizing of production, the process of the creation of surplus value, as a specific category of bourgeois society, ceases."[138]

Bukharin held that although the "new rich" under the NEP were bourgeoisie, they should not be destroyed, but be used and eventually beaten by state-owned enterprises.[139] He reasoned that the state would incorporate small producers into socialism, since the increased productive forces would adapt to a higher level of relations of production, that is, socialism.[140] This was also true for the peasantry. Bukharin remarked,

> [T]his [NEP policy] isn't frightening at all, because in the final analysis, on the basis of this very same economic growth, the peasant will be moved along the path of our transformation of both himself and his enterprise into a particle of our general state socialist system—just as he grows into capitalist relations under a capitalist regime.[141]

To further dilute the class consciousness of society, Bukharin saw a more pluralistic society, a vision distinct from the ultraleftist approach that divided society rigidly into two antagonistic classes, the proletariat and the bourgeoisie. He remarked,

The basic powers and basic forms of the common economy are capitalism, small-scale production of commodities, communism. The basic powers are: bourgeoisie, petit bourgeoisie (especially the peasantry), and proletariat.[142]

Bukharin's words were consistent with Lenin's viewpoint.[143]

The concept of the state was also at the center of theoretical debates for the Thaw. The reformists' logic was that since classes no longer existed in the Soviet Union in the early 1960s, the state did not have to worry about one class oppressing the other. In other words, the Soviet productive forces were advanced enough in the 1960s to replace "dictatorship of the proletariat" with "state of the whole people," that is, to move from primary-stage socialism to mature-stage socialism, which was closer to communist society.[144] According to Burlatsky, this theory was "the biggest contribution made after Lenin to the theory of the state."[145]

Burlatsky summarized this theory of the "state of the whole people" as follows: (1) The Soviet state had become an instrument of the will of the whole people instead of representing the will of the proletariat. (2) The functions of the Soviet state included the building of socialism and developing the economy, education, and culture. (3) The state relied on persuasion for governance instead of force against a class, although coercion was still used against criminals. (4) Institutionally, the whole people got more and more actively involved in running the state, unlike in the early days when only a tiny proportion of the population was involved in politics.[146]

This chapter shows that the NEP and the Thaw had similar historical backgrounds, political strategies adopted by reformers, and philosophical and theoretical justifications used by reformers. As discussed in Chapter 6, the Gorbachev Reforms by and large followed the pattern of the earlier Soviet reforms. In the setting of Russian culture, the reforms tended to go in the opposite direction of communist ideals: various degrees of decentralization in institutions, market relations and private ownership in economics, individualism in terms of values, and pluralism in politics.

Chapter 5

Reforms within Communism: China

During his years in power, Mao Zedong initiated three policies which could be described as radical departures from Soviet and Chinese Communist practice: the Hundred Flowers of 1956–1957, the Great Leap Forward of 1958–1960, and the Cultural Revolution of 1966–1976.

—Roderick MacFarquhar[1]

Never before has a nation so industrially backward and with so large and poor a population attempted so strenuously to acquire the military strength and stature of a major world power.

—U.S. Central Intelligence Agency[2]

The origins of the Great Leap Forward (GLF) and the Cultural Revolution (CR) have always been a source of controversy among scholars. For the GLF, contributing political factors cited included China's underdeveloped institutions that were unable to prevent leaders' errors;[3] the initial success of the People's Republic of China, which led to people's blind confidence in the Chinese Communist Party (CCP);[4] the communist experience of mass mobilization during World War II;[5] the international environment, including the containment policy by the Western bloc against China;[6] and the humiliations suffered by the Chinese in modern times that led to people's impatience for modernization.[7]

Economic factors for the GLF included the problems produced by China's first Five-Year Plan (FYP) (1953–1957), modeled after Joseph Stalin's development strategy;[8] the lack of scientific knowledge by China's leaders, who were mostly former peasants or professional revolutionaries;[9] Mao Ze-dong's lack of experience in running the country's economy;[10] and China's poverty, which fueled people's impatience for rapid social change.[11]

Cultural factors contributing to the GLF included China's cultural traditions, such as the datong ideal and the peasant rebellions' egalitarianism,[12] and the persistence of the petit bourgeois mentality of those who wanted to change things overnight.[13]

Regarding the origins of the CR, although scholars have noted ideological, personality, political, and international factors, they have not focused on economic ones. One major issue is whether it was a power struggle or an ideological one.[14] Scholars such as Yan Jiaqi believe that Mao started the CR to solidify his power,[15] while others like Hong Yung Lee believe that it was more of an ideological struggle between Mao's radical leftist line and Liu Shaoqi's moderate one.[16] Mao's personal role in the CR has also been emphasized. The U.S. Central Intelligence Agency believed during the CR period that China's policies would become moderate if Mao died suddenly,[17] a view that was shared by some scholars.[18]

Scholars from mainland China cited at least three factors for the CR. First was a perceived lack of control by true believers of Marxism. Mao believed that one-third of the rural population was outside the influence of Marxists. In factories, the majority of the leadership was not Marxist. Finally, schools were monopolized by bourgeoisie intellectuals, and most people in the arts and letters were not true believers of communism. Second was one-man rule of the CCP. Party members did not challenge Mao's judgment, even when they believed he was wrong. The third major factor was the international environment, which included China's split with Khrushchev and its conflicts with the United States.[19]

In this chapter, I focus on the ideological and cultural dimensions of the GLF and the CR, arguing that the two Maoist reforms were structural adjustments to the communist system. The direction of these reforms was heavily influenced by China's cultural traditions. Although the parallels between the GLF and CR have been noted,[20] no systematic, parallel comparative study of these reforms has been done.

Thus, the current study deemphasizes the role played by individuals. For instance, Mao was not the only leader in China who disagreed with Nikita Khrushchev on the way he treated Joseph Stalin. Actually, upon learning of Khrushchev's Secret Report in 1956 against Stalin, Deng Xiaoping showed his resentment toward Khrushchev even before he reported to Mao and other top Chinese leaders.[21] Regarding the GLF, Deng recalled many years later that everybody was "hot-headed" at the time, not just Mao.[22] Utopianism was on everyone's mind. On June 30, 1958, Liu Shaoqi, who later became president of the People's Republic of China, said to the editors of *Beijing ribao,* the official newspaper in Beijing, that "we should now see whether it is feasible to establish the basic-level organizations of communist society."[23] Regarding the origins of the CR, Mao was not alone in believing that the "class enemy" was inside the party. Actually, it was Wang Guangmei, Liu's wife, who first brought up the idea that representatives of the bourgeoisie were in the Central Party Committee, a notion that was almost surely endorsed by Liu at the time.[24]

In addition, in the course of researching this parallel comparative study, the limitations of certain existing studies were revealed. For instance, if it is true that the two reforms shared much in common in political strategies and philosophical underpinnings, then some of the previously presented interpretations about the origins of the GLF that focused on the immediate historical backgrounds lose credibility because the historical circumstances in which the GLF and CR both emerged were drastically different. These incomplete interpretations included the professional backgrounds of CCP members[25] and the Chinese people's initial enthusiasm for communism after 1949.[26]

Finally, this study highlights the role played by the official theoretician Chen Boda in the two reforms.[27] As Mao Zedong's political secretary for thirty-one years before he fell from power in 1970, Chen personified the Maoist reforms of the GLF, including the Hundred Flowers, the People's Commune,[28] and the CR. Chen was born in Huian, Fujian Province, in 1904. He joined the CCP in 1927 and then studied in Moscow for three years. When he returned to China, Chen first taught at Zhongguo University in Beijing. In 1937, with the pending Japanese invasion, he moved to Yanan. In 1945, at the Seventh Party Congress, among the 77 members and candidate members of the CCP Central Committee, Chen was the only theory specialist.[29]

After 1949, Chen Boda not only invented many Maoist slogans, but also theorized them. These slogans include, "Let a Hundred Flowers Blossom, Let a Hundred Schools of Thought Contend,"[30] "People's Commune,"[31] and "the Great Leap Forward."[32] As the head of the Great Cultural Revolution Leadership Group, Chen played an even more important role during the CR. Mao recommended Chen for the position. The three most important documents of the movement came from Chen: the *Renmin ribao* editorial, "*Heng sao yiqie niu, gui, she, shen*" ("Wipe out all enemies"), published on June 1, 1966, in which he asserted the need for the CR; "Wu yao liu tongzhi" (the May 16 announcement), which comprised theoretical guideline of the CR; and the so-called "Sixteen Items" (The Resolution of the CCP Central Committee on Cultural Revolution) published on August 9, 1966.[33]

The concept of the "two of lines struggle" was first raised by Chen.[34] So was the rhetoric of naming the February 1967 veteran cadres' counterattack on the CR, "er yue ni liu" (the February Counter-Trend).[35] During the CR, Zhang Chunqiao, a leftist radical from Shanghai, wanted to establish the so-called Shanghai Commune, modeled after the Paris Commune of 1871. This was also Chen Boda's idea.[36] Chen was put under house arrest on October 18, 1970, for supporting Lin Biao against Mao, and on September 13, 1971, he was thrown into prison.[37]

The format of this chapter parallels that of Chapter 4. Key structural concepts examined in the first two sections include centralization, development priority of heavy industry versus light industry, accumulation versus consumption, market forces, collectivization, and political control. In the first section, I discuss the Stalinist model of the first five-year plan (FYP) and the Khrushchev model formulated at the Eighth Party Congress in 1956 that was put into practice during the so-called 1961–1965 "adjustment period." Next, the Maoist GLF and CR model is examined in the second section by focusing on similar structural issues discussed previously. Key theoretical and philosophical concepts, including stage theory, dialectics, and state theory, following the format of Chapter 4, are examined in the third section.

Structure: Historical Background of the Great Leap Forward (1958–1960) and the Cultural Revolution (1966–1976)

The Chinese communist experience differs from the Soviet one in certain crucial areas. First, while two Soviet communist models have been identified—the Stalinist model and the reform model of New Economic Policy (NEP) and the Thaw—at least three models have been identified in Maoist China: (1) the Stalinist model, which is largely reflected in the First FYP (1953–1957) and collectivization; (2) the Khrushchev model formulated at the Eighth Party Congress in 1956, which was put into practice from 1961 to 1965 after the failure of the GLF; (3) and the Maoist model of the GLF and CR.

Among the three models, the Maoist one was dominant during the entire period of Mao Zedong's rule. For instance, although the CR emerged against the background of the "adjustment policy" of 1961–1965 that contained elements of the Khrushchev model, Khrushchevism was never as influential as the Maoist and Stalinist models. That's why Roderick MacFarquhar believed that Maoist China never really adopted a "Khrushchev model" because the policy of the Eighth Party Congress only stayed on paper in 1956, and the "adjustment policy" of 1961–1965 was not that different from the Stalinist model of the first FYP.[38]

Even when China practiced the Stalinist model in economics, the politics were different. For instance, the Hundred Flowers in 1956, a departure from the Stalinist model, occurred during the first FYP period (1953–1957) of Stalinism. The Chinese were more concerned than the Soviets about the so-called "bureaucratism" problem, which also triggered popular protests against the communist government in Hungary in 1956. "Bureaucratism" largely referred to the cadres' increasing loss of touch with the masses and the waning of their revolutionary zeal.[39] In May 1957, the Central Committee repeatedly issued instructions accusing certain Party members of having "anti-people tendencies."[40] The waning of revolutionary enthusiasm occurred not only within the party, but also in society.[41]

Similarly, when China practiced the Khrushchev model in economics during the "adjustment period" of 1961–1965, the politics were once again different. Mao at that time believed that many leaders were not true communists, and thus the CR was necessary.

The dominance of the Maoist model during the entire period of Mao's rule from 1949 to 1976 was also reflected in China's economic policy, which stressed the collective good at the expense of the individual. For instance, during this entire period, China was less developed than the Soviet Union and other Eastern European communist countries in the areas of labor force mobility, enterprise autonomy, and control of the surplus produced by the People's Communes.[42] Maoist China (with the exception of the first FYP and the "adjustment period" of 1961–1965) also stressed capital investment at the expense of consumption. From the end of the first FYP in 1957 through 1976 when Mao died, the salary for the average worker was increased only once. Low consumption also led to a seller's market in the sense that demand was always greater than supply.[43]

In addition, while the Soviet reforms emerged largely from socioeconomic crisis, that is, the difficulties of War Communism and Stalinist rule, the Maoist reforms were prompted largely by political crises, albeit real or perceived. In the first few years after 1949, especially during the first FYP period, the Chinese economy was stable and growing. During that period, Chinese industrial output increased by 10.9 percent per year, according to official sources.[44] The U.S. Central Intelligence Agency's estimate of China's annual industrial growth was as high as 16 percent during the first FYP period, which compared favorably with that of the Soviet Union (1928–1932).[45] From 1949 to 1957, China's average annual growth in agriculture was 8.5 percent.[46]

Similarly, 1965, when the CR emerged, had been the best year since 1949, according to Kang Shien, a former petroleum industry minister.[47] Apparently, Kang was referring to China's socioeconomic situation at the time. Favorable socioeconomic conditions were precisely the reason for Mao's over-estimation of political crisis at the time, which ultimately led to the CR.

Thus, it was not surprising that entirely different events were occurring in China and the Soviet Union in 1958: While China bombed Jinmen and Mazu,[48] Khrushchev was speaking about the peaceful coexistence between socialist and capitalist countries; while Mao reflected on the intensity of class struggle at the Chengdu Conference on April 1–9, 1958,[49] Khrushchev was talking about "the state of the whole people" that deemphasized class struggle; while the GLF and the People's Communes left individuals with even less freedom than the Stalinist model of the first FYP, Khrushchev was letting his people have more freedom and material incentives than Stalin had.[50] Not surprisingly, both Bukharin and Khrushchev were the main targets of criticism by Mao during the CR. For instance, the official media sources *Hong qi* and *Renmin ribao*[51] in their joint editorial on May 18, 1967 condemned Bukharin.[52] Liu Shaoqi was described by Chen and Mao as "China's Khrushchev."[53]

The Stalinist Model

China adopted the Stalinist model of development soon after the end of the Korean War (1950–1953). In December 1953, the Propaganda Department of the CCP Central Committee claimed that "the path that USSR traveled in the past is the example for us today."[54] China's first FYP was designed with the assistance of Soviet experts.[55] In many ways, the Chinese went further than the Soviets in following the Stalinist model in terms of their haste for industrialization and collectivization, an emphasis on heavy industry at the expense of light industry and agriculture, centralized control at the expense of local autonomy, and high levels of capital accumulation at the expense of consumption.

On September 3, 1952, Stalin told Zhou Enlai that China's plan to achieve a 20-percent annual increase in industry was excessive.[56] In the Soviet

Union, collectivization (1929–1943) and agricultural mechanization (1929–1932) took place more or less simultaneously, while in China, mechanization followed collectivization. That is to say, China's political and economic reform preceded technological development.[57] This was the reverse of the late Qing reform, in which efforts for technological modernization in the 1860s preceded the political reform of 1898. Under Mao, collectivism, unlike the Western orientation emphasized in the late Qing period, was the focus.

During China's first FYP period, the ratio of light industry to heavy industry was 1 to 7.3, while that of the Soviet Union during the first FYP was 1 to 6.[58] China's central government accounted for 80 percent of total public sector revenue and 75 percent of all public sector spending. Regarding capital construction projects, the central government controlled 79 percent, compared to local governments' 21 percent.[59] During China's first FYP, the Chinese devoted nearly 48 percent of their public capital investment to industrial development compared with that of the Soviet Union at 42 percent.[60]

The Khrushchev Model

China's development strategy departed from the Stalinist model in 1956 after Khrushchev's "secret report" against Stalin was presented at the Twentieth Party Congress of the Soviet Union. The new model of development was formulated at the CCP's Eighth Party Congress in 1956 and was put into practice during the so-called "adjustment period" of 1961 to 1965 when the Chinese government was trying to save the country's economy from the damage brought about by the GLF by adopting incentive-based policies.

As a rational response to the Stalinist model, China's first reaction in 1956 was similar to Khrushchev's Thaw: (1) agricultural development had first priority, followed by light industry and then heavy industry; (2) the management style should stress decentralization, giving power to local governments and enterprises; (3) in contrast to an exclusive focus on the state, collectives and individuals should receive greater attention; (4) the CCP should adopt more flexible policies toward other "democracy parties";[61] and (5) more moderate policies should be adopted with regard to social classes, in the sense that the bourgeoisie would not be treated as the enemy of the state.[62] We will call this the "Khrushchev model."

The Khrushchev model was embodied in three major documents: an editorial in *Renmin ribao,* the official newspaper of CCP Central Committee, the Political Report of the Eighth Party Congress,[63] and Mao's "On Ten

Great Relationships." The editorial drafted by Chen Boda but published in the name of the editorial board signaled China's departure from the Stalinist model. It criticized Stalin's personality cult, his over-emphasis on heavy industry at the expense of light industry and agriculture, and concentration of power in the central government. The article instead advocated mobilization of the masses, greater emphasis on light industry and agriculture, decentralization, and the importance of autonomous communist parties throughout the world.[64]

The Political Report from the Eighth Party Congress in September 1956, also drafted by Chen, theorized the argument in the *Renmin ribao* editorial. In addition to points embodied in the *Renmin ribao* editorial, the document also pointed out that modernization had replaced class struggle as the main task of the party.[65]

Mao's "On Ten Great Relationships" was the third important document along with the Khrushchev model. It was first circulated among the top leadership of the CCP on April 25, 1956,[66] and was published on October 26, 1976 in *Renmin ribao,* one and a half months after Mao died. Like many other Chinese leaders, Mao's initial reaction to the Stalinist model was similar to that of Khrushchev[67] and Bukharin.[68] Mao repeated his criticism of Stalin for over-emphasizing heavy industry, neglecting individual incentives, and excessive centralization.[69] Mao also criticized Stalin for the USSR's one-party monopoly and devastation of the legal system, adding that these things would not be permitted in Great Britain, France, and the United States.[70]

The Khrushchev model remained an idea in 1956, because the Maoist regime changed its policies before the model could be put into practice.[71] The CCP's departure from the orientation of the Eighth Party Congress was due to a combination of social and political factors. The reduced emphasis on class struggle was reversed because of the "rightist" attack on the party.[72] Accelerated collectivization culminating in the establishment of the People's Communes was partly in response to Khrushchev's desire to realize communism in the USSR by 1980. The Chinese simply wanted to beat the Soviets. It was relatively easier for the CCP to make this switch, because its commitments to the moderate policies adopted at the Eighth Party Congress were not firm.[73]

Although the Khrushchev model was not implemented in 1956, some ingredients of the same were applied during the so-called "adjustment period" from 1961 to 1965, because the Chinese government was compelled to make policy adjustments in response to the failure of the GLF. At the CCP

Work Conference attended by some 7,000 cadres—the so-called "7,000 People Conference"—which took place on January 1–February 7, 1962, four tendencies were criticized: utopianism in terms of unrealistically lofty goals, egalitarianism in terms of income distribution, decentralized leadership, and rapid urban population growth due to emigration from the countryside.[74]

The conference introduced the so-called "responsibility system" (*bao chan dao hu*) in the countryside, which encouraged individual incentives over the GLF's extreme collectivism.[75] In addition, 40 percent of the villages nationwide were decollectivized in 1962,[76] including in Hunan Province, where Mao was born.[77] Tian Jiaying, another of Mao's political secretaries, suggested that since de-collectivization was a trend, the party should encourage the peasants to do it by themselves instead of relying on the government's instruction.[78]

Although socioeconomic policies during this time period were more in line with those of Khrushchev, politics were very different. That's probably why MacFarquhar considered the period similar to the Stalinist model in his study. Again, the Chinese communists were more concerned with cadres' so-called "bureaucratism" than were the Soviets. This disparity between politics and economic policies was identical to that of 1956 when the socioeconomic policy reflected in the Eighth Party Congress report mirrored the Thaw in the Soviet Union, and the politics of the Hundred Flowers[79] was very different.

Mao attributed "bureaucratism" to the facts that the land reform[80] was not complete and therefore power was not in the hands of real communists, and the degeneration of cadres who had lost their revolutionary zeal.[81] In 1963, Mao said that "bad" cadres comprised perhaps less than 1 percent of all cadres.[82] This was a modest estimate, because Mao did not want to destabilize the country's economy by political upheaval.

By the end of 1963, China's economy had been consolidated. From 1963 to 1965, the output of industry and agriculture together increased annually at an average rate of 15.7 percent and workers' salaries increased by 34.5 percent over three years.[83] With a more stable economy, Mao became more daring regarding class struggle. In early 1964, Mao announced that China's entire cultural system was not in the hands of real communists.[84] At a conference in mid-May, 1964, Mao said that one-third of the CCP's influence was not in the hands of true believers of Marxism, adding that it was possible some of China's top leaders had become representatives of the bourgeoisie class, which was how he described Khrushchev.[85]

Mao's voice was first echoed by leaders in Hunan and Hebei provinces. In 1964, reports from more provinces confirmed Mao's estimate. Shanxi

Province reported that when the "work teams" entered the villages, they were overwhelmed by opposition from the class enemy.[86] Meanwhile, Chen went to Xiao Zhan in Hebei Province, and claimed that 80 percent of the cadres there were not true believers of Marxism.[87] In 1966, Chen said these "capitalist roaders" and intellectuals were the social base for Liu Shaoqi and Deng Xiaoping.[88]

Political Strategies

The GLF is a loose term describing the mass mobilization of production and collectivization begun around 1958. The term *Da yue jin,* or Great Leap Forward, first appeared in a *Renmin ribao* editorial on November 18, 1958, commenting on the party's ongoing collectivization endeavors.[89] The GLF can be divided into three stages: (1) from the Second Session of the Eighth Party Congress of May 1958 to the Zhengzhou Conference in November 1958, when the GLF was fully underway; from the Zhengzhou Conference to the Lushan Conference in July 1959, when China's leadership tried to address the problem of leftist utopianism; (3) and from the Lushan Conference to January 1961, at the Ninth Plenum of the Eighth Party Congress, when the GLF increased its utopian momentum, due to the failure of the Lushan Conference to correct leftist utopian tendencies.[90] The GLF ended in failure.[91]

The Cultural Revolution began with Yao Wenyuan's article, "On the Historical Drama: Hai Rui Who Was Fired" (*Lun xinbian lishi ju, Hai Rui ba guan*),[92] published on November 10, 1965, in *Wenhui bao,* a newspaper largely read by intellectuals. Hai Rui was an official in the Qing Dynasty who dared to criticize the emperor on behalf of the people. The purpose of publishing this article was to counterattack the attempts by those who wanted to rehabilitate Marshall Peng Dehuai, Hai Rui's contemporary peer, who had criticized Mao for his leftist policies during the GLF at the 1959 Lushan Conference. This implies that the CR was the continuation of the GLF.

The CR can be divided into roughly three stages. The first was described as the most "fanatic," beginning with the publication of Yao's article and ending with the Ninth Party Congress in 1969 when Mao consolidated his power by ousting opposition to the CR. The second stage was bracketed by the Ninth Party Congress to the death of Lin Biao in 1971,[93] a period characterized by rivalry among the leftists. The third period, 1971 to 1976, when Mao died, was characterized by the waning of leftist fanaticism. The CR ended in disaster.[94]

Parallel themes have been identified in the GLF and CR. Included here are the decentralization of power in political and economic institutions, mass mobilization, an emphasis on heavy industry at the expense of light industry, high capital accumulation at the expense of consumption, and the tendency to combat market forces. This is what is referred to as the Maoist model of development.

The only strategy that the Maoist GLF and CR reforms shared with their Soviet counterparts was the decentralization of power. Regarding the GLF, Mao repeated his criticism of the Stalinist model for its concentration of power in 1958,[95] a position echoed by Chen.[96] Mao called upon local governments and organizations to resist the central government's incorrect policies.[97] Accordingly, in 1958, of the 1,165 enterprises run by the central ministries, 885 (76 percent) were delegated to local government authorities in the provinces.[98] Decentralization in light industry and heavy industry was 98.5 percent and 70 percent, respectively.[99] Intellectuals and military officers were also encouraged to work in grassroots units.[100]

Decentralization continued under the CR. Mao remarked on March 12, 1966 that "the practice that everything was controlled by the central government is not good."[101] Prominent Chinese economist Liu Guoguang pointed out that during the CR, the economy was decentralized again, just like during the GLF.[102]

The GLF and CR did not follow the Stalinist model, and both represented departure from the Khrushchev model politically and economically.

Political Perspective

Politically, both the GLF and CR endorsed mass mobilization in processes and self-governance by the masses in institutions. This strategy was adopted in response to so-called "bureaucratism," a term describing the leadership losing touch with the masses. Referring to this phenomenon, Mao pointed out that the so-called "bourgeois ideology" started to develop within the party immediately after the Korean War ended in 1953. He also criticized China's "indiscriminate introduction of the experience of the Soviet Union," which brought bourgeois advisors to China to assist in the country's modernization process.[103]

Equating populism with democracy, Mao believed that China's democratic tradition surpassed that of the Soviet Union:

[O]ur democratic tradition has a long history. Promoting democracy at our base, with no money, food, weapons or outside aid, we had no choice but to rely on the people. The party had to become one with the people, the troops with the masses, and the officers with the soldiers.[104]

Thus, the Hundred Flowers program was launched by the Chinese government. This method of mobilizing intellectuals outside the party to purify it differed not only from the Stalinist model but also from the Khrushchev one, and naturally it made the Soviet leadership unhappy.[105] Typically, the Soviet regime under Stalin had relied on purges to purify the party, but, under Khrushchev, the Soviet government often took a passive position by allowing some degree of freedom among the populace.

The strategy of mass mobilization, rather than bureaucratic administration, was used for the purpose of achieving modernization during the GLF. The masses were mobilized not only to perform typical activities that are part of agricultural production, but also unusual ones such as killing sparrows and rats that were reportedly competing with humans for food. For instance, in 1958, the people of Tunliu County in Shanxi Province were determined to kill all sparrows and rats within their territory.[106] Accordingly, *Renmin ribao,* the Party organ, printed columns by specialists, teaching people various techniques to catch sparrows and rats.[107]

For Mao, the enthusiasm of the masses should be encouraged at all costs. In response to reports from local governments that certain People's Commune leaders exaggerated about the amount of grain that the communes had produced, Mao said that "reporting 100 catties as 50 does not matter, but reporting 50 catties as 100 is serious."[108] Mao also criticized Stalin for his mistrust of the masses.[109]

Chen elevated the importance of Mao's view of "from the masses and return to the masses"[110] to whether it was Marxist or not. Chen said,

> Following in the footsteps of the great teachers—Marx, Engels, Lenin and Stalin—Comrade Mao Tse-tung [Zedong] likewise pays the utmost attention to the great creative power of the revolutionary masses in revolutionary China. Comrade Mao Tse-tung has never separated his Marxist-Leninist theoretical work from the revolutionary movement of the masses.[111]

Regarding the ideal form of governance, the Maoist reformers believed that the ideal basic political unit in the countryside where most Chinese lived should be the People's Commune, which performed not only political functions, but also economic and social ones.[112] In 1958, Mao told Chen Boda that the People's Commune was communism in its embryo form.[113] For Mao, the Weixing Commune, one of the first People's Communes, was designed to mimic the Paris Commune, the model of true democracy for Karl Marx.[114] Chen explained that the commune combined industry, agriculture, commerce, education, and militia.[115]

Like the GLF, the strategy of mass mobilization was also used during the CR by the Maoist reformers.[116] In response to Mao's call, hundreds of thousands of "Red Guard" organizations were established nationwide beginning in 1966.

Echoing Mao's remarks during the GLF that people who inflated their numbers were guilty of technical errors, but those who discouraged the masses for their enthusiasm were guilty of inappropriate political attitudes, Chen said that the key to distinguishing genuine communists from fake ones was whether they trusted the masses or not.[117]

Regarding governance, the Maoist reformers during the CR also drew inspiration from the Paris Commune. According to Mao, the first "big character poster" (*da zi bao*) during the Cultural Revolution by Nie Yuanzi, a radical theorist in Beijing, in which she condemned moderate leader Liu Shaoqi, was in the tradition of the Paris Commune.[118] Nie criticized Liu because his policies were close to Khrushchev's. *Wen Hui Bao*, an important newspaper based in Shanghai, reported that the Shanghai Commune —the form of government that the CR rebels hoped would replace the Shanghai government—was modeled after the Paris Commune.[119]

In 1966, *Hong qi,* another party organ, carried two major articles introducing the organizational principles of the Paris Commune. One of them discussed the direct democracy election system and the principle that government officials could be recalled at any time. The salaries of government officials would be the same as those of average workers.[120] Following the model of the Paris Commune, during the CR members of the Revolutionary Committee were directly elected and subject to removal by the masses.[121] The Revolutionary Committee was comprised of rebels as well as military personnel and veteran cadres.[122]

Economic Perspective

Economically, both the GLF and CR favored collectivization, heavy industry at the expense of light industry, accumulation for capital investment at the expense of consumption, egalitarianism at the expense of self-interest, and planning as opposed to market forces. Except for decentralization, Maoist economic policy almost completely matched the Stalinist model.

During the GLF, China's collectivization proceeded quickly. In 1953, privately owned farms and factories produced about two-thirds of all output. By the end of 1956, more than 95 percent of peasants had been organized into cooperatives.[123] China's collectivization was originally planned to be accomplished in 18 years, but actually took only seven years.[124] By August 1958, a total of 26,000 People's Communes were established nationwide and over 99.1 percent of peasant households were organized into communes.[125] From September 4, 1958 through the end of October 1958, 2.65 million public dining halls, to which all commune members had access, were established in China. The proportion of peasants who ate at the dining halls was estimated at 70 to 90 percent nationwide. In Henan Province, 100 percent of the population ate their meals in these facilities.[126]

Regarding development priority, heavy industry came first, light industry second, and agriculture third. In 1958, heavy industrial output comprised 52.1 percent of gross national product (GNP), light industry, 26.1 percent, and agriculture, 21.8 percent. In 1960, heavy industry accounted for 66.6 percent of GNP.[127]

The People's Communes also became a way to squeeze the peasants for the purpose of accumulation. From 1958 to 1961, the People's Communes were asked to turn over their goods to the central government at a price set by the government for a total of 25 billion yuan. At that time, the peasantry numbered 531.52 million people, which would equate to 48.89 yuan per person. Average per capita consumption then was only 68 yuan per year.[128]

Chen Boda in 1958 stressed that the party should not rely on material incentives to mobilize the masses. He also advocated the idea of gradually abolishing the differences between the cities and countryside and of letting rural collectives run the factories.[129] Mao justified the abolition of salaries by saying that although during wartime, there was no salary, a tradition continued through 1952, the communist forces were triumphant. He asked, "How come we cannot use the same system, that is, without salaries, in times of peace?" One of the goals of the People's Commune was to gradually abolish salaries. If mass dining halls worked in the armed forces, they should also work in the countryside, Mao added.[130] In 1958, Mao criticized the large salary differences in the Soviet Union.[131] In 1958, Zhang Guangnian, a well-known Chinese musician, described individualism as a cancer that was dangerous to communism.[132]

Although some of the issues in the GLF such as development priority and accumulation for capital investment were not at the top of Chinese leadership's agenda during the CR, because the movement was largely a political event instead of an economic one like the GLF, parallels in economic policies can still be found. First, collectivization was intensified in the sense that ownership of the means of production moved from smaller units to larger ones.[133] In 1967, Xiyang County, in Shanxi Province, ownership of the means of production was transferred from the "production brigade" to the "big brigade." In 1962, "big brigade" ownership accounted for only 5 percent of the total, compared to 14 percent in 1970. "Private plots," the small pieces of land reserved for the peasant families' use to generate additional income, decreased during the CR.[134]

In addition, more egalitarian policies were adopted. For instance, equal income distribution started with Dazhai village in Xiyang County, Shanxi Province. Furthermore, private market functions were restricted. Sales of agricultural products on the private market accounted for 21.4 percent of total output in 1962, compared to 10 percent in 1970. There were also restrictions placed on peasants' sideline production. For instance, in 1966, peasant farmers sold the government 539,000 tons of fresh eggs, but in 1968, the total declined to 381,000 tons, a drop of 29.3 percent.[135] This implies that the number of peasants who privately raised chickens had significantly decreased in only two years.

The moderate economic policy during the period from 1961 to 1965 was condemned during the CR. A village party secretary said that because of the so-called "responsibility system" promoted by moderate leader Liu Shaoqi, the land of the collective was not properly farmed to the extent that the harvest from one *mu* (equal to 0.0667 hectare) averaged only 40 kilograms of grain.[136] The Chinese also criticized Khrushchev's reformist policies, especially in the area of limited privatization. China's official media charged that in Moscow alone, there were 40 private markets,[137] and during the Soviet Union's seventh FYP, 20 percent of the Soviet labor force was not engaged in public sector production.[138]

The attempt to abolish the differences between white-collar and blue-collar workers, cities and countryside, and coastal areas and landlocked regions continued during the CR.[139] In 1966, Mao spoke to Lin Biao, the leftist defense minister, about the possibility of abolishing the division of labor, salary differentials, and differences between the cities and the countryside. As late as 1975, Mao still spoke about abolishing commodities.[140]

Philosophical Underpinnings

Just as the Maoist development model departed from both the Stalinist and Khrushchev models, the philosophical underpinnings that justified the Maoist reforms were very different from their Soviet counterparts. This was reflected in the Maoist reformers' treatment of the Marxist theoretical framework, such as the ontological issue of the so-called "stage theory," the methodological issue of "dialectics," and "state theory" to justify their drastically different political agendas during the GLF and CR.

Stage Theory

An essential difference between the Chinese reformers and their Soviet counterparts regarding "stage theory" is that while the former such as Chen Boda believed that China could skip not only the stage of capitalism, but also the stage of socialism, by jumping right into communist society, Soviet reformers such as Bukharin and Suslov reinterpreted the theory to promote gradual change. The economic-determinist Marxist theory of historical materialism had been nominally accepted by the Chinese communists long before the GLF and CR. As early as 1936, Chen Boda claimed that he believed in historical materialism.[141] In his book, *On the Cultural Front,* Chen discussed such key concepts of historical materialism as productive forces, relationship of production, progress, and class.[142] In 1953, Chen repeated his commitment to historical materialism.[143]

Nevertheless, the Chinese Marxists never felt completely comfortable with economic-determinist Marxism. In a drastic departure from historical materialism, which held that the productive forces were the driving power of history, Mao wrote in 1953, "People, only people, are the driving force of the development of history."[144] Mao also added that "man's role is more important than technology in human history development"[145] and "man's ability to know and to change nature is unlimited."[146] Not surprisingly, in his book, *Selections of Mao Zedong,* Mao cited Confucius five times as much as Marx and Engels.[147]

Chen Boda noted the "sinolization" of Marxism in China. He was keenly aware that although China's cultural transformation in modern times was inspired by the Western ideas of freedom, equality, and fraternity, they were quickly turned into something different, such as egalitarianism, which had been demonstrated in the Taiping Rebellion.[148]

During the GLF, the stage theory of historical materialism was completely dismissed, as the regime relied on utopian ideals for social transformation. Chen wrote in 1958 that, for real communists, one day equates to twenty years in terms of achievements, and communism was not far away.[149] According to Mao, China could catch up with Great Britain in steel production in seven years and with the United States in fifteen years.[150]

Accordingly, the regime increased its steel production target from 6.248 million tons in February 1958 to 10.7 million tons in June 1958.[151] A *Renmin ribao* editorial claimed on August 3, 1958 that "the land will yield whatever amount of grain as long as man can imagine [it]."[152] In Mao's words,

> Probably in about ten years our production will be very bountiful [and the people's] morality will be very noble; then we can practice communism in eating, clothing and housing.[153] There's a document that says the transition to communism will start from the third FYP; I added [or the] fourth or fifth FYP.[154]

The Maoist reformers not only chose a different path toward communism by giving up historical materialism, they also created their own vision of communism, a vision inspired by Chinese tradition. Long before their takeover in 1949, the Chinese communists including Chen Boda were inspired by datong.[155] Mao first read Kang Youwei's *Datongshu* in 1917 when he was twenty-four. In a letter to his friend, Li Jinxi, in the same year, Mao wrote, "Datong is our goal."[156] In 1919, he created his utopian blueprint for a "new society." Mao's new society was characterized by public ownership of everything: "public kindergarten, public elderly homes, public schools, public libraries, public banks, public farms, public workplaces, public shops, public theaters, public hospitals, public parks, and public museums."[157]

Chen was also inspired by the idea of datong. He argued that although datong had limitations, it should be the general direction for China's future. China should not model itself after Western Europe or North America.[158]

The datong tradition continued after the communist takeover in 1949. In March 1958, Mao said that Kang's *Datongshu* was a continuity of China's datong tradition in ancient times. In May 1958, while the Propaganda Department of the Central Party Committee was compiling utopian ideas, the editors included Kang's *Datongshu*.[159] On August 4, 1958, Mao visited the People's Commune in Xushui County, Hebei Province. The leaders from the CCP Central Committee's Department of Peasant Affairs were asked to bring Kang Youwei's *Datongshu* with them "as the guideline for the People's Commune."[160]

Mao said, "We can't rule the majority of the people by relying on law. The majority of people [can be ruled only] by relying on the cultivation of [good] habits."[161] In one of his well-known poems, "Qin Yuan Chun-Snow," he wrote: "*Huan qiu tong ci liang re* (The whole world shares the common warmth and coolness)."[162]

The Maoist vision of communism was also inspired by Zhang Lu's peasant rebellion. In annotating *Zhang Lu Zhuan,* the biography of Zhang Lu, Mao said that the People's Commune had its origins in Chinese history. Under Zhang Lu, free medical treatment was similar to that of the present People's Commune. Also, under Zhang Lu, free meals were similar to the big dining halls of the People's Communes. Formally designated government officials did not exist under Zhang Lu; instead, *ji jiu* (literally, ritual persons), who effectively organized ceremonies, ruled. Mao also praised Zhang Lu's practice that the soldiers were also workers.[163] Mao's annotated *Zhang Lu Zhuan* was distributed to participants in the Sixth Session of the Eighth Party Congress on December 10, 1958. It was also distributed to the participants at the Zhengzhou Conference and Wuhan Conference at the end of 1958.[164]

In addition to datong and the self-governance tradition of the peasant rebellion, the GLF was also inspired by the Taoist utopia in the book *Tao Hu a Yuan* (Peach Blossom Shangri-la), as discussed earlier in Chapter 2. In October 1958, Fan Xian County in Shandong Province planned the realization of communism in just two years, based on *Tao Hua Yuan,* with the goal of abolishing the use of money. In response, Mao wrote, "This is interesting. It is a poem. It may also be realizable."[165] Mao later wrote in his poem, "Qi Lu": "Dao Shaoshan, 'Where are you, Tao Yuanming? Can we cultivate land in your *Tao Hua Yuan?'* (*Tao ling bu zhi he chu qu, Tao hua yuan li kegeng tian?*)" Mao wanted to demonstrate that the People's Commune was better than the utopian *Tao Hua Yuan.*[166]

Regarding the CR, the thesis of stage theory was also challenged. Mao criticized Stalin's book, *Economic Problems of Socialism in the Soviet Union* (1959), for its over-emphasis on economics at the expense of politics.[167] The media also criticized Liu Shaoqi's emphasis on productive forces. The moderate Liu was put in the same category as Nicolai Bukharin and Karl Kautsky, the two Marxist theoreticians whose philosophical perspective was in line with the economic-determinist version of Marxism. Because of Liu's economic determinism, the Maoist propaganda machine claimed that Liu's prediction that it would take another forty to fifty years before China could start building socialism was too conservative.[168] The Chinese media claimed that politics should be in command and Liu Shaoqi's economism was wrong.[169]

The sinolization of Marxism was so thorough during the CR that when social scientists at the May Seventh Schools, a relatively mild form of labor camp, wanted to study the works of Marx and Lenin, their request was rejected. Mao's works were the only "Bible" of the time.[170]

Dialectics

The Chinese reformers' interpretation of Marxian dialectics resembles the Taoist yin/yang, an approach that was responsible for justifying the generalized chaos of the GLF and the CR, as well as the relationship of heavy industry versus light industry, and various definitions of class struggle, freedom, and science. A key problem of the so-called "dialectics" was that it could justify or delegitimize anything. According to the official interpretation, a dialectical understanding of the relationship between the economic base and superstructure was that although the base was decisive in the final analysis, the superstructure could sometimes prevail over the base. The failure to offer a definite answer as to which one was more decisive left the reader in the dark regarding the final cause of social phenomena.

Although this way of understanding differed significantly from the mainstream scientific method in the West,[171] it was very close to the Taoist yin/yang. For the Tao, "to bend is to become straight,"[172] "humility is the basis for nobility, and the low is the basis for the high,"[173] "the softest things in the world overcome the hardest,"[174] and "good fortune leans on bad fortune, bad fortune hides behind good fortune."[175]

To justify the chaos during the GLF, Mao explained that a balanced situation was always temporary, and that imbalance was the constant.[176] Mao's remark equated to saying that the chaotic situation during the GLF was normal, and therefore no one should be alarmed by it. This is a departure from Bukharin's "equilibrium theory."

In terms of the relationship between heavy and light industry, this way of thinking allowed Chen to adopt completely opposite positions without risking contradiction. On one page of his article, "Under the Banner of Comrade Mao Zedong," he said that heavy industry should be given more attention, although in the previous two pages he criticized the tendency to pay too much attention to heavy industry.[177]

Two concepts in dialectics were used to interpret class: "the unity of opposites" and "change." The former refers to the situation that although the bourgeoisie and the working class were in antagonistic positions, one could not live without the other.[178] Mao criticized Stalin for his metaphysical way of thinking and for his failure to understand dialectics, charging that Stalin emphasized conflict too much, and failed to see that opposites could also coexist.[179] This allowed Mao to accuse Stalin of over-stressing "class struggle." However, on another occasion, he accused Stalin for not paying enough attention to "class struggle."[180]

"Change" refers to the impermanence of everything. Mao used the Chinese classic tale, "A Dream of Red Mansions," to explain the notion of change;[181] thus, under certain circumstances, contradictions among friends could be transformed into contradictions among enemies.

Contradictory or confused theory pronouncements continued throughout the CR. Chen Boda said that in a dialectical way the dictatorship of the masses during the CR was not the opposite of freedom. Quoting Mao, Chen asserted that

> there are only concrete freedoms, concrete democracies, and no abstract ones. In a class society, if the exploiting classes have the freedom to exploit the working people, there will be no freedom for the working people to be free from being exploited.[182]

With this understanding of the methodological issue of dialectics, it is not surprising that the Maoist discourse about empiricism was also far-fetched. On March 1, 1975, the radical leftist leader Zhang Chunqiao attacked veteran cadres who had more work experience than the CR rebels, charging them with "empiricism."[183]

Theory of the State

Unlike Bukharin and Khrushchev, who believed that under state socialism the interests of the proletariat or the interests of all people were protected since the communist party was in control of the state, the Maoist reformers believed that it was possible for the bourgeoisie to usurp state power in a communist country and to use it against the interests of the people. This was the theoretical basis for Mao to launch the Hundred Flowers campaign in 1956 and the Cultural Revolution in 1966.

The analysis of social class has new meanings in comparison with the classical Marxist interpretation, which was based on the ownership of the means of production. For the Maoists, the class enemy no longer comprised those who possessed the means of production such as capitalists and landlords, but rather communist cadres whose revolutionary zeal had waned. In 1958, Mao raised the issue of the "bourgeois right,"[184] referring to the privileges that some cadres enjoyed at the expense of the people.

On May 16, 1966, Mao remarked that "from 'the center' to lower level institutions, provinces, municipalities and autonomous regions, there are representatives of the bourgeoisie. China's 'Khrushchev' is sleeping right beside us."[185] Mao argued that since many party members have become "slave masters,"[186] the goal of the CR was to purge them.[187]

In 1967, Chen said that

> most of the literary associations and journals, with the exception of a few, had not followed the policies of the party, satisfying themselves as being elitist. They lost touch with the workers, peasants, and soldiers. These journals do not reflect socialist revolution and socialist construction.[188]

On May 18, 1967, at the one-year anniversary of the publication of the "May 16 Announcement," *Hong qi* and *Renmin ribao* published a joint editorial. It said that world communism had already undergone three stages: that of Marx and Engels who established the scientific socialism theory; that of Lenin and Stalin, who created the theory that socialism could happen in one country in the age of imperialism; and that of Mao who continued the revolution under the dictatorship of the proletariat.[189] This was the theoretical foundation of the CR.

In summary, the Maoist GLF and CR reforms were similar in terms of political strategies and philosophical underpinnings. In response to the deficiency of state socialism, the Maoist reformers radicalized the Chinese revolution. These reforms are in contrast to reforms undertaken in the Soviet Union in response to similar structural problems, in which the Soviets veered away from communist ideals.

Chapter 6

Reforms out of Communism: China and the Soviet Union

The [Chinese] revolutionary Marxist emphasis on "victory over nature" has a technological dimension imported from the West, but the main business of the ancient sages had been to think up and carry out economic projects like river dredging in order to "control the ten thousand things" and to "put in order heaven and earth." Most crucial here is the fact that the Western promise of material progress was welcomed not by people with just the normal human desire for rising living standards but by people for whom this very question of "the people's livelihood" was philosophically of the utmost importance.

—Thomas A. Metzger[1]

Unlike the Chinese tradition, Christianity is not monistic, because matter and spirit are believed to be distinct.

—Donald W. Treadgold[2]

The reforms by Deng Xiaoping and Mikhail Gorbachev took different courses that have in turn brought about different results. While the Chinese reforms focused on economics, a strategy that led to China's sustained growth over the last thirty years, the Soviet reforms were aimed at both economics and politics, a strategy that led to the disintegration of the Soviet Union in 1991. Although many scholars seem to believe that political control made a major difference in the outcomes of the two reforms, they have failed to explain why the Soviets reformed both economics and politics while the Chinese chose to stay on the track in the area of economics.

81

Steven Solnick argued that organizational reforms greatly weakened authority linkages within Soviet hierarchies, while in the case of China, those same linkages remained largely intact. The Chinese government preserved "both its capacity for monitoring and its reputation for disciplining transgressions."[3] Viewing the Chinese reform from the perspective of centralization, Barry Wingast made a similar argument by saying that China's economic reform succeeded because of the government's political control.[4] Frederick Barghoon blamed Gorbachev's mishandling of ideology, that is, "democratic centralism," for the collapse of the Soviet system. Marxism is an ideology of organization and an organization of ideology. The basis of this ideology is that the top leaders possessed the truth. Gorbachev depicted all previous leaders, except Lenin, as fundamentally bad. This delegitimized the Communist Party and led to the collapse of the organization.[5]

For those who have tried to explain the dichotomy of politics versus economics, interpretations vary. Yan Sun argued that it was China's initial success in economics that reinforced the determination of the Chinese leadership to stay on track for reforming the country's economic system first. Initial Soviet setbacks in economic reform may have contributed to their switch of policy emphasis to politics.[6] This is only part of the story, because when the Chinese economic reforms met with great difficulty after the mid-1980s, which eventually led to the popular uprising at Tiananmen in 1989, the Chinese leaders still chose to focus on economic, but not political reform.

Nancy Tucker observed that Chinese decentralization was more far-reaching than that of the USSR because the Soviet system, in comparison to the Chinese one, was harder to reform. The Soviet bureaucracy, established in 1917 instead of 1949, was more entrenched than its Chinese counterpart, and the USSR never had a Cultural Revolution that shook the bureaucracy in fundamental ways. She also argued that implementing the Chinese-style responsibility system in the Soviet countryside was more difficult because of larger-scale and more modernized Soviet agricultural production. In addition, only 20 percent of Russians lived in the countryside. So, even if the Soviet leaders had used the Chinese-style responsibility system, it would still not have been significant.[7] This interpretation may explain why the Soviet economic reform experienced great difficulties. However, it does not explain why, in spite of institutional entrenchment, the Soviet political reform proceeded rapidly after 1987.

The dynamics of the two reforms were complex, and multiple factors must have been at play. Thus, previously presented interpretations were all valid to various degrees. More independent variables may be added to the list as well, such as generational politics. Chinese leaders succeeded in re-taining political control because, unlike Mikhail Gorbachev, Deng, as a first-generation revolutionary, had more charisma and firmer commitment to communist ideology. In accordance with the general thesis of this book, I argue that the reforms by Deng and Gorbachev were prompted by struc-tural factors that resulted in economic slowdown in China and the Soviet Union in the 1980s. However, the direction the reforms took was influenced by the dynamics of their ideological and political-cultural transformations.

An analysis of the writings and speeches by reform leaders reveals that although both reforms included decentralization, the Soviet leaders in-tended to have both economic and political reforms from the very begin-ning, while the Chinese leaders emphasized economic reform at the expense of the political one, in spite of small-scale twists and turns. Accordingly, the dynamics of the ideological and cultural transformations of the two coun-tries were different as well. These differences resulted in Soviet reform leaders being highly critical of Marxism as well as Russia's Asian linkages, while Chinese leaders justified their reforms by resorting to Marxist histor-ical materialism and tried to combine communism with China's Confucian datong tradition.

This study is based on a combination of surveys and analysis of the writ-ings of the two countries' reform leaders, especially Hu Qiaomu (1912–1992) and Alexander N. Yakovlev (1923–2005), the two ideology czars dur-ing respective time periods. Hu was Mao Zedong's political secretary for twenty-five years from 1941 to 1966, and served as deputy minister of the Propaganda Department of the CCP Central Committee from 1956 to 1966. Hu became a Politburo member in 1982, thus making him not only the de facto, but also the de jure ideology czar for China in the early 1980s. In two of the most important articles he wrote during the period, Hu attacked the trend of "liberalization" in 1980 and the theories of "humanism" and "alienation" in 1984, declaring that he was representing the "center," that is the CCP Central Committee.[8]

Similarly, Yakovlev became the de facto ideology chief of the Commu-nist Party of the Soviet Union (CPSU) from 1965 to 1973, at which time he was first deputy minister of the party's Propaganda Department.[9] He was sent to Canada for ten years after that. In 1985, when Gorbachev came to power, he was again put in charge of the party's ideology work and became a Politburo member in 1987. Yakovlev "almost single-handedly invented the concept of perestroika and persuaded Gorbachev to pursue it."[10] He is also known as the "father of glasnost,"[11] and was one of the three "most important politicians of the Gorbachev era."[12] In the introduction to the Chinese version of a book by Yakovlev, the editors wrote, "Yakovlev's views are completely identical to those of Gorbachev."[13] Regardless of the accuracy of these evaluations, his role as a major spokesman of the Gorbachev regime is beyond doubt.

Key structural factors that will be examined in subsequent sections include centralization in both political and economic structures, ownership of the means of production, and democracy. The main theoretical and philosophical issues to be discussed include historical materialism, dialectics, and cultural traditions of China and Russia. The time-frame examined in this chapter is 1976, when Mao Zedong died, to 1997, when Deng Xiaoping died.

Structure: Historical Background of Deng's Reform (1978–1997) and Gorbachev's Reform (1985–1991)

Although Deng's reforms emerged from the Cultural Revolution (CR), the political structure of China in the later stages of the ten years of chaos resembled that of the Stalinist structure more than that of the first three years of the CR, when the Red Guards and other mass organizations took control of the country. The Revolutionary Committees that became the leadership entities of China in the late stage of the CR consisted of veteran cadres, the military, and the rebels. Although the composition of the Revolutionary Committees was different, the function they played was similar to that of the Stalinist-style organizations in the sense that they listened to the top leadership in Beijing on the one hand and had absolute control of local governments on the other.

The economic system of public ownership of the means of production and central planning was not changed during the CR, in spite of some decentralization. By 1978, the output of state owned enterprises was 77.6 percent and that by the collectives was 22.4 percent. The output produced by individuals was almost zero.[14]

Gorbachev inherited the Stalinist structure from Konstantin Chernenko, the Soviet leader who died in office in 1985. On the eve of Gorbachev's reforms, conservatism prevailed. A *Pravda* editorial attacked pluralism by stating, "Recently bourgeois propaganda has been especially active in counter-posing the concept of ideological and political pluralism to socialist democracy."[15] Similarly, the Party's ideological control over literature was also emphasized.[16] Chernenko viewed the road to communism as a lengthy one, stressing the Party's guiding role and calling for discipline.[17] The Soviet media restrained from commenting on China's capitalist-oriented reforms in 1984.[18]

At the start of the two reforms, both China and the Soviet Union were faced with a major problem: widespread lack of incentives for workers led to low productivity. By 1976, one-third of state-owned enterprises in China lost money. As a result, average salaries of employees decreased by 6 percent from 1966 to 1976.[19] In 1978, the Chinese Communist Party called for correcting the practice of paying the same amount to those who worked and those who did not. Because of the lack of incentives, in some enterprises, the average workday was only 5 to 5.5 hours. Some enterprises relied on temporary workers since regular employees refused to work. Hu Qiaomu noted that during the first five-year plan period (1953–1957), productivity increased annually by 8.7 percent. If this growth rate had continued, by 1977 the productivity in industry, infrastructure, and transportation should have trebled and the number of workers in these occupations reduced by two-thirds.[20] China's per capita food production in 1977 was the same as in 1955.[21]

Low productivity was caused partly by the irrational nature of the Chinese economic system. Prereform China gave priority to industry at the expense of agriculture. For example, because of the government's practice of setting lower prices for agricultural products and higher prices for industrial products such as fertilizer, sometimes an increase of agricultural production would actually reduce peasants' income.[22]

The lack of incentives was also due to a high concentration of power. In spite of the fact that power was decentralized to certain degrees during the CR, Hu complained that the system no longer encouraged economic development in the 1980s because of excessive centralization.[23]

The situation on the eve of the reform in the Soviet Union was similar. In 1985, the country's growth rate was zero.[24] Gorbachev pointed out that productivity was higher in the 1930s through the 1960s compared to the 1970s and 1980s.[25] Gorbachev wrote,

Why does it happen that an enterprise produces outdated output on a low technical level or consumer goods for which there is no demand, but lives normally and sometimes even prospers? Our economic mechanism allows such phenomena to occur.[26]

A survey in the Soviet Union found that although 98 percent of the respondents considered "industriousness and a conscientious attitude toward labor to be highly important factors in achieving success and well-being in life," most admitted that there was "an obvious contradiction here between words and deeds, between our consciousness and our real actions."[27] Russian scholar Tatyana Zaslavskaya wrote, "The situation in which it [restructuring] began was essentially a pre-Revolutionary situation, in which the 'lower classes' were unwilling or refused to do good-quality work, while the 'upper crust' was no longer able to make them."[28]

Gorbachev cited public ownership of the means of production as a major cause for people's lack of incentives; he pointed out that 96 percent of the country's wealth belonged to the government.[29] Yakovlev said that all social evils lay in government ownership of everything.[30]

Centralization of power was also blamed for the low productivity. Burlatsky wrote:

We know how acute the problems of overcoming excessive centralization and departmentalism are in our country. Eighteen million people in the administrative apparatus—that's too high a price to pay for the hypertrophied principle of centralization. . . . The central apparatus of departments and ministries could profitably be reduced by half or even by two-thirds.[31]

On the eve of the reforms, there was a consensus for change in both countries. In the case of China, the most widespread popular protest against the communist regime occurred in the spring of 1976 when thousands of people in Beijing used the opportunity of mourning the moderate leader Premier Zhou Enlai to condemn the radical "Gang of Four."[32] In the Soviet Union, a similar consensus for change was expressed by Gorbachev: "None of us can continue living in the old way."[33] Polls show that in May 1987, over 90 percent of Soviet citizens were in favor of restructuring, while only 0.6 percent were opposed.[34] Y. K. Ligachev, generally perceived as a "conservative," sounded much like everyone else. At the sixty-ninth anniversary of the October Revolution on November 6, 1986, he "stressed 'irreversible restructuring' and 'radical' reform of economic management."[35]

Political Strategies

The common strategy adopted by leaders of the Deng Reform and Gorbachev Reform was decentralization of the countries' economic structure in an attempt to boost incentives at the level of enterprises and individual workers. Beginning in 1979, the Chinese government instituted a number of policies to decentralize the country's economy. Enterprises assumed more responsibilities so that many state-imposed production quotas were lowered, and the profits could be retained by enterprises rather than being turned over to the state. By 1981, a total of 86.7 percent of Chinese communes had adopted the responsibility system.[36]

In addition, the percentage of industrial output produced by state-owned enterprises had declined, and by 1989, they accounted for about 60 of total output.[37] Hu insisted in 1981 that a certain amount of private enterprise could be tolerated. Under current circumstances, socialism meant that there would be a certain amount of centralized planning, enterprise self-management, democratization of enterprises, various types of responsibility systems, and a role for market dynamics.[38]

After two years of adjustments, at the CPSU Central Committee conference in November 1987, the Gorbachev Reform commenced the democratization of society and economic reforms focusing on decentralization and accountability.[39] Gorbachev said, "We will not solve the problem of autonomy if directors have to get approval from dozens of people every time something comes up and discuss everything from A to Z. Decisions on every question cannot be passed on to the central bodies."[40] The official newspaper, *Pravda,* reported that the economic reform was "a changeover from an excessively centralized, command system of management to a democratic one based primarily on economic methods and on an optimal combination of centralism and self-management."[41]

Although reformers in the two countries shared a commitment to decentralization in the economic realm, which was connected to ownership of the means of production to promote incentives, they differed on political reform, democracy, relations between politics and economics, and how to understand or evaluate the communist experiences in the past.

Generally speaking, for the Chinese reform was largely socioeconomic;[42] for the Russians, political reform surged ahead of economic reform.[43] This occurred in spite of the fact that the Chinese leaders may have been fragmented during the reform period,[44] and may have adopted some liberal moves,[45] such as allowing multicandidate elections at the village level.

Hu said that it was absurd to support democratic ideology one-sidedly while neglecting the concentration of power (*jizhong*) and authority. This was similar to saying that any problems, no matter whether significant or trivial, had to be settled through ballots. He wrote,

If we believe this, we would have to assume that every person is an encyclopedia, thus having the capacity for correct judgment. Consequently, the masses would be buried in ballots by this kind of democracy. . . . This absurd "democracy" is not only inconceivable now, but unimaginable in the remote future.[46]

In criticizing the so-called "bourgeois liberalization,"[47] Hu wrote in 1981 that in a capitalist society, freedom meant that capitalists can freely exploit the workers. Hu criticized leaders who wanted to implement certain practices that seem to accompany a capitalist economy, such as parliamentary democracy, the two-party system, freedom of press, freedom of assembly, and individualism.[48] Hu said that

> freedom and responsibility cannot be separated from each other. Freedom is not everything. The so-called "liberalization" is the belief that freedom is above everything. This is against socialism. I support freedom on the condition that it is not against the interest of society.[49]

The Chinese government's de-emphasis on political democratization was partly a reflection of the attitudes of the Chinese public at the time. Surveys performed in the 1980s and 1990s showed that although China did not comprehensively introduce democracy, the Chinese people's sense of the mastery of their destiny was comparable to citizens of democratic nations in the 1960s.[50] In village-level elections, the process for the majority of the Chinese peasants in some areas was entirely different from local elections in the West. Rather than choosing a leader based on candidates' competition with one another, the villagers sought to build consensus through selecting local leaders.[51]

The situation in the former Soviet Union was different. According to Gorbachev, "When I began perestroika, it was precisely politics that I had to keep in mind. This of course meant changing the politics of the CPSU, which had led our country into a blind alley."[52] Gorbachev seemed to be serious about political reform. Beginning in mid-1985, the Soviet media were full of shocking headlines about reshuffling of high-level government officials.[53]

Political reform was also at the top of Yakovlev's agenda. In 1991, he wrote that the party's organizational principle of so-called "democratic centralism" did not do justice to its name. There was "centralism" only, and no "democracy."[54] Yakovlev believed that the party should turn over "all the power to soviet,"[55] a slogan shared by Gorbachev.[56]

Gorbachev asserted that political reform should move in the direction of democracy. He stated,

We proceed from the premise that socialism is a society of growing diversity in people's opinions, relationships and activities. Each person has his own social experience, his own level of knowledge and education, his own special way of perceiving what is happening. . . . [W]e are in favor of diversity in public opinion, of richness in spiritual life.[57]

Gorbachev believed that democratic procedure was an effective way to give people freedom and to control the *nomenklatura* (bureaucracy). In contrast, when the same structural problem was presented to the post-Mao leaders, they adopted different means, such as retiring the veteran cadres and introducing a civil service system based partly on merit instead of relying totally on political loyalties.

Yakovlev agreed with Gorbachev in believing that

perestroika's central goal was democracy. It was precisely a central goal, not a tactical one. It was seen as a strategic task, which stemmed from the understanding that it is precisely the lack of a democratic beginning that is the source of all the difficulties, all the troubles, and all the problems that we have in the country.[58]

Gorbachev believed that without democracy, economic success was not possible. In the West, many people thought that between the two slogans of "perestroika" and "glasnost," the former was about economics, while the latter was about politics. But, according to Gorbachev, "the conception of perestroika was aimed at a profound qualitative change in society by linking socialism with democracy."[59] He continued,

We had first of all to accelerate scientific and technological progress, but that presupposed democratization in the economic sphere, managerial autonomy for individual enterprises, placing them on a self-financing basis (without government subsidies), making them profitable, and so forth.[60]

In a similar vein, Yakovlev criticized the slogan of "[s]av[ing] the country through economics" by saying that "if human relations are not handled properly, i.e., politics, we cannot develop our economics successfully."[61] In a separate piece, he said, "Even the introduction of the market economy was considered not a goal in itself but as a kind of guarantee for the establishment of democracy."[62]

Although he seemed to be committed to political reform, Gorbachev's economic strategy was inconsistent. In a major report delivered to members of the Central Party Committee in 1985, Gorbachev seemed to want to do everything in economics without first establishing priorities. At times, he put emphasis on machine-building industries:

> We are planning to improve the use of capital investments, to give priority to the development of such highly important branches as machine-building, the electrical equipment and electronics industries, power engineering, transportation and others.[63]

Several months later, he contradicted himself by calling for the streamlining of machine-building industries.[64]

Policy differences by reformers in the two countries were related to their distinctive treatments of the past. Soviet reformers glorified the Thaw. As a demonstration, the liberal-minded Soviet theoretician Fyodor M. Burlatsky was an adviser to both Khrushchev in the 1960s and Gorbachev in the 1980s. Burlatsky writes,

> The names we see on the surface of perestroika today [in the 1980s] are almost without exception people of my generation. The most crucial period will arrive with a new wave of young enthusiasts and reformers, who will have the same passionate faith in the need for change and be as fanatical in implementing it as the children of the Twentieth Party Congress.[65]

Gorbachev referred to Khrushchev in a positive light in November 1987. In fact, those Soviet authors who viewed Khrushchev positively were "uniformly supportive of the perestroika" in the Gorbachev era.[66]

The Soviet reformers also harshly criticized the human rights abuses of Stalin, including the gulags and killings. Actually, all previous leaders, except Lenin, were depicted in a negative light. Although Russian scholars realized that Soviet authoritarianism was partly caused by unusual historical conditions, such practices had to be terminated in the current situation. B.P. Kurashvili, of the USSR Academy of Sciences, called the economic practices before the 1960s the result of extraordinary conditions, such as social turbulence and wars. Under these circumstances, it was natural for the government to give priority to collective interests at the expense of individual interests and to directly control the country's production apparatus. Under "normal conditions," such as after the 1960s, things could be run in a reverse way with more emphasis on individual incentives and interests rather than collectives ones, and on self-management instead of direct state management.[67]

This perspective was not shared by their Chinese counterparts who, although critical of the Maoist reforms of the Great Leap Forward (GLF) and the CR, were far more moderate in characterizing the communist experience in general. The post-Mao leadership generally painted Mao in a positive light by claiming that 70 percent of Mao's policies were constructive, while only 30 percent were mistakes. In an apologist tone for Mao, Hu Qiaomu argued that many of China's policies after the founding of the People's Republic were responses to extraordinary situations, such as the challenging international environment. For instance, with the containment policy of the United States, it was hard for China to adopt an open-door policy. For Hu, some of those authoritarian policies had worked well under such extraordinary historical conditions. For instance, the first five-year plan (1953–1957) was successful.[68] The nationalization of privately owned companies in 1957 was also necessary, because the capitalists were guilty of tax evasion and sabotage.[69]

Those who were most critical about Maoist China were on the margins of political power. For instance, post-Mao dissident intellectuals such as Wang Ruoshui and Zhou Yang attempted to use the theories of humanism and alienation to address the political problems of Chinese communism. The theory of alienation implied that the party bureaucrats had become the masters of the people instead of their servants, an issue that first emerged in 1956, triggered the Hundred Flowers, and then reemerged during the CR. Humanist theory was a critique of past communist practices of using whatever means necessary to justify "good ends," in reference to persecutions and purges during the so-called "Anti-Rightist Movement" in 1957 and the CR. In addition, humanism emphasized individualism, such as human dignity, values, needs, and freedom. In the 1980s, Wang and Zhou were purged from the party for their comments.[70] Hu Qiaomu criticized Wang and Zhou's humanism argument that the human being "is the starting point of Marxism." For Hu, there was no such a thing as an "abstract" person. People were concrete and their existence was based on class relations.[71]

Philosophical Underpinnings

The different strategies adopted by reform leaders in China and the Soviet Union were based on distinctive theoretical bases, a situation that is connected with the dynamics of the ideological and cultural transformation of the two nations during that time period. Reform leaders of the two countries treated differently authoritarian systems inherited not only from the communist past, but also from the ancient past. This situation had an impact on their treatment of certain critical theoretical and philosophical issues such as historical materialism, dialectics, and cultural traditions of both countries.

The theoretical basis of Deng's political strategy was the so-called "primary-stage socialism." Grounded in Marxist historical materialism, it was first mentioned in June 1981 at the Sixth Plenum of the Eleventh Party Congress and then fashioned into a comprehensive theory at the Thirteenth Party Congress in 1987. Su Shaozhi, former director of the Political Science Institute, the Chinese Academy of Social Sciences, was widely believed to have contributed to this theory.[72]

Departing from the Maoist voluntarist slogan that "[r]evolution is the locomotive of the development of productivity,"[73] the post-Mao theoretical premise went back to classical Marxism, that is, that productive forces were the driving force of history. Arguing from historical materialism that there were five stages in the evolution of human society (primitive society, slavery society, feudalism, capitalism, and communism), the post-Mao official line contended that Mao had made the mistake of skipping the stage of capitalist development and prematurely jumped into the communist practices of the GLF and the CR. Now it was time to make up the skipped capitalist stage by adopting such practices as making use of market forces, less-central planning, and a commodities exchange.[74] Criticizing Mao's betrayal of the Marxist philosophy of historical materialism and dialectical materialism,[75] Hu believed that beginning with the socialist transformation in the 1950s, it would take at least a hundred years to realize socialist modernization.[76]

Taking a drastically different position, Yakovlev attacked Marxist historical materialism in particular[77] and economic determinism in general.[78] Yakovlev believed that Marx's idea about the relations between base and superstructure was mechanical.[79] From the perspective of materialism, the human being was a functional phenomenon, merely a particle of nature, one of the ways that material systems function.[80] He argued,

Material production must serve and be subordinate to spiritual creativity to have meaning and value. The economy is a value but the value of the lawful organization of society stands above it, for it cannot exist without it or outside it. . . . Even higher stands the value of the system of free ideas, freedom of science, freedom of art. But the most sacred, the most important of all criteria for progress is human freedom of choice.[81]

For the Chinese, however, the emphasis on economics was not only in accordance with the final goal of communism, as explained by historical materialism, but also consistent with the Chinese holistic way of thinking: "[M]aterial progress was welcomed not by people with just the normal human desire for rising living standards but by people for whom this very question of 'the people's livelihood' was philosophical of the utmost importance." Traditionally, "the main business of the ancient sages had been to think up and carry out economic projects like river dredging in order to 'control the ten thousand things' and to 'put in order heaven and earth.'"[82]

Besides historical materialism, another Marxist concept at the center of theoretical discussions was dialectics, a concept debated during other communist reforms such as the NEP, the Thaw, GLF and the CR. Hu used the so-called "dialectical method" to argue that nothing was absolute, such as freedom and non-freedom. In the tone of Taoist yin/yang, Hu remarked that freedom was not a universal value endorsed by all, because some people's freedom was always obtained at the expense of the non-freedom of other people.[83]

For the Soviet reformists, however, dialectics was part of "German idealism,"[84] which was ideologically related to authoritarianism.[85] Yakovlev criticized dialectics as follows:

Marx's lack of desire to delve into an isolated fact was a consequence of the version of Hegelian dialectics with which he armed himself in an effort always to keep the analysis of reality on a philosophical plane. If the concrete is only a concrete movement in the eternal movement of essence, there is no point in spending time and effort to understand a butterfly that lives only for a day in that eternal movement of time, in that eternally changing world.[86]

Because of this deficiency, according to Yakovlev, Marxism was more of an ideology than a science: "The method of ideology is contrary to the method of science in every way, since ideology does not tolerate scientific knowledge but fears it."[87] As an alternative, Yakovlev endorsed empiricism as a scientific method.[88] This was also shared by A. Tsipko, another Soviet intellectual leader during the same time period.[89]

This situation was similar to the contrast between Chinese intellectuals and their Japanese counterparts during the Late Qing Reform and the Meiji

Restoration in the sense that while the Chinese tended toward monistic materialism that provided intellectual support to political authoritarianism, the Japanese found empiricism and positivism more appealing, as discussed in Chapter 3. This situation was also a continuation of the Chinese intellectual development in the early twentieth century when most Marxist intellectuals such as Chen Duxiu (1879–1942) found monistic materialism and the dialectical method appealing, while most Chinese liberal intellectuals such as Hu Shi (1891–1962) endorsed some kind of empiricism and positivism as a methodological approach. The Marxists won the battle at that time.[90]

When the reforms in both countries experienced problems in the late 1980s, the leadership realized that a deeper cause was a cultural one. In China, people's enthusiasm about culture was demonstrated by the fact that one million people in the Chinese city of Guangzhou participated in discussions over the pro-Western TV series *He Shang (Yellow River Elegy)*. The city had a population of six million at the time. The authors traced the communist authoritarian system to its Asian roots. The hope of China was the "Blue Ocean," that is, the West.[91] But these authors were on the margins of political power. This anti-Asian tradition never prevailed over the official ideological line.

To endorse the Chinese datong tradition, which is connected to authoritarianism, Hu Qiaomu praised a Confucian-type character rather than a communist one in the 1984 film *Gaoshan xia de huahuan* (Garland at the Foot of the Mountain). Liang Sanxi, a character in the film, is a better representation of a good Confucian peasant than a communist. As a communist theoretician, Hu was self-conscious about his compliment of Liang Sanxi. Unlike communist characters in CR literary works, Liang is not noted for his "class consciousness." Instead, he is recognized for his good-heartedness and unselfishness.[92] In a slightly different tone from communism, Hu praised "the common spirit, common soul, and common morality of the Chinese nation." He refused to define "common," which sounded like a lack of the Marxist "class character."

A more straightforward advocate of Chinese tradition among the top leadership was Li Ruihuan, a standing member of the Politburo. Li praised the popular soap opera, *Kewang* (Yearnings), which depicted "a new model of relationship that is sincere, honest, equal, mutually supportive, united, friendly and harmonious," instead of competitive, a hallmark of capitalism.[93]

Hu's and Li's promotion of Chinese traditional culture was partly a reflection of the Chinese political culture in the 1980s and early 1990s in the sense that the Chinese people were exploring various cultural paths for the country's modernization drive. As a demonstration, a pro-Chinese-tradition soap opera *Kewang* was just as popular as the pro-Western documentary *River Elegy*. The streets of Beijing were vacant when *Kewang* episodes were broadcast.[94] Broadcast in 1990, *Kewang* was described as Chinese television's first major successful soap opera.[95] Joseph Fewsmith noted that in a departure from the May Fourth tradition,[96] starting in the late 1980s, some Chinese intellectuals also began to look at the positive aspects of Chinese tradition.[97]

Also turning his attention to culture, Yakovlev stated that "[r]eform in USSR and in Russia turned out to be a difficult process politically and economically, and even more so psychologically." He felt that the Soviet reformers had under-estimated the role of cultural traditions toward reforms. The psychological condition of the society turned out to be more inert, indifferent, and dependent than the reformers had imagined.[98]

Yakovlev traced Russian authoritarianism to its Asian roots:

> As we know, the land of Rus accepted Christianity from Constantinople in 988 A.D. Characteristics of Byzantine rule of that era—baseness, cowardliness, venality, treachery, over-centralization, apotheosis of the ruler's personality—dominate in Russia's social and political life to this day. In the twelfth century, the various fragmented Russian principalities from the Volga to the Carpathians were conquered by the Mongols. Asian traditions and customs, with their disregard for the individual and for human rights and their cult of might, violence, despotic power, and lawlessness became part of the Russian people's way of life. . . . The people existed for the government, not the government for the people.[99]

Yakovlev insisted that oriental psychology and religion were more congruent to various utopias than the more pragmatic, rationalist culture of European Christian civilization.[100] His views were shared by another Soviet thinker who described the Asiatic character of Russia as a "lack of restraint against maximalism and extremism."[101] Chinese hopefulness toward the future, as demonstrated in the writings of Kang Youwei, was noted as "utopian socialism" by the Russian historian, S.L. Tikhvinskii.[102] Critics of Asian traditions also held that the belief in the perfectibility of human nature was a source of authoritarianism.[103] Yakovlev believed that human nature was not perfect,[104] a view shared by the Chinese dissident philosopher, Wang Ruoshui, during the reform period.[105] Wang was purged by the party because of his liberal ideas.

Believing that it was high time to abandon authoritarian and utopian practice, Yakovlev argued that pluralism was consistent with the twentieth century, which contrasts with the nineteenth century when progress was viewed as simplified.[106] Yakovlev believed that as human civilization reaches a higher level, freedom starts to become more important and the individual capacity to defend and explain the uniqueness and sovereignty of spiritual life takes on greater meaning.[107] "A centrifugal historical trend is replaced with a centripetal one....[108] The real historical process abandoned false constructions of one-dimensionality, universalism, and qualitative homogeneity in social existence."[109]

To summarize, Deng's reforms (1978–1997) and Gorbachev's reforms (1985–1991) did not occur accidentally, and the strategies adopted were not random. Both sets of reforms were prompted by structural deficiencies of state socialism. The communist leaders in the two countries seemed to have addressed the technical problem of the system in similar ways, that is, decentralization. They addressed the problem of attitude, such as the political culture problem, differently in the sense that the Chinese emphasized collectivist values more than their Soviet counterparts. The Chinese holistic way of thinking, which sees politics and economics as inseparable, also had an impact on the reform agenda.

Conclusion

Hopefulness toward the Future as Natural, Supernatural, and the Product of Human Endeavor

As a discourse analysis, this study has tried to explain how political culture impacted on the political strategies and philosophical perspectives of reforms in Japan, Russia, and China in the twentieth century. The importance of political discourse in social transformation was demonstrated by the fact that Fukuzawa invented a vernacular to popularize Western ideas to the Japanese, while Kang Youwei started schools to enlighten the Chinese. Political discourse played an even more important role in communist societies, as was demonstrated by the Soviet regime engaging in attempts to brainwash the public in the Thaw and Chen Boda's use of news media to convey leftist messages to the people during the Cultural Revolution.

In Deng's reform, Hu's "primary-stage socialism theory" as official discourse was more effective for China in the sense that datong was not abandoned, just postponed. This discourse enabled the Chinese government to reorient China in the direction of quasi-capitalism without having to abandon Marxism. The official discourse by the Soviet reformers was less effective in remolding the new political culture in that it totally negated the past without providing a feasible future blueprint for social change. Gorbachev's rejection of the Soviet past, except Lenin, contributed to the collapse of the communist system.[1] For the future, Yakovlev never adequately explained why the Soviet Union needed to have a two-party system model[2] rather than the European multiparty system. He also never explained why the U.S. style of government including checks and balances and the separation of power among the legislature, the judiciary, and the executive[3] was better than the "fusion of power" of the British system. His criticism about nonliberal democracies' utopian trust of human nature was also open to debate.[4] Yakovlev's blueprint was apparently the U.S. model, which is quite unique among Western democracies.

The effectiveness of official discourse has little to do with truth. Neither Hu's nor Yakovlev's theory was academically sound. Hu's "primary-stage socialism" theory was misinformed as a Marxist theory. Numerous works have been published in the West criticizing historical materialism, as an economic determinist reading of Karl Marx's works on which the so-called "primary-stage socialism" was based.[5] Yakovlev's theory was equally superficial. His blaming of Asian traditions for the communist system was not accepted by Western scholars who believe that totalitarian ideas, including communism, were rooted in European thought, including Christianity.[6]

Through a discourse analysis of these comparative case studies, we have seen similarities as well as differences in the strategies adopted and the philosophical underpinnings endorsed in these reforms. While the Meiji Restoration and the Late Qing Reform centralized the power of their respective countries, all six reforms in the Soviet Union and communist China, the New Economic Policy (NEP), the Thaw, the Great Leap Forward, and the Cultural Revolution, Deng's reform, and Gorbachev's reform shared the common strategy of decentralization.

The differences among these reforms were just as obvious. Regarding the Meiji Restoration and the Late Qing Reform, while the Japanese intended to save Japan in the face of modernization, the Chinese wanted to save not only China, but also the world.

Similarly, two parallel Soviet reforms of the NEP and the Thaw contrasted with the two parallel Maoist reforms of the Great Leap Forward and the Cultural Revolution. While the Soviet reforms moved in the direction of more incentives, political relaxation, and pluralism, the Maoist reforms went in the opposite direction—less incentives, political monism, and collectivist values.

Gorbachev's reform moved in the same direction of the earlier Soviet reforms. David Nordlander regarded the Gorbachev reforms as the fruition of Khrushchev's "unkept promises," and interpreted the Khrushchev era as an "early stage of perestroika."[7] Burlatsky contended that the antecedents for Gorbachev's perestroika were in the NEP of the 1920s, thus effectively linking all three Russian reforms, that is, the NEP, the Thaw, and the Gorbachev Reform.[8]

The Deng Reform inherited elements of the two Maoist reforms of the Great Leap Forward and the Cultural Revolution in the sense that the Chinese society and intellectuals seem still to endorse the datong vision, as China scholar Suzanne Ogden has argued.[9] Thomas Metzger also remarked in the 1990s that anti-selfishness was at the center of Chinese utopianism, a mentality that was still very much alive among intellectuals not only in China but also in Taiwan.[10]

Among Chinese intellectuals, the word "freedom," which often runs against the datong concept was viewed negatively until the late 1990s.[11] Philip Huang noted,

Indeed, to this day, despite all the references to *ziyou* [freedom] in the many constitutions of the successive regimes of twentieth century China, *ziyou* has never quite been able to shake its associated negative connotations of selfishness, with obvious consequences for Chinese conceptions of "democracy."[12]

The Chinese understanding of "freedom" is shared by other Asians as well such as Lee Kuan-Yew, a former Prime Minister of Singapore. The resistance by the Vietnamese against the Americans during the 1960s and early 1970s was the fight for "freedom." But that "freedom" was a collective one —the freedom of Vietnam.[13] For the Asians,

the principle of freedom is never sufficient, and therefore it is necessary to introduce a second principle, that is, the principle of differentiation, to protect those who, for a range of reasons, are disadvantaged.[14]

These different political strategies as well as the philosophical underpinnings endorsed in the reforms of Japan, Russia, and China in the twentieth century had roots in different respective understandings of human hope. The Japanese notion of hope seems to lie in "the natural" in the sense that life is accepted as it is. Thus, in premodern times, the Japanese felt comfortable borrowing from China, because of Chinese power and prosperity at that time. In modern times, however, the Japanese feel comfortable borrowing from the West because of Western dominance of the modern world. This mentality contributed to the successes of the Taika Reform (645 CE) as well as the Meiji Restoration (1868).

The Russian hope seems to lie in "the supernatural," such as a savior. This pessimistic understanding of human hope contributed to the fact that the Russians had the tendency to retreat from communist ideals during the three reforms of the NEP, the Thaw, and that of Gorbachev.

The Chinese sense of hope, however, lies in humankind's endeavor to change the world. The Confucian datong and xiaokang can serve as a key to understanding the political culture of the four Chinese reforms discussed in this book. The leaders of the Late Qing Reform (1898) and the Dengist Reform (1978–1992) such as Kang Youwei and Hu Qiaomu intended to first reach the stage of xiaokang on their way toward datong. The leaders of the Maoist reforms of the Great Leap Forward (1958–1961) and the Cultural Revolution (1966–1976) such as Chen Boda wanted to realize datong immediately by demanding total egalitarianism.[15] In the view of Lucian Pye, "the two seemingly contradictory political cultures of Maoism and Dengism are, in fundamental respects, acceptable for the Chinese."[16] All four Chinese reforms were driven by the desire to change the world for the better.

This situation was consistent with the general observation that China's modernization process in which the reforms were an important part took different paths in comparison with other countries, partly due to the country's cultural traditions. In the words of Brantly Womack, "[t]he relative autonomy of China's process of modernization can be attributed to her massiveness as a nation and as a culture."[17]

China's datong tradition is connected with the Chinese monistic way of thinking. This way of thinking is partly a result of the geography in which Chinese civilization originated: China is a closed system, separate from other parts of the world by the Pacific to the east and southeast, by the Himalayas to the southwest, by the great desert to the west, and by highlands to the north. China was also large enough to be self-sufficient.

This situation contrasts with Western Europe whose civilization originated in and around the Mediterranean. Unlike China, the Mediterranean is geographically an open system in the sense that peoples of different linguistic and ethnic backgrounds have always been aware of and interacted with each other. This is because the Mediterranean is more like an inland lake, and it was relatively easier for the people around it to travel from one place to another even in premodern times. Thus, it was easier for Europeans to develop a pluralistic understanding of the world.[18]

As with the case of Russia whose civilization was part of the West that originated from the open geographic system of the Mediterranean, Japan's geography also differs significantly from that of China, a situation that influenced cultural transformation. Living under the shadow of China, the Japanese traditionally had never viewed Japan as the center of the universe as did the Chinese. Instead, it was easier for the Japanese to endorse pluralism, because the high mountains in Japan made it harder for the Japanese from different regions to communicate with each other in premodern times.[19] Unlike the Chinese datong, the Japanese parochial "groupism" is not universalistic. Japanese policies after World War II inherited this non-universalistic tradition in the sense that, until recently, Japan had enjoyed the benefits provided by the global system maintained by other countries, especially the United States, without worrying about its own contribution to system maintenance.[20]

Living under the shadow of China also contributed to a lack of confidence by the Meiji leaders who adopted moderate strategies during the reforms. Ironically, these moderate policies contributed to the success of the reforms, because social transformation needs to be gradual. This situation parallels the American Revolution when the framers of the U.S. Constitution were also driven by a lack of confidence in the inevitable success of their new ideas that nevertheless turned out to be hugely successful. In contrast, the overconfident and impatient Chinese in the Late Qing Reform, like the leaders of the French Revolution, turned their social experiments into disasters.

In addition to different understandings of hope and expectations about the future, political, and historical factors may have also accounted for differences in strategies and philosophical underpinnings of the reforms. The most important political factor is the formation of the state. Japan and Russia historically had weak states, while China traditionally had a strong state that reinforced the Chinese ambition to transform society and nature.

In Chapter 3, I briefly discussed the feudal political structure of Togukawa Japan. In fact, the entire premodern Japanese political structure since the Taika Reform had little mobilization power.[21] In the words of Fukuzawa Yukichi, "[W]e might even say that Japan has never been a single country,"[22] as the common people were separated from the ruling class. When one kingdom conquered another, the Japanese usually showed little concern over the change in rulers. Japan's lack of a powerful central government in premodern times made it unlikely to support grand transformations in nature and society.

Similar to Japan's premodern political system, Russia historically also lacked effective central administrative capabilities. Premodern Russia was not so much a society as an agglomeration of tens of thousands of separate rural settlements.[23] As late as the sixteenth century, the boyars and the Church resisted power from the center, and the Church continued to struggle against such power until 1721 when the centralized system was entrenched in the Russian state.[24]

Premodern Russia's lack of centralized control was due not to constitutional reasons—given the country's authoritarian tradition—but to administrative ones.[25] The Russian empire was too large to be centrally controlled.[26] This lack of central government control in premodern times was also partly due to its cultural and ethnic diversity. Theodore H. Von Laue noted that "[t]he Russian Empire thus faced among its inhabitants the deep cultural cleavages which the other European states encountered only in their contact with colonial peoples overseas."[27] While most people in China had always been Han, as late as 1897, the majority (55.7 percent) of those living in Russia had been non-Russians.[28] Until recently, Russian peasants were more likely to identity themselves as Orthodox Christians than as Russians.[29]

Although China's premodern political structure was not as powerful as that of modern nation-states, its all-encompassing system (*da yi tong*) was more effective in administration in comparison with Japan and Russia during the time period, as was mentioned briefly in Chapter 3.[30] "State" in the modern sense was taking shape in China during the Spring–Autumn period (77–476 BCE) and government intervention also began at that time. Although the "legalist school" of the period was better known for state intervention,[31] the Confucian school also held that the government was meant to assist the economy and society.[32]

During the reign of Emperor Xuan in the Han dynasty (206 BCE–24 CE), the Chinese government established grain storage facilities so that it could help the peasants by buying grain at regular prices during bumper harvests and selling them at lower prices to the peasants during times of famine. Emperor Wu, also in the Han dynasty, established a government loan system with very low interest rates. Emperor Taizong, during the Tang dynasty (618–906 CE) distributed free food to peasants during periods of famine. Chancellor Wang Anshi in the Song Dynasty (960–1279 CE) gave loans to poor peasants during the spring who could then pay back the loans in the fall during the harvest. Emperor Yongzheng of the Qing Dynasty (1644–

1911 CE) made the rich contribute more money to support the government's administrative costs and public projects.[33]

Premodern Chinese governments were active not only in transforming society, but also in transforming nature. Western scholars noted that the governments of premodern China were responsible for producing the vast network of dikes, irrigation ditches, and waterways that crisscrossed the Chinese realm, which exceeded in scale and scope any public-works construction by their counterparts in premodern Europe, even at the height of the Roman Empire.[34] The two most impressive construction projects that premodern China produced—the Great Wall, which runs from the east coast of China to the west, and the Grand Canal, which runs from Beijing in the north to Hangzhou in the south—served the pragmatic purposes of agricultural production, national defense, and transportation, unlike the Egyptian pyramids, which were built mainly for religious ceremonial purposes.[35]

Accompanying effective central control was China's authoritarian political culture. Although Japan and Russian were authoritarian societies as well, their authoritarian cultures were of different kinds. The Japanese were noted for their "groupism," which, although it differs from individualism, was distinct from a one-man dictatorship at the top level such as China's.[36] Therefore, the Japanese felt comfortable with the post–World War II situation in which the average tenure of prime ministers was roughly two years. Russian authoritarianism was also rooted at the lower levels, such as the family and commune.[37] Chinese authoritarianism, however, was primarily found at the state level. Important Confucian values such as monism, supremacy of the state, or benevolence, were not valued by the Japanese or the Russians.

Besides the role played by the strong state, historical factors have also contributed to China's "outbursts" of utopianism in the twentieth century. The utopian attempts of mass mobilization to change nature such as the Great Leap Forward and to change society such as the Cultural Revolution were unprecedented in Chinese history.

Chinese philosopher Jin Guantao offered the following explanations. In ancient times, according to Jin, datong was understood to have existed in the primitive era. Thus, the Confucian gentry looked backward for utopia. However, in modern times, with the acceptance of social Darwinism by Chinese intellectuals, people looked to the future for their utopian goals. This progressive orientation was therefore more action oriented than the regressive one. Jin also wrote that in ancient times, self-cultivation, rather than social reconstruction, was the goal of the Confucian gentry, since the basic political system was not to be questioned. Therefore, the elites looked inward for a better future. In modern times, the feudal system came under attack and Chinese intellectuals sought a utopian future through social transformation. Finally, in premodern times, Confucianists believed that it was the gentry, not the masses, who carried the virtues of society. In modern times, especially under the Maoist regime, the masses were supposed to carry the virtues of society. Thus, there were more utopian actions in the twentieth century than in the past.[38]

National salvation was another factor for the unleashing of massive utopian actions in twentieth-century China. Chinese economist Liu Guoguang wrote that the driving force of China's economic prosperity since the 1980s has been the people's desire for change in compensation for the humiliations suffered by the Chinese since the mid-nineteenth century.[39] Thomas Metzger critiqued Chinese utopianism and its central idea of anti-selfishness, writing that this attitude was connected with national salvation, the main concern of Chinese leaders during the twentieth century.[40] National salvation was not a serious concern for Japan and Russia during the same time period.

Due to these cultural, political, and historical factors, Chinese utopianism has persisted to the present. In all likelihood, this particular type of hopefulness toward the future will continue to influence Chinese society. David Elkins and Richard E.B. Simeon write, "Culture may not be able to explain why any one alternative was chosen over another, but it may explain why certain alternatives were never considered at all."[41]

How will this unique Chinese tradition of hopefulness impact on the country in the future? As the twentieth century was drawing to a close, several influential publications appeared, each presenting a vision of the world in the new millennium. In the summer of 1989, Francis Fukuyama published an article in *National Interest* entitled, "The End of History."[42] Fukuyama had predicted, even before the collapse of the communist system in the former Soviet Union and the Eastern European bloc, that liberalism as the ultimate human value had been victorious and that the current challenge of humankind was the materialization of liberal values. Fukuyama's argument was supported by the progress of democratization in Latin America and East Asia in recent decades and the fact that both the former Soviet Union and China started capitalist-oriented reforms in the last quarter of the twentieth century. This was surely a rosy utopian vision for the West.

In response, in 1993, Samuel Huntington published an article entitled, "The Clash of Civilizations," in *Foreign Affairs*. Taking a drastically different position, Huntington warned that the collapse of communism in the former Soviet bloc did not bring human conflicts to an end. In fact, he predicted that the new century would be full of conflicts not in terms of clashing ideologies but rather of cultural traditions. The West would have to face challenges from other cultural traditions, and particularly Confucianism and Islam. He claimed that the decline of the West began as early as 1900 and it would take another four hundred years to hit bottom.[43] This vision was certainly not far from a dystopian one for the West.

Huntington's argument was fueled by the relative decline of Western power versus the rest of the world. In the last three decades of the twentieth century, the average salary increase received by U.S. workers was close to zero. If current trends continue, in 2010, 90 percent of the world's scientists will be living in Asia, home to one-half of humankind.[44] Huntington's prediction was also strengthened by the September 11, 2001, terrorist attacks on the World Trade Center in New York City.

Benjamin Barber disagreed with both Fukuyama and Huntington. In his *Jihad vs. McWorld,* Barber argued that nothing is static and everything is interrelated. This situation was more obvious in the modern age, especially from the perspective of globalization. For instance, there is no such a thing as an integrated American culture. The new century would be one in which all cultural traditions must adjust to the challenge of globalization. Barber's prediction was neither utopian nor dystopian for the West, but rather distinctly un-utopian.[45]

A less well-known position has been adopted by Arnold J. Toynbee, the British historian. Toynbee argued that Chinese culture was all-encompassing, tolerant, resilient, and pragmatic.[46] In a world that is not only globalized but also threatened with massive destructive weapons, the Chinese universalistic mentality was constructive toward building a new global order. His position was supported by China's healthy economic performance in the last three decades. By some indicators, China may overtake the United States in the next twenty or thirty years. For those who worry about the rise of China, this could be a nightmare.

Where does our interpretation of Chinese utopianism fit into this picture? In other words, in which direction will China move: the Western utopia of Fukuyama, the Western dystopia of Huntington, the un-utopia of Barber, or a nightmare for those who worry about China's rise, as Toynbee suggested?

In the foreseeable future, Fukuyama's Western utopia will not be applicable to China. The outbursts of Chinese utopianism in the twentieth century were not accidental. Utopianism is deeply rooted in China's past, especially in the tradition of an all-encompassing state, an official ideology centered on the idea of benevolence, and the tendency against rationality in ways of thinking. These characteristics differ significantly from both the Japanese and the Russian traditions.

Toynbee's Chinese unification of the world is unlikely as well. Among others, one factor that militates against such a future is that, in spite of the continuity of Chinese culture, profound changes have actually taken place in China's political culture in the last century, and especially in the last two decades.[47]

Wang Hui divided the ideological transformation of China after 1989 into three stages. In 1989–1993, political discourse was noted for its anti-radicalism. With its roots in the failure of the 1989 Tiananmen Square protest, criticism extended to the twentieth-century Chinese experience, starting from the 1898 Late Qing Reform. Such criticism targeted the pace, not the direction of capitalist-oriented reforms, which was also in accordance with the regime's "primary-stage socialism." In 1993–1997, Chinese political discourse favored Deng's Southern Tour in 1992, which deepened the reform and ignored official corruption and other social evils. Next, in 1997–2003, because of the U.S. government's condemnation of the Tiananmen Square incident of 1989—while overlooking Yeltsin's armed attack on the democratically elected Duma in 1993, as well as the bombing by the United States of the Chinese embassy in Belgrade in 1999—Chinese intellectuals started to question the datong view as well as the general direction of reform. During this period, an increasing number of Chinese intellectuals started to talk about personal freedom.[48]

Jiwei Ci challenged the notion of a monolithic Chinese culture by noting the phenomena of hedonism and nihilism after 1989. For Ci, nihilism "represents a disoriented condition of existence, one in which the connection between action and meaning is severed, but that condition may be experienced whether, and regardless of the degree to which, those involved have the ability or desire to raise it to the level of conscious reflection and appraisal."[49] In other words, if one listens to what the Chinese say, it is utopian; if one looks at what they do, it is dystopian.

At this juncture, it appears that Huntington and Barber may provide us with more useful insights regarding the future of China. While tradition will continue to exert a major influence on Chinese society, Chinese culture is undergoing changes as well, especially in the context of globalization. Although it is difficult to predict exactly how Chinese society will evolve, many scholars look to Asia's other Confucian societies, such as Taiwan and South Korea, for clues. The continuity of the datong mentality is visible in these societies in the sense that the income gap between rich and poor is not as great as that of many Western countries. However, the emphasis on the collective good often parallels some form of authoritarian rule. While Taiwan and South Korea took several decades before embarking on the path toward political democratization, China may take longer, given the official communist ideology and the size and diversity of the country. The datong tradition will be part of China's struggle toward modernity for a long time to come, for better or for worse.

Notes

Notes to the Preface

1. Eric Hobsbawm, *The Age of Extremes: A History of the World, 1014–1991* (New York: Vintage Books), 1996, 2.

2. Hu Xiwei and Tian Wei, "Er shi shi ji zhongguo wenhua jijin zhuyi sichao fu yi" (On Cultural Radicalism of Twentieth-Century China), *Tianjin shehui kexue*, no. 1 (2002), 25–30.

3. Zhang Letian, *Gao Bie Lixiang: Renmin gongshe zhidu* Yanjiu (Farewell, Idealism: A Study of People's Communes) (Beijing: Dongfang Chubanzhongxin, 1998).

4. Wu Yannan, et al., eds., *Gudai wu-tuo-bang yu jindai shehui zhuyi sichao* (Utopia in Ancient Times and Socialist Trends in Modern Times) (Chengdu: Chengdu chubanshe, 1995).

5. Li Zehou and Liu Zaifu, *Gaobie Geming: Huiwang ershi shiji zhongguo* (Farewell, Revolution: Retrospective of Twentieth-Century China) (Hong Kong: Tiandi Tushu youxian gongsi, 1995).

6. Jin Guantao, "Zhongguo wenhua de u-tuo-bang jingshen" (The Utopian Spirit of the Chinese Culture), in *Ershiyi shiji* (Twenty-First Century) (December 1990), 16–32.

7. Li Dao, ed., *Gaobie u-tuo-bang* (Farewell, Utopia) (Lanzhou, China: Gansu renmin chubanshe, 1998).

8. Le Nong, *Li xiang guo de tan qiu: zhongguo datong shihua* (Look for Utopia: China's Datong Tradition) (Zhengzhou: Henan reminchubanshe, 1981).

9. Zhou Ning, *Kong Jiao U-tuo-Bang (Confucian Utopia)* (Beijing: Xueyuan chubanshe, 2004), 27–31.

10. Maurice J. Meisner, *Marxism, Maoism and Utopianism: Eight Essays* (Madison: University of Wisconsin Press, 1982).

11. Stuart R. Schram, "To Utopia and Back: A Cycle in the History of the Chinese Communist Party," *The China Quarterly*, no. 87 (September 1981): 407–39.

12. Thomas A. Metzger, "Modern Chinese Utopianism and the Western Concept of the Civil Society," in *Kuo T'ing-I hsien sheng 9 chih tan ch'en chi nien lun wen chi: hsia ts'e* (Taipei: Chung yang yen chiu yuan chin tai shih yen chiu so fa hsing, 1995);

Metzger, *Escape from Predicament: Neo-Confucianism and China's Evolving Political Culture* (New York: Columbia University Press, 1986).

13. Kung-Chuan Hsiao, *A Modern China and a New World: K'ang Yu-wei, Reformer and Utopian, 1858–1927* (Seattle and London: University of Washington Press, 1975).

14. Zhang Longxi, "Utopian Vision, East and West," *Utopian Studies* 13 (2002).

Notes to Chapter 1

1. David Elkins and Richard E.B. Simeon, "A Cause in Search of Its Effect, or What Does Political Culture Explain?" *Comparative Politics,* no. 11 (January 1979), 125–45.

2. Theda Skocpol and Margaret Sommers, "The Uses of Comparative History in Macrosocial Inquiry," *Comparative Studies in Society and History,* no. 22 (1980), 180.

3. Bruce J. Dickson, "What Explains Chinese Political Behavior? The Debate over Structure and Culture," *Comparative Politics* 25, no. 1 (October 1992), 103–18.

4. John T. Kautsky divides the Marxist enterprise into the Western European type, which he calls "Marxism," and the practices of revolutionary Marxist countries such as the former USSR and China, which he calls "Leninism," a term which is identical to "Marxism-Leninism," "classical Marxism," or "orthodox Marxism." For Kautsky, "Marxism" was the inspiration of Western European intellectuals who intended to empower the working class. "Decentralization" in terms of institutional alternatives was a key feature of this endeavor. In contrast, "Leninism" was the inspiration of intellectuals in less-developed countries, such as the former Soviet Union and China, that intended to modernize their countries as soon as possible. For them, "centralization," which was believed to be more effective in modernization, was a key institutional feature. John H. Kautsky, "Centralization in the Marxist and Leninist Tradition," *Communist and Post-Communist Studies* 30, no. 4 (1997), 379–400.

5. Robert C. Tucker, *Marx Engels Reader,* 2nd ed. (New York: W. W. Norton & Company, 1978), 490.

6. "When, in the course of development, class distinctions have disappeared, and all production has been concentrated in the hands of a vast association of the whole nation, the public power will lose its political character. Political power, properly so called, is merely the organized power of one class for oppressing another." Ibid., 490.

7. Ibid., 713.

8. The Paris Commune, a workers' movement in 1871, practiced direct democracy in the sense that officials were directly elected by the people, the standing army was abolished, and officials received salaries similar to those of ordinary workers. It failed in two months.

9. Janos Kornai, *The Socialist System* (Princeton, NJ: Princeton University Press, 1992).

10. David Nordlander, "Khrushchev's Image in the Light of Glasnost and Perestroika," *The Russian Review* 52 (April 1993), 248–62.

11. Gabriel A. Almond, "The Study of Political Culture," in Lane Crothers and Charles Lockhart, *Culture and Politics: A Reader* (New York: St. Martin's Press, 2000), 10.

12. Political scientists can be divided into two camps with regard to their methodological departures: the "hard," which emphasizes the impact of economics on the political process, and the "soft," which emphasizes the relative independence of politics

and ideology. See Ronald H. Chilcote, *Theories of Comparative Politics: The Search for a Paradigm* (Boulder, CO: Westview Press, 1981). Those who emphasize the relative independence of politics and ideology include Francis Fukuyama, and, in the China field, Edward Friedman. Francis Fukuyama, *The End of History and the Last Man* (New York: Avon Books, 1993); Edward Friedman, "Immanuel Kant's Relevance to an Enduring Asia-Pacific Peace," in Edward Friedman and Barrett L. McCormick, eds., *What If China Doesn't Democratize?* (Armonk, NY: M.E. Sharpe, 2000), 224–58.

13. Max Weber, *Protestant Ethic and the Spirit of Capitalism* (London: Routledge, 2001).

14. Robert D. Putnam, "Studying Elite Political Culture: The Case of 'Ideology,'" *American Political Science Review* 65, no. 3 (September 1971), 652.

15. Almond, "The Study of Political Culture," 23–24.

16. David Elkins and Richard E.B. Simeon, "A Cause in Search of Its Effect, or What Does Political Culture Explain?" *Comparative Politics*, no. 11 (January 1979), 125–45.

17. Shang Huipeng, *Zhongguo ren yu ribenren* (The Chinese and the Japanese) (Beijing: Beijing daxue chubanshe, 2000), 6.

18. Joseph R. Levenson, *Confucian China and Its Modern Fate: The Problem of Intellectual Continuity* (Berkeley: University of California Press, 1958), 118–20.

19. Shiping Hua, "Political Cultures," in *Encyclopedia of Government and Politics,* 2nd ed., ed. Mary Hawkesworth and Maurice Koga (London: Routledge, 2004), 491–501; Richard W. Wilson, *Compliance Ideologies: Rethinking Political Culture* (Cambridge: Cambridge University Press, 1992); Roy C. Macridis, *Contemporary Political Ideologies: Movements and Regimes* (New York: HarperCollins Publishers, 1992), 2.

20. Giovanni Sartori, "Politics, Ideology, and Belief Systems," *American Political Science Review* 63 (1969), 398.

21. Carl J. Friedrich and Zbigniew K. Brzezinski, *Totalitarian Dictatorship and Autocracy* (Cambridge, MA: Harvard University Press, 1965), 88.

22. Brantly Womack, "The Phases of Chinese Modernization," *Collected Papers of History Studies,* no. 4 (1999), 1–15.

23. "It was Marxist theory which first achieved a fusion of the particular and total conceptions of ideology." Karl Mannheim, *Ideology and Utopia* (New York: Harcourt, Brace & World, Inc., 1936), 147.

24. Dickson, "What Explains Chinese Political Behavior?" 103–18.

25. Tony Saich, "Negotiating the State: The Development of Socialist Organizations in China," *China Quarterly,* no. 161 (March 2000), 138–39.

26. Theda Skocpol and Margaret Sommers, "The Uses of Comparative History in Macrosocial Inquiry," *Comparative Studies in Society and History,* no. 22 (1980), 180.

27. William G. Rosenberg and Marilyn Young, *Transforming Russia and China: Revolutionary Struggle in the Twentieth Century* (New York: Oxford University Press, 1982).

28. Mark Selden, with Chad Raymond and Kate Zhou, "The Power of the Strong: Rural Resistance and Reform in China and Vietnam," *China Information* 14, no. 2 (2001).

29. Yanqi Tong, *Transition from State Socialism: Political and Economic Changes in Hungary and China* (Lanham, MD: Rowman & Littlefield, 1997).

30. When I presented the chapter that compares the Late Qing Reform and the Meiji Restoration at the Unirule Institute in Beijing in June 2004, my commentator, Gao Hong from the Institute of Japan Studies at the Chinese Academy of Social Science, said that someone once told him in a joking manner that "if anybody attempts to compare China with another country, I will shoot him."

31. Michel C. Okenberg, "The American Study of Modern China: Toward the Twenty-First Century," in *American Studies of Contemporary China,* ed. David Shambaugh (Washington, DC: Woodrow Wilson Center Press, 1993), 315.

32. "A case is an instance of a more general category. The analysis is made within a comparative perspective which mandates that the description of the particular be cast in terms of broadly analytic constructs." H. Scarrow, *Comparative Political Analysis* (New York: Harper & Row, 1969), 7.

33. Their model can be described as follows: the historical and social structural backgrounds against which the reforms emerged were similar, but with one crucial difference: the cultural determinants that impacted on the processes of reform. Theda Skocpol and Margaret Sommers, "The Uses of Comparative History in Macrosocial Inquiry," *Comparative Studies in Society and History,* no. 22 (1980)174–97. See also Charles C. Ragin, *The Comparative Method: Moving Beyond Qualitative and Quantitative Strategies* (Berkeley: University of California Press, 1987).

34. Benjamin Schwartz's lecture in 1969 at Harvard, titled, "Why Did Japan 'Make It' During the Meiji Period, Whereas China in the Late 19th Century Did Not?" cited in Stuart R. Schram, "To Utopia and Back: A Cycle in the History of the Chinese Communist Party," *The China Quarterly,* no. 87 (September 1981), 408.

35. Li lists several differences between Japan and China in the nineteenth century: (1) China's feudal system was stronger than Japan's; (2) Japan's reform was accomplished through civil wars, while China's reform was performed by a small elite; (3) at the time of Japan's reform, the United States had just concluded the Civil War, and thus was too preoccupied to intervene in Japan, and Britain and France were too busy in China. Li Qingting, "Mingzhi weixin yu Wuxu bianfa chengbai yinyou zhi bijiao" (Why Did the Meiji Restoration Succeed and the Late Qing Reform Fail?), *Journal of the Teacher's College, Qingdao University* 12, no. 2 (June 1995), 56–58.

36. Schrecker focused on the Ching-I, or movement for renovation. Although these scholars functioned outside power centers, they had some patrons who worked inside government. In Meiji, the *hirazamurai* resembled the Chinese Ching-I in the sense that they were morally committed, but were outside the power center. There were similarities and differences between the two reforms. In terms of motivations and the composition of the two groups, both were outside the center of power and consisted of people who were enraged by foreign invasions. Differences included the following: The Qing elites feared peasant rebellions more because they were stronger than the Japanese protests from below, and the ideological drive within the Japanese group was stronger, because the semireligious Shinto and the rigor of Bushido bolstered it. John Schrecker, "The Reform Movement of 1898 and the Meiji Restoration as Ch'ing-I Movement," in *The Chinese and the Japanese: Essays in Political and Cultural Interactions,* ed. Akira Iriye (Princeton, NJ: Princeton University Press, 1980).

37. In general terms, War Communism can be categorized as typical of the communist system. However, it was more radically communistic because of the civil war.

38. Nordlander also mentioned that Burlatsky was indeed a representative of Khrushchev's ideas. In the article, the author mentioned that Leonid Brezhnev (1906–1982) criticized Khrushchev for his "subjectivism" and "voluntarism," but Gorbachev referred to Khrushchev in a positive light. Nordlander noted that "Soviet authors participating in the forum on Khrushchev were almost uniformly supportive of perestroika" (p. 249). "[A]side from Bukharin, who never held leadership in either the party or state, Khrushchev was the only significant reformer in Soviet history" (p. 249). For Soviet re-

form-oriented intellectuals, "Khrushchev stoked their hopes for change but did not fulfill their aspirations. Nearly thirty years later, they looked to Gorbachev's reforms as the fruition of Khrushchev's unkept promises" (p. 250). "Khrushchev's Image in the Light of Glasnost and Perestroika," by David Nordlander, *The Russian Review* 52 (April 1993), 248–62.

39. Roderick MacFarquhar: "Had he [Mao] died as soon after the revolution as Lenin, none would have taken place." MacFarquhar, "The Secret Speeches of Chairman Mao," in *The Secret Speeches of Chairman Mao: From the Hundred Flowers to the Great Leap Forward,* ed. Roderick MacFarquhar, Timothy Cheek, and Eugene Wu (Cambridge, MA: Harvard University Press, 1989), 3.

40. Stuart Schram, "To Utopia and Back: A Cycle in the History of the Chinese Communist Party," *The China Quarterly,* no. 87 (September 1981), 407–39. This was also noted by Wolfgang Bauer, *China and the Search for Happiness* (New York: Seabury Press, 1976), 400.

41. Yan Sun, "The Chinese and Soviet Reassessment of Socialism: The Theoretical Bases of Reform and Revolution in Communist Reforms," *Communist and Post-Communist Studies* 27, no. 1 (1994), 39–58; "Reform, State and Corruption: Is Corruption Less Destructive in China than in Russia?" *Comparative Politics* 32, no. 1 (October 1999), 1–20.

42. Minxin Pei, *From Reform to Revolution: The Demise of Communism in China and the Soviet Union* (Cambridge, MA: Harvard University Press, 1994).

43. Yasheng Huang, "Information, Bureaucracy, and Economic Reforms in China and the Soviet Union," *World Politics,* 47, no.1 (October 1994), 102–34.

44. Steven Lee Solnick, "The Breakdown of Hierarchies in the Soviet Union and China," *World Politics* 48, no. 2 (January 1996).

45. As will be explained in Chapter 2, the Chinese characters "da tong" are an idea found in the Confucian *The Analects.* Literally, it means, "grand harmony," or "great reunion of harmony." It is a paradise in which everybody loves one another.

46. According to the monistic way of thinking, power has one source, and so does truth. This idea is part of the Chinese tradition.

47. Burlatsky noted that the precedent of Gorbachev's reform was the NEP. Fyodor M. Burlatsky, "New Thinking about Socialism," in *Breakthrough: Emerging New Thinking,* ed. Anatoly Gromyko and Martin Hellman (New York: Walker & Company, 1988), 256–66.

48. For the challenges of making comparative culture studies from a theoretical perspective, see David G. Horn, "Reading History: Toward Comparative Cultural Studies: A Review Article," *Comparative Studies in Society and History* 39, no. 4 (1997), 734.

49. William G. Rosenberg and Marilyn B. Young's *Transforming Russia and China: Revolutionary Struggle in the Twentieth Century* (New York: Oxford University Press, 1982), deserves mention, although these authors only focus on the similarities of the communist experiments of the two countries. David Law summarizes the study by Rosenberg and Young by listing similarities in both revolutions: (1) they emerged from enormous social chaos and dislocations; (2) they had to solve the problems of economics, because both countries were poor; and (3) they had to stick to their socialist commitment as an ideology. Law, "Revolutions Compared: Russia and China: A Review Article," *Comparative Studies in Society and History* 28, no. 3 (July 1986), 545–51.

50. See James Paul Gee, *An Introduction to Discourse Analysis: Theory and Method* (London and New York: Routledge, 1999), 1.

51. Vivien A. Schmidt, "Does Discourse Matter in the Politics of Welfare State Adjustment?" *Comparative Political Studies* 35, no. 2 (March 2002), 169–70.

52. Friedrich and Brzezinski, *Totalitarian Dictatorship and Autocracy,* 108–10.

53. "Zi Lu," in Confucius, *The Analects,* translated with an introduction and notes by D.C. Lau (London: Penguin Classics, 1979).

54. For the control of communication in communist countries, including official discourse, see Friedrich and Brzezinski, *Totalitarian Dictatorship and Autocracy,* 129–47.

55. Shiping Hua, "One Servant, Two Masters: The Dilemma of Chinese Establishment Intellectuals," *Modern China* 20, no. 1 (January 1994), 92–121.

56. David Shambaugh, ed., *American Studies of Contemporary China* (Washington, DC: Woodrow Wilson Center Press, 1993), 14–42.

57. Thomas Metzger, *Escape from Predicament: Neo-Confucianism and China's Evolving Political Culture* (New York: Columbia University Press, 1986), 14.

58. Gloria Davies, "Introduction," in Gloria Davies, ed., *Voicing Concerns: Contemporary Chinese Critical Inquiry* (Lanham, MD: Roman & Littlefield Publishers, 2001), 2.

59. Anthony J. Kane, "The Humanities in Contemporary China Studies: An Uncomfortable Tradition," in David Shambaugh, ed., *American Studies of Contemporary China* (Washington, DC: Woodrow Wilson Center Press, 1993), 7.

60. Li Junru, "China under the New Leadership of Hu Jintao," lecture, Center for Asian Studies, American University, Washington, DC, November 8, 2004.

61. Neil Renwick and Qing Cao, "China's Political Discourse toward 21st Century: Victimhood, Identity and Political Power," *East Asia: An International Quarterly* 17, no. 4 (Winter 1999), 112–43.

62. Shu-Yun Ma, "Chinese Discourse on Civil Society," *The China Quarterly,* no. 137 (March 1994), 180–93.

63. He Ping, *China's Search for Modernity: Cultural Discourse in the Late 20th Century* (Houndmill, Basingstoke, Hampshire; New York: Palgrave MacMillan in association with St. Anthony's College, Oxford, 2002).

64. W.L. Chong, ed., *China's Great Proletarian Cultural Revolution: Master Narratives and Post-Mao Counternarratives* (Lanham, MD: Roman & Littlefield, 2002).

Notes to Chapter 2

1. Delmer M. Brown, "The Early Evolution of Historical Consciousness," in *The Cambridge History of Japan,* ed. John Whitney Hall, vol. 1, *Ancient Japan* (New York: Cambridge University Press, 1993), 537–48.

2. Wolfgang Bauer, *China and the Search for Happiness: Recurring Themes in Four Thousand Years of Chinese Cultural History* (New York: Seabury Press, 1976), xii, 6.

3. Lewis Mumford, *The Story of Utopias* (New York: Viking Press, 1962), 1.

4. Barbara Goodwin, "Utopianism," in *The Blackwell Encyclopedia of Political Thought,* ed. David Miller (New York: Basil Blackwell, 1987), 533.

5. Ibid., 534–35.

6. Karl Mannheim, *Ideology and Utopia: An Introduction to the Sociology of Knowledge* (New York: Harcourt, Brace and World, 1936), 192.

7. Howard White, *Peace among the Willows: The Political Philosophy of Francis Bacon* (The Hague: Martinus Nijhoff, 1968).

8. B.F. Skinner, *Walden Two* (New York: Macmillan, 1962).

9. Frederick Engels, *Socialism: Utopian and Scientific* (New York: International Publishers, 1972).

10. Cited in Mannheim, *Ideology and Utopia,* 126.

11. V.I. Lenin, "Two Utopias," in Lenin, *Collected Works* (Moscow: Progress Publishers 1975), vol. 18, 355–59.

12. Andrzej Walicki, *Marxism and the Leap to the Kingdom of Freedom: The Rise and Fall of the Communist Utopia* (Stanford, CA: Stanford University Press, 1995).

13. Plato, *The Republic* (New York: W.W. Norton and Company, 1985).

14. For instance, a major textbook in political science views the various forms of utopia as the foundation of political theory. Thomas M. Magstadt and Peter M. Schotten, *Understanding Politics: Ideas, Institutions and Issues,* 5th ed. (New York: Worth Publishers, 1999). Utopia differs from regular political theory in three aspects: (1) Utopia pictures the good society in its entirety. (2) Utopia pictures the best society and is therefore more ambitious. (3) Utopia negates the undesirable elements of the current society and makes it a sharper critical tool than regular political theory. Goodwin, "Utopianism," 537.

15. Bauer, *China and the Search for Happiness,* ix.

16. Buddhism, imported from China in 552 CE, was not influential among the Japanese people until the thirteenth century. This chapter focuses on Confucianism and the indigenous culture since they were the most influential at the end of the Tokugawa period. Edwin O. Reischauer, *Japan: The Story of a Nation* (New York: McGraw-Hill Publishing Company, 1990), 16. See also Jack Seward, *The Japanese* (New York: William Morrow and Company, 1972), 190.

17. W.G. Beasley, *The Rise of Modern Japan* (New York: St. Martin's Press, 1995), 1–14.

18. Marius B. Jansen, "The Meiji Restoration," in *The Cambridge History of Japan,* ed. Marius B. Jansen, vol. 5, *The Nineteenth Century* (New York: Cambridge University Press, 1989), 313.

19. Beasley, *Rise of Modern Japan,* 1–14.

20. Reischauer, *Japan: The Story of a Nation,* 7.

21. Beasley, *Rise of Modern Japan,* 1–14.

22. Harry D. Harootunian, "The Function of China in Tokugawa Thought," in *The Chinese and the Japanese: Essays in Political and Cultural Interactions,* ed. Akira Iriye (Princeton, NJ: Princeton University Press, 1980), 21.

23. Ibid., 23.

24. Beasley, *Rise of Modern Japan,* 1–14.

25. Jansen, "The Meiji Restoration," 313.

26. Brown, "The Early Evolution of Historical Consciousness," 537–48.

27. Ibid., 537–48.

28. S.N. Eisenstadt, *Japanese Civilization: A Comparative View* (Chicago: University of Chicago Press, 1996), 320.

29. Shintoism had almost no ethical content, except for an emphasis on ritual purity. Edwin O. Reischauer, *Japan: The Story of a Nation* (New York: McGraw-Hill Publishing Company, 1990), 14.

30. Tuetuo Janita, *The Intellectual Foundations of Modern Japanese Politics* (Chicago: University of Chicago Press, 1974), 7.

31. Shang Huipeng, *Zhongguo ren yu ribenren (The Chinese and the Japanese)* (Beijing: Beijing daxue chubanshe, 2000), 349. Also, Frederick Wakeman, "All the Rage in China," *New York Review of Books,* March 2, 1989.

32. Edwin O. Reischauer, *The Japanese Today: Change and Continuity* (Cambridge, MA: Harvard University Press, 1996).

33. "Russian philosophy must be viewed as an indispensable part of the Western intellectual tradition since it provides perhaps the most elaborated footnotes to the most mature and comprehensive dialogues of Plato: *The Republic* and *The Laws*. Questions of social ethics and political philosophy, of an individual's relationship to a State, of adequate knowledge and virtuous behavior, of wisdom and power, of religious and aesthetic values, of ideas and ideals as guidelines for human life—all of these are central to Russian philosophy and exemplify its continuing relevance vis-à-vis Plato's legacy and the Western tradition in its broadest sense. Moreover, the very status of ideas in Russian philosophy mirrors Plato's vision of them as ontological entities, 'laws,' or ideal principles—as opposed to mere epistemological units. In discussing Russian philosophy, especially that of its Soviet period, we are bound to consider the practical fate of such Platonic conceptions as we explore the final outcome of an ideocratic utopia, wherein philosophy was designated to rule the republic." Mikhail Epstein, "An Overview of Russian Philosopy" (Atlanta, GA: Emory University, 1995), http://www.emory.edu/INTELNET/rus_thought_overview.html.

34. This is based on a conversation with Blair Ruble, director of the Kennan Institute, Woodrow Wilson International Center for Scholars, in Louisville, Kentucky, on May 26, 2006. In 1918, Russian peasants were more likely to identity themselves as Orthodox Christians than as Russians. Richard Pipes, "Flight from Freedom," *Foreign Affairs* 83, no. 3 (May/June 2004), 9–15. Depending on how the question is asked, as many as 90 percent of ethnic Russians today identify themselves as Russian Orthodox. Wikipedia, http://en.wikipedia.org/wiki/Russian_Orthodox Church (accessed November 29, 2005).

35. The three paths of Western utopianism are summarized by Zhou Ning in *Kong Jiao U-tuo-Bang* (Confucian Utopia) (Beijing: Xueyuan chubanshe, 2004), 5. The influence of Plato's philosophy is described as follows: "For 'the safest general characterization of the European philosophical tradition,' according to Alfred North Whitehead, is that it consists of a series of footnotes to Plato." Robert D. Cumming, "Introduction: The Trial and Death of Socrates," in Plato, *Euthyphro, Apology, Crito,* trans. F.J. Church (Upper Saddle River, NJ: Prentice Hall, 1948), vii.

36. St. Augustine, *The City of God* (Garden City, NY: Image Books, 1958).

37. Thomas More, *Utopia* (Cambridge: Cambridge University Press, 2002).

38. Plato, *The Republic* (New York: W.W. Norton and Company, 1985).

39. John 18:36 (King James version).

40. James Reeve Pusey, *China and Charles Darwin* (Cambridge, MA: Harvard University Press), 166.

41. St. Augustine, *The City of God* (Garden City, NY: Image Books, 1958).

42. This book was representative of Western utopian thought during the time period. Frank E. Manuel and Fritzie P. Manuel, *Utopian Thought in the Western World* (Cambridge: Belknap Press of Harvard University Press, 1979), 3–18.

43. Utopia parallels the emergence of Protestantism, which is essentially the individualization and pluralization of Christianity. The faithful were able to worship without having to rely on a unified church. For example, one year after Sir Thomas More

(1478–1535) published his *Utopia* (1518), Martin Luther (1483–1546) nailed his Ninety-Five Theses to the door of Wittenberg Church.

44. More, *Utopia.*

45. Bauer, *China and the Search for Happiness,* xii, 6.

46. "No one has fewer dreams than the citizen of a democracy; and few are ever known to indulge in those idle and solitary contemplations which normally anticipate and end up in great agitations of the heart. They do, it is true, set great store on obtaining that sort of deep, reliable, and peaceful affection which adds charm and security to one's life. But they do not pursue those violent and capricious emotions which disturb and shorten one's life." Alexis de Tocqueville, *Democracy in America and Two Essays on America,* trans. Gerald E. Bevan (New York: Penguin Books, 2003), 694.

47. Ibid.

48. Utopias before the seventeenth century were not aimed at action. Manuel and Manuel, *Utopian Thought in the Western World,* 2. Prior to the end of eighteenth century, utopia in the West was not intended to be realized. Maurice J. Meisner, *Marxism, Maoism and Utopianism: Eight Essays* (Madison: University of Wisconsin Press, 1982), 4, 8.

49. Unlike the premodern Russian government that did not have effective control of the country, modern nation-states' mobilization power is enormous. Manuel and Manuel, *Utopian Thought in the Western World,* 16.

50. The three types of Chinese utopianism were summarized by Wu Yannan. In addition to the three kinds examined in this chapter, China also experienced the Christian utopia of the Taiping Rebellion and various socialist utopian movements in modern history. Wu Yannan, et al., eds., *Gudai wu-tuo-bang yu jindai shehui zhuyi sichao* (Utopia in Ancient Times and Socialist Trends in Modern Times) (Chengdu: Chengdu chubanshe, 1995), 12–20.

51. Linguistically, utopia can refer to both a "non-place" and a "better place." Meisner, *Marxism, Maoism and Utopianism,* 3, 13; Kung-Chuan Hsiao, *A Modern China and a New World: K'ang Yu-wei, Reformer and Utopian, 1858–1927* (Seattle and London: University of Washington Press, 1975), 412.

52. Thomas A. Metzger, *Escape from Predicament: Neo-Confucianism and China's Evolving Political Culture* (New York: Columbia University Press, 1986).

53. Bauer, *China and the Search for Happiness.*

54. The translator did a superb job in using both the sound of utopia and the literary meaning of the three Chinese characters: *wu* means "no," and *bang* means "place." But *tuo* just mimics the sound.

55. Andrzej Walicki, *Marxism and the Leap to the Kingdom of Freedom: The Rise and Fall of the Communist Utopia* (Stanford, CA: Stanford University Press, 1995).

56. Xiao Tangyan, et al. *Gudai U-Tuo-Bang yu Jindai Shehuizhuyi Sichao* (Ancient Utopianism and Socialism in Modern Times) (Chengdu, China: Sichuan chubanshe, 1994), 64.

57. Peng Ming, ed., *Cong kongxiang dao kexue: zhongguo shehui zhuyi sixiang fazhan de lishi kaocha* (From Utopia to Science: Historical Overview of the Development of China's Socialist Thought) (Beijing: Zhongguo renmin daxue chubanshe, 1986), 43.

58. *Li Ji,* in which datong is described, was compiled by a Confucian scholar named

Dai Sheng in the West Han period (206 BCE–220 CE). It has forty-nine chapters that are believed to contain statements by Confucius and his disciples. One of the chapters is *Li Yun,* which, according to Dai Sheng, is the statement made by Confucius when he was talking to one of his students. Cited in Le Nong, *Lixiang guo de tan qiu—Zhongguo datong sixiang shihua* (Looking for Utopia) (Zhengzhou: Henan renmin chubanshe, 1981), 14. Also see Chen Zhengyan and Lin Qiyan, *Zhonguo Guodai datong sixiang* (Utopian Thought in Premodern China) (Shanghai: Shanghai renmin chubanshe, 1986), 84–85.

59. The issue was called into question by Kong Yingda during the Tang dynasty (618–907 CE), and then by Chen Hao and Huang Zhen in the Song synasty (42–479 CE). These scholars attributed the idea of datong to Lao Tzu and Mo Tze. See Jiang Jianshe, *Zhou qin shidai lixiangguo tansuo* (Exploring Utopias in the Zhou and Qin Periods) (Zhengzhou, Henan: Zhong Zhou guji chubanshe, 1998), 204. Also see Chen Zhengyan and Lin Qiyan, *Zhonguo Guodai datong sixiang,* 84–85.

60. In 1921, Liang Shuming said that *Li Yun* was not consistent with the philosophy of Confucius. In terms of tone and philosophy, it is more like Lao Tzu. Liang cited a letter from Wu Yu to Chen Duxiu in which Wu cited observations by Lu Donglai, Zhu Xi, and Li Bangzhi in the Song dynasty to argue that these three scholars opposed the idea that *Li Yun* was Confucian in nature. They felt that the philosophical tone of datong was more consistent with the tradition of Lao Tzu and Chuangzi rather than Confucius. Liang Shuming, *Dontxi wenhua jiqi zhexue* (The Cultures and Philosophies of the East and West) (Beijing: Shangwu yinshuguan, 2003), 140. Le Nong, a contemporary scholar, believes that the author was a Confucian who lived between the Qin and Han dynasties. *Li Yun* was born under the influence of the peasant rebellions at the end of the Qin dynasty. Cited in Le Nong, *Lixiang guo de tan qiu,* 14.

61. Hong Kong scholar Zhang Longxi said that Confucius argued for self-restraint and favored restoring the rituals of Zhou (1027–221 BCE). But Zhou is not datong. Therefore, Zhang noted elements of Chinese utopianism from other sources, such as *The Analects* and Mencius. Zhang cited the example of Confucius seeking paradise during a sea voyage. Zhang also cited literary works, such as *Jing Hua Yuan,* Cao Cao's literary works, and Tao Yuanming's *Tao Hua Yuan Ji* (Peach Blossom Shangri-la). Zhang Longxi, "Utopian Vision, East and West," *Utopia Studies* 13 (2002).

62. Meisner, 1–5.

63. Peng Ming, ed., *Cong kongxiang dao kexue: zhongguo shehui zhuyi sixiang fazhan de lishi kaocha* (From Utopia to Science: Historical Overview of the Development of China's Socialist Thought) (Beijing: Zhongguo renmin daxue chubanshe, 1986), 46.

64. Wu Yannan, et al., eds., *Gudai wu-tuo-bang yu jindai shehui zhuyi sichao,* 62.

65. For the translation, see W.T. de Bary, ed., *Sources of Chinese Tradition,* vol. 1 (New York: Columbia University Press, 1960), 176.

66. *The Analects,* XVI. I. 10, cited in K'ang Yu-wei, *Ta T'ung Shu: The One-World Philosophy of K'ang Yu-wei* (London: George Allen and Unwin Ltd., 1958), 211.

67. Jiang Jianshe, *Zhou qin shidai lixiangguo tansuo (Exploring Utopias in the Zhou and Qin Periods)* (Zhengzhou, Henan: Zhong Zhou guji chubanshe, 1998), 211.

68. Wu Yannan, et al., eds., *Gudai wu-tuo-bang yu jindai shehui zhuyi sichao,* 552.

69. V.I. Lenin, *The State and Revolution* (New York: International Publishers, 1932), 52.

70. For a discussion about Chinese anarchists, see Wolfgang Bauer, *China and the*

Search for Happiness: Recurring Themes in Four Thousand Years of Chinese Cultural History (New York: Seabury Press, 1976), 131–52.

71. *Mencius,* edited by D.C. Lau (New York: Penguin Books, 1970), 49.

72. Ibid., 168.

73. Ibid., 167.

74. There seems to be a conflict between rationality and Chinese culture. Li Zehou said that Confucian thought is not rational. Li Zehou and Liu Zaifu, *Gaobie Geming: Huiwang ershi shiji zhongguo* (Farewell, Revolution: A Retrospective of Twentieth-Century China) (Hong Kong: Tiandi Tushu youxian gongsi, 1995), 82. Similarly, Stuart Schram observes that, for the Chinese, "the subjective creates the objective." Stuart R. Schram, "To Utopia and Back: A Cycle in the History of the Chinese Communist Party," *The China Quarterly,* no. 87 (September 1981), 422.

75. For Plato, wisdom and morality are the same, and the bottom line of his wisdom is logic, rationality, and consistency. Plato believed that humans are not kind by nature. Good people often do not have a good ending. Plato, *The Republic,* 48–49, 56–61.

76. In the words of Roger Ames, Greek thought is rational, while traditional Chinese thought is "biographical." Roger Ames, "New Confucianism: A Native Response to Western Philosophy," in Shiping Hua, *Chinese Political Culture* (Armonk, NY: M.E. Sharpe, 2001), 70–102. In Greek philosophy, truth comes from one's head and logic is the key. The death of Socrates is the best testimony of Plato's belief in the integrity of morality and rationality. Socrates was arrested by the Athenian authorities on false charges and had the opportunity to escape. However, he chose to stay to be executed, because he felt that his actions had to be consistent with his words: He had already pledged loyalty to the Athenian government and had to accept the government's judgment, right or wrong. Plato, *Euthyphro, Apology, Crito* (Upper Saddle River, NJ: Prentice-Hall, 1948).

77. Metzger, *Escape from Predicament,* 154–58, 220.

78. Li Zehou and Liu Zaifu, *Gaobie Geming: Huiwang ershi shiji zhongguo,* 82.

79. "The fundamental equation of an ideal world order, calm and equality can thus already be found in Confucius, although its form rather reminds us of a uniform stabilization of inequality. The period where this kind of government seems to have been fully realized in Confucius's opinion was the western (or 'earlier') Chou dynasty (about 1050–770 BCE)." Bauer, *China and the Search for Happiness,* 22.

80. Chen Zhengyan and Lin Qiyan, *Zhongguo gudai datong sixiang yanjiu,* 84.

81. For the translation, see William Theodore de Bary and Irene Bloom, *Sources of Chinese Tradition,* 2nd ed., vol. 1 (New York: Columbia University Press, 1999), 343.

82. Lao-Tzu, *Tao Te Ching,* translated by Stephen Addiss and Stanley Lombardo (Indianapolis: Hackett Publishing Company, 1993), chapter 80.

83. Ibid., chapter 57.

84. Ibid., Chapter 5.

85. Ibid., 13.

86. Wu Yannan, et al., eds., *Gudai wu-tuo-bang yu jindai shehui zhuyi sichao,* 22–30.

87. The text of the translation follows: "During the Tai-yuan period of the Chin [Qin] dynasty a fisherman of Wuling once rowed upstream, unmindful of the distance he had gone, when he suddenly came to a grove of peach trees in bloom. For several hundred paces on both banks of the stream there was no other kind of tree. The wild flowers growing under them were fresh and lovely, and fallen petals covered the ground—it made a

great impression on the fisherman. He went on for a way with the idea of finding out how far the grove extended. It came to an end at the foot of a mountain whence issued the spring that supplied the stream. There was a small opening in the mountain and it seemed as though light was coming through it. The fisherman left his boat and entered the cave, which at first was extremely narrow, barely admitting his body; after a few dozen steps it suddenly opened out onto a broad and level plain where well-built houses were surrounded by rich fields and pretty ponds. Mulberry, bamboo and other trees and plants grew there, and criss-cross paths skirted the fields. The sounds of cocks crowing and dogs barking could be heard from one courtyard to the next. Men and women were coming and going about their work in the fields. The clothes they wore were like those of ordinary people. Old men and boys were carefree and happy.

"When they caught sight of the fisherman, they asked in surprise how he had got there. The fisherman told the whole story, and was invited to go to their house, where he was served wine while they killed a chicken for a feast. When the other villagers heard about the fisherman's arrival they all came to pay him a visit. They told him that their ancestors had fled the disorders of Chin [Qin] times and, having taken refuge here with wives and children and neighbors, had never ventured out again; consequently they had lost all contact with the outside world. They asked what the present ruling dynasty was, for they had never heard of the Han, let alone the Wei and the Chin [Qin]. They sighed unhappily as the fisherman enumerated the dynasties one by one and recounted the vicissitudes of each. The visitors all asked him to come to their houses in turn, and at every house he had wine and food. He stayed several days. As he was about to go away, the people said, 'There's no need to mention our existence to outsiders.'" T'ao Ch'ien, *The Poetry of T'ao Ch'ien,* trans. James Robert Hightower (Oxford: Clarendon Press, 1970), 254–55.

88. Wu Yannan, et al., eds., *Gudai wu-tuo-bang yu jindai shehui zhuyi sichao,* 89–93.

89. Chen Zhengyan and Lin Qiyan, *Zhongguo gudai datong xixiang yanjiu,* 182–89.

90. In the view of Jin Guantao, Confucianism and Taoism as value systems complement each other. For instance, Confucianism is participatory in the country's politics while Taoism is nonparticipatory. For details of his theory, see Jin Guantao, *Zhongguo Fengjian Shehui de Chaowending Jiegou.*

91. Wu Dou Mi Dao, a Taoist sect, was created by Zhang Ling during the period. In order to join the organization, each member was required to submit five *dou* of rice. A *dou* is roughly a decaliter. The sect was modified by Zhang Xiu. In February 184 CE, the so-called Yellow Turban Rebellion led by Zhang Jiao broke out. Many peasant rebellions, including the Yellow Turban Rebellion and the Taiping Rebellion, shared traits with millenarianism, especially before the peasant governments were established, because the peasant rebellions were aimed at mobilization. Zhang Jiao considered himself a follower of the Way of Supreme Peace, or *Tai Ping Dao.* The teaching of *Tai Ping Dao* is the so-called *Taiping Jing,* with multiple authors, including Gan Ji and Gong Chong. Both were Taoist priests. Zhang Lu surrendered to Cao Cao, the leader of Wei, during the Three Kingdoms period (220–280 CE), and that was the end of the experiment.

92. Theda Skocpol and Margaret Sommers, "The Uses of Comparative History in Macrosocial Inquiry," *Comparative Studies in Society and History,* no. 22 (1980), 182.

93. Jin Guantao and Liu Qingfeng, *Xingsheng yu weiji—lun zhongguo fengjian shehui de chao wenting jiegou* (Prosperity and Crisis—on the Ultrastability of China's Feudal System) (Changsha, China: Hunan renmin chubanshe, 1983), 115–16.

94. *Mencius,* edited by D.C. Lau (New York: Penguin Books, 1970), 144.

95. Ibid.

96. Gao Min, *Qin-han shi lun ji* (Historical Works on Qin-Han) (Zhengzhou: Zhongzhou shuhua she, 1982), 344–69. Also see Wu Yannan, et al., eds., *Gudai wu-tuo-bang yu jindai shehui zhuyi sichao,* 75–77.

97. Liu Zehua, ed., *Zhongguo gudai zhengzhi sixiang shi* (A History of Chinese Political Thought in Premodern Times) (Tianjin: Nankai daxue chubanshe, 1994), 381–95.

98. The Taiping Rebellion (or Rebellion of Great Peace) was led by Hong Xiuquan, who claimed to be the younger brother of Jesus Christ. The peasant rebellion against the Qing government failed, causing as many as 20 million deaths.

99. Karl Marx, "On International Events," in *Marx, Engels Quanji* (Works by Marx and Engels) (Beijing: Renmin chubanshe, n.d.), vol. 7, 265. Cited in Wu Yannan, et al., eds., *Gudai wu-tuo-bang yu jindai shehui zhuyi sichao,* 13.

100. Li Zhenzhong, *Taiping tianguo de xingwang* (The Rise and Fall of the Kingdom of Heavenly Peace) (Taipei: Cheng Chun Book Co., 1999), 199–206.

101. Kung-Chuan Hsiao, *A Modern China and a New World: K'ang Yu-wei, Reformer and Utopian, 1858–1927* (Seattle and London: University of Washington Press, 1975), 500.

Notes to Chapter 3

1. Lin Daizhao, et al., *Zhongguo Jindai Zhengzhi Zhidushi* (A History of Modern China's Political System) (Chongqing, China: Chongqing chubanshe, 1988), 178.

2. Douglas Howland, "Society Reified: Herbert Spencer and Political Theory in Early Meiji Japan," *Comparative Studies in Society and History,* no. 42 (2000), 67–86.

3. Edwin O. Reischauer, *Japan: The Story of a Nation* (New York: Alfred A. Knopf, 1970), 121–23.

4. Yao Fenglian and Zheng Yushuo, eds., *Jian ming zhongguo jindai zhengzhi sixiang shi* (A Concise History of Modern Chinese Political Thought) (Lanzhou, China: Gansu renmin chubanshe, 1986), 127–60.

5. Marius B. Jansen, "The Meiji Restoration," in *The Cambridge History of Japan,* vol. 5, ed. Marius B. Jansen (New York: Cambridge University Press, 1989), 360–66. Li Qingting, "Mingzhi weixin yu Wuxu bianfa chengbai yinyou zhi bijiao" (Why Did the Meiji Restoration Succeed and the Late Qing Reform Fail?), *Journal of the Teacher's College, Qingdao University* 12, no. 2 (June 1995), 56–58.

6. George M. Wilson, "Plots and Motives in Japan's Meiji Restoration," *Comparative Studies in Society and History* 25, no. 2 (1983), 407–27.

7. Luke S.K. Kwong, "Chinese Politics at the Crossroads: Reflections on the Hundred Days Reform of 1898," *Modern Asian Studies* 34, no. 3 (2000), 691.

8. "Far from an informed reformer, he [Kang] knew very little about the West, limited as his knowledge was to the few phrases that he could glean from published Chinese writings." Ibid., 670.

9. Wilson, "Plots and Motives in Japan's Meiji Restoration," 407–27.

10. Takashi Koizumi, "Fukuzawa Yukichi and Religion," *Asian Philosophy* 4, no. 2 (1994), 109.

11. Albert Craig, "Preface to Library of Japan Edition," in Fukuzawa Yukichi, *The Autobiography of Fukuzawa Yukichi* (New York: Madison Books, 1992), vii.

12. David Dilworth and Umeyo Hirano, Introduction to Fukuzawa Yukichi, *An Encouragement of Learning* (Tokyo: Sophia University, 1969), x.

13. Ibid., xi.

14. Li Sizhen, "Kang Youwei yu Datongshu" (Kang Youwei and Datongshu), in Kang Youwei, *Datongshu: Chuantong waiyi xia de jinshi lixiang guo* (Datongshu: Modern Utopia Wrapped up in Traditions), ed. Li Sizhen (Zhengzhou: Zhongzhou guji chubanshe, 1998), 5.

15. Carol Gluck, *Japan's Modern Myths: Ideology in the Late Meiji Period* (Princeton, NJ: Princeton University Press, 1985), 27.

16. Conrad Totman, *The Collapse of the Tokugawa Bakufu, 1862–1868* (Honolulu: University of Hawaii Press, 1980), 190.

17. W.G. Beasley, *The Rise of Modern Japan* (New York: St. Martin's Press, 1995), 1–14.

18. David L. Howell, "Visions of the Future in Meiji Japan," in *Historical Perspectives on Contemporary East Asia,* ed. Merle Goldman and Andrew Gordon (Cambridge, MA: Harvard University Press, 2000), 91.

19. Jansen, "The Meiji Restoration," 215.

20. Carol Gluck, *Japan's Modern Myths: Ideology in the Late Meiji Period,* 11–15.

21. Jin Guantao and Liu Qingfeng, *Xingsheng yu weiji—lun zhongguo fengjian shehui de chao wending jiegou* (Prosperity and Crisis—On the Ultrastability of China's Feudal System) (Changsha, China: Hunan renmin chubanshe, 1983).

22. Tang Zhijun, *Wuxu zhengbian shi* (A History of the Hundred-Day Reform in 1898) (Beijing: Renmin chubanshe, 1984), 4–10.

23. The term *xiang* refers to Hunan Province, Zeng Guofan's place of origin.

24. The term *huai* refers to Anhui Province, Li Hongzhang's place of origin.

25. The "boxers" (Righteous and Harmonious Society Movement) were organized initially as semireligious sects in the provinces. They later evolved into paramilitary units to fight foreigners. The Qing government tried to make use of the "boxers" to resist foreigners. When the attempt failed, the government turned against these paramilitary fighters.

26. Lin Daizhao, et al., *Zhongguo Jindai Zhengzhi Zhidushi,* 166.

27. Fukuzawa Yukichi, *An Encouragement of Learning,* translated with introduction by David A. Dilworth and Umeyo Hirano (Tokyo: Sophia University, 1969), 65.

28. Li Sizhen, "Kang Youwei yu Datongshu," 2.

29. Hao Chang, "Intellectual Change and the Reform Movement, 1890–8," in *The Cambridge History of China,* eds. Denis Twitchett and John K. Fairbank, vol. 11, *Late Ch'ing, 1800–1911* (New York: Cambridge University Press, 1989), 384.

30. David L. Howell, "Visions of the Future in Meiji Japan," in *Historical Perspectives on Contemporary East Asia,* ed. Merle Goldman and Andrew Gordon (Cambridge, MA: Harvard University Press, 2000), 92.

31. Carol Gluck, *Japan's Modern Myths: Ideology in the Late Meiji Period,* 31.

32. Hao Chang, "Intellectual Change and the Reform Movement, 1890–8," 274–338.

33. Fukuzawa Yukichi, *An Encouragement of Learning,* 65.

34. Kang Youwei, *Kang Youwei Quanji* (Works of Kang Youwei), vol. 2, ed. Jiang Yihua and Wu Genliang (Shanghai: Guji chubanshe, 1990), 33–36.

35. Kang Youwei, "Shang qingdi di er shu" (Second Letter of Appeal to the Emperor), in *Kang Youwei Quanji*, vol. 2, 75.

36. Kang Youwei, "Shanghai Qiang xue hui hou xu" (Shanghai Strengthening China Society Constitution), in *Kang Youwei Quanji* (Works of Kang Youwei), vol. 2, 194.

37. Fukuzawa Yukichi, *An Outline of a Theory of Civilization*, 107.

38. Zhang Yanru and Zou Xiaoxiang, "Lun Riben Mingzhi Chuqi de Qimengsixiang" (On the Enlightenment Thought of the Early Japanese Meiji Period), *Riben Wenti Yanjiu* (Japan Studies, Beijing), no. 122 (2002), 53–59.

39. Carol Gluck, *Japan's Modern Myths*, 18.

40. Kang Youwei, "Kongzi gaizhi" (Confucius's Reform), in *Kang Youwei Quanji* (Works of Kang Youwei), ed. Jiang Yihua and Wu Genliang (Shanghai: Guji chubanshe, 1990), vol. 2, 293.

41. Ibid., 298.

42. Ibid., 295.

43. Ibid., 345.

44. Ibid., 293.

45. Hao Chang, "Intellectual Change and the Reform Movement, 1890–8," 276.

46. Jansen, "The Meiji Restoration," 312.

47. Cited in Lin Daizhao, et al., 176.

48. Kwong, "Chinese Politics at the Crossroads," 672.

49. Kung-Chuan Hsiao, *A Modern China and a New World: K'ang Yu-wei, Reformer and Utopian, 1858–1927* (Seattle and London: University of Washington Press, 1975), 481.

50. Lin Daizhao, et al., *Zhongguo Jindai Zhengzhi Zhidushi*, 178.

51. David Philing, "Two Giants of Asia Must Find a New Way of Co-Existing," *Financial Times,* April 5, 2004, p. 3.

52. Fukuzawa Yukichi, *An Outline of a Theory of Civilization*, 18.

53. See Luke S.K. Kwong, "The Ti-Yung Dichotomy and the Search for Talent in Late-Ch'ing China," *Modern Asian Studies* 27, no. 2 (1993), 253–79.

54. Shiping Hua, *Scientism and Humanism: Two Cultures in Post-Mao China (1978–1989)* (Armonk, NY: M.E. Sharpe, 1995).

55. Fukuzawa Yukichi, *An Outline of a Theory of Civilization*, 15.

56. Ibid., 17.

57. "From teachings about knowledge and morality down to government, economics and the minute details of daily life, there are none who do not propose emulation of the ways of the west. . . . How superficial they are in uncritically believing things western and doubting things Eastern." Fukuzawa Yukichi, *An Encouragement of Learning,* 95.

58. Frank Gibney, "The Great Teacher Fukuzawa," in Mark Borthwick, *The Pacific Century: The Emergence of Modern Pacific Asia,* 2nd ed. (Boulder, CO: Westview Press, 1998), 133.

59. Fukuzawa Yukichi, *The Autobiography of Fukuzawa Yukichi,* 135.

60. Kang Youwei, *Datongshu: Chuantong waiyi xia de jinshi lixiang guo* (Datongshu: Modern Utopia Wrapped Up in Traditions), ed. Li Sizhen (Zhengzhou: Zhongzhou guji chubanshe, 1998).

61. Li Sizhen, "Kang Youwei yu Datongshu," 17.

62. Li Zehou, "Lun Kang Youwei de Datongshu" (On Kang Youwei's Datongshu), *Wen, Shi, Zhe,* no. 2 (1955).

63. Kung-Chuan Hsiao, *A Modern China and a New World,* 481.

64. In the New Democracy, the means of production was largely in the private sector, although the Communist Party was in control. In socialism, the means of production was publicly owned.

65. Mao Tsetung, *Selected Works of Mao Tsetung,* vol. 5 (Beijing: Foreign Languages Press, 1977), 284–307.

66. The writing of *Datongshu* started in 1884 when Kang was twenty-seven years old. It contains 210,000 Chinese characters, and ten parts. The first two parts were published in *Bu Ren* magazine in 1913. The 1935 draft, reportedly the first complete draft of the book, was only a copy sent by Qian Dingan, not the handwritten draft by Kang. Therefore, some scholars doubted whether Kang had actually written the book. In 1961, Kang's relatives sent some handwritten manuscripts by Kang to the Shanghai Museum. It was not until in the early 1980s that the museum found among those handwritten manuscripts four volumes of Kang's *Datongshu*. These four volumes later joined another three volumes of Kang's handwritten manuscripts of *Datongshu* kept in the Tianjin Library. This complete handwritten draft of *Datongshu* was published by Jiangsu Guji Chubanshe in 1985. This version differs from the previous editions not only in terms of format, but also in terms of content. The current study is mainly based on this version of *Datongshu*. Li Sizhen, "Kang Youwei yu Datongshu," 24, 27–28.

67. Lin Keguang, *Lun Da Tong Shu* (On Da Tong Shu) (Beijing: Sanlian shudian, 1957).

68. Kang Youwei, *Datongshu.*

69. He gave up the ideas, because the blueprint depicted in Da Tong Shu differs from Western utopias in the sense that Kang's grand harmony is realizable. Laurence G. Thompson, *Ta T'ung Shu: The One-World Philosophy of K'ang Yu-wei* (London: George Allen and Unwin, Ltd., 1958), 30.

70. Cited in Kung-Chuan Hsiao, *A Modern China and a New World,* 499.

71. In addition, some scholars failed to understand Kang's thought. In the words of Qian Mu (1895–1990), "In present-day China, there is neither need for the establishment of *Datong* nor the means through which to reach it. Where did Kang's *Datong* idea come from?" Ibid., 25.

72. However, socialism was an exception; it was not acceptable. Carol Gluck, *Japan's Modern Myths: Ideology in the Late Meiji Period* 16.

73. Fukuzawa Yukichi, *An Outline of a Theory of Civilization,* 21–22.

74. Ibid., 22.

75. Thompson, *Ta T'ung Shu,* 214–16.

76. Yusheng Lin, *The Crisis of Chinese Consciousness: Radical Anti-Traditionalism in the May Fourth Era* (Madison: University of Wisconsin Press, 1979).

77. Fukuzawa Yukichi, *An Outline of a Theory of Civilization,* 21–22.

78. Tsuda Sokichi, "Preface" to Fukuzawa Yukichi, *An Outline of a Theory of Civilization,* translated by David A. Dilworth and G. Cameron Hurst (Tokyo: Sophia University, 1973), xv.

79. Fukuzawa Yukichi, *An Outline of a Theory of Civilization,* 6.

80. Ibid., 9.

81. Sokichi, "Preface" to Fukuzawa Yukichi, *An Outline of a Theory of Civilization*, xviii.

82. Hiroko Willcock, "Traditional Learning, Western Thought, and the Sapporo Agricultural College: A Case Study of Acculturation in Early Meiji Japan," *Modern Asian Studies,* no. 34 (2000), 977–1017.

83. Donald W. Treadgold, *The West in Russia and China*, vol. 2, *China, 1582–1949* (New York: Cambridge University Press, 1973), 174–75.

84. Kang Youwei, "Chunqiu Dong Shi Xue" (Dong Zhongshu on Spring–Autumn Period) in *Kang Youwei Quanji* (Works of Kang Youwei), ed. Jiang Yihua and Wu Genliang (Shanghai: Guji Chubanshe, 1990), vol. 2, 827–28.

85. Mencius, *Mencius,* translated with an introduction by D.C. Lau (New York: Penguin Books, 1970), 169.

86. Thompson, *Ta T'ung Shu,* 216.

87. Chang Hao also describes the late Qing intellectual tradition as quite preoccupied with the problem of how to create a world based on *jen* (*ren*), the highest Confucian virtue of compassion and total benevolence. This preoccupation, in turn, as illustrated most vividly by the highly influential thought of T'an Ssu-t'ung (Tan Sitong), was basic to the vision of democracy that developed in China at the turn of the century under Western influence. Thomas A. Metzger, "Modern Chinese Utopianism and the Western Concept of the Civil Society," *Kuo T'ing-I hsien sheng 9 chih tan ch'en chi nien lun wen chi: hsia ts'e* (Taipei: Chung Yang yen chiu yuan chin tai shih yen chiu so fa hsing, 1995), 300–305.

88. Fukuzawa Yukichi, *An Encouragement of Learning,* 71.

89. Fukuzawa Yukichi, *An Outline of a Theory of Civilization,* 80–81.

90. Plato, *The Republic* (New York: W.W. Norton & Company, 1985).

91. Zhang Yanru and Zou Xiaoxiang, "Lun Riben Mingzhi Chuqi de Qimengsixiang," 53–59.

92. Pacific Basin Institute, "Reinventing Japan," in *The Pacific Century,* The Annenberg/CPB Collection (Seattle, WA: Pacific Basin Institute, 1992), part 5.

93. Ibid., part 4.

94. *He Shang* is nationalistic in orientation. However, rather than suggesting that the Chinese should despise Westerners for having forced China open via military conquest, the authors blame the local cultural tradition for China's weakness. See Xiaokang Su, "Yellow River Elegy," *Chinese Sociology and Anthropology* 24, no. 2 (Winter 1991–1992).

95. Shang Huipeng, *Zhongguo ren yu ribenren* (The Chinese and the Japanese) (Beijing: Beijing daxue chubanshe, 2000), 280, 350–52.

96. Kang Youwei, *Datongshu,* 79.

97. Edward X. Gu, "Who Was Mr. Democracy? The May Fourth Discourse of Populist Democracy and the Radicalization of Chinese Intellectuals (1915–1922)," *Modern Asian Studies* 35, no. 3 (2001), 589–621.

98. Fukuzawa Yukichi, *An Outline of a Theory of Civilization,* 6.

99. Tsuda Sokichi, Preface to Fukuzawa Yukichi, *An Outline of a Theory of Civilization,* xvii.

100. Fukuzawa Yukichi, *An Encouragement of Learning,* 22.

101. Charles Hauss, *Comparative Politics: Domestic Responses to Global Challenges,* 4th ed. (Belmont, CA: Wadsworth, 2003), 198.

102. Tsuda Sokichi, Preface to Fukuzawa Yukichi, *An Outline of a Theory of Civilization,* xiv.

103. Fukuzawa Yukichi, *An Encouragement of Learning,* 116.

104. Douglas Howland, "Society Reified: Herbert Spencer and Political Theory in Early Meiji Japan*," Comparative Studies in Society and History,* no. 42 (2000), 67–86.

105. Metzger, "Modern Chinese Utopianism," 300, 305.

106. Wang Rongzu, "Ziyouzhuyi zai zhongguo," *Er Shi Yi Shi Ji (21st Century),* 2nd ed. (December 1990), 33–37.

107. Li Sizhen, "Kang Youwei yu Datongshu," 20.

108. Liao Yuren, "Ruhe jiasu sanminzhuyi quanmian dengshang dalu" (How to Quicken the Process during Which the Three Principles of the People Conquer Mainland China), in Qi Fang, *Heping Yanbian zhanlue de chanseng jiqi fazhan* (The Origin and Development of the Strategy of Peaceful Restoration of Capitalism) (Beijing: Dengfang chubanshe, 1990), 197.

109. Sun Zhongshan, "Zhi Quan Yang Yi" (To Quan Yang Yi), in *Sun Zhongshan quan ji* (Works of Sun Zhongshan), vol. 8 (Shanghai: Zhonghua Shujiu, 1986), 405.

110. Fukuzawa Yukichi, *An Encouragement of Learning,* 9.

111. Ibid., 2, 105–109.

112. Ibid., 76. Also see Tsuda Sokichi, Preface to Fukuzawa Yukichi, *An Outline of a Theory of Civilization,* xiv.

113. Fukuzawa Yukichi, *An Encouragement of Learning,* 2, 76. Also see Zhang Yanru and Zou Xiaoxiang, "Lun Riben Mingzhi Chuqi de Qimengsixing," 53–59.

114. Tuetuo Janita, *The Intellectual Foundations of Modern Japanese Politics* (Chicago: University of Chicago Press, 1974), 87–91.

115. Shiping Hua, *Scientism and Humanism,* 10–20.

Notes to Chapter 4

1. David Nordlander, "Khrushchev's Image in the Light of Glasnost and Perestroika," *The Russian Review* 52 (April 1993), 248–62.

2. Sergei Roy, "Yesteryear," *Moscow News,* February 23, 2000.

3. The word "thaw" was first used in 1855 after the death of Czar Nicholas, and there was a relaxed atmosphere. Serge Petroff, *The Red Eminence: A Biography of Mikhail A. Suslov* (Clifton, NJ: Kingston Press, 1988), 240.

4. Studies such as those by Moshe Lewin noted the "swing of the pendulum" of the reforms in a general sense. Lewin, *Political Undercurrents in Soviet Economic Debates* (Princeton, NJ: Princeton University Press, 1974).

5. Alfred J. Rieber, "The Reforming Tradition in Russian and Soviet History: Commentary," in *Reform in Modern Russian History: Progress or Cycle?,* ed. and trans. Theodore Taranovski (Washington DC: Woodrow Wilson Center Press and Cambridge University Press, 1995), 237–46.

6. Alfred G. Meyer, Introduction to Nikolai Ivanovich Bukharin, *Historical Materialism: A System of Sociology* (Ann Arbor: University of Michigan Press, 1969), 5a.

7. Stephen F. Cohen, "The Friends and Foes of Change: Reformism and Conservatism in the Soviet Union," *Slavic Review* 38, no. 2 (June 1979), 195–96.

8. Fyodor Burlatsky, *Khrushchev and the First Russian Spring: The Era of Khrushchev through the Eyes of His Adviser* (New York: Charles Scribner's Sons, 1988), 62.

9. Alfred G. Meyer, Introduction, 5a.

10. Alec Nove wrote, "Bukharin in 1917–1920 was one of those who suggested an extremely radical line of instant socialism . . . a Utopian and optimistic set of ideas concerning a leap into socialism, which would seem to have little to do with the reality of hunger and cold." Nove, *An Economic History of the USSR* (East Rutherford, NJ: Penguim Books, 1969).

11. Stephen F. Cohen, "Friends and Foes of Change," 193.

12. Khrushchev's efforts in the first three years after the death of Stalin were described as "neo-economic Stalinism." Lazar Volin, "Khrushchev's Neo-Economic Stalinism," *American Slavic and East European Review* 14, no. 4 (December 1955), 445–64.

13. Without mentioning the NEP, Mikhail Suslov, the ideology czar of the former Soviet Union from 1955 to 1982, referred to Bukharin only once in public speeches during the 1965–1977 period. Suslov, *Selected Speeches and Writings* (Oxford: Pergamon Press, 1980).

14. "Socialism was built in the USSR under the conditions of bitter struggle against class enemies and their agents in the party—Trotskyites, Zinovievites, Bukharinists and bourgeois nationalists." Nikita Khrushchev, "For Close Ties between Literature and Art and the Life of the People," *Current Digest of Soviet Press (CDSP)* 9, no. 35 (1957), 4–10.

15. Nikita Khrushchev, *Khrushchev Remembers: The Glasnost Tapes,* trans. and ed. Jerrod L. Schecter, with Vyacheslav V. Luchkov (Boston: Little, Brown and Company, 1990), 41–42.

16. Nikita Khrushchev, *Khrushchev Remembers: The Last Testament,* trans. and ed. Strobe Talbott (Boston: Little Brown and Company, 1974).

17. In 1962, Khrushchev pointed his finger at Suslov and said, "How can we fight against remnants of the cult of personality if Stalinists of this type are still in our midst?" Petroff, *The Red Eminence,* 135.

18. Lenin died in 1924. From 1924 through 1928, the NEP continued and it was a period of power consolidation for Stalin. Not until 1928 did Stalin feel that he was firmly in control to stop NEP and to return to the policies of state socialism.

19. Fyodor M. Burlatsky viewed War Communism as one of the two models to build state socialism, rather than a response to historical contingencies. The other model was the NEP. Burlatsky, "New Thinking about Socialism," in *Breakthrough. Emerging New Thinking: Soviet and Western Scholars Issue a Challenge to Build a World beyond War,* ed. Anatoly Gromyko and Martin Hellman (New York: Walker and Company, 1988), 256–66. For Lars T. Lih, "the Bolsheviks escalated the military communism of the Civil War emergency into a militant and millenarian communism, one that was designed to endure." Lih, "The Mystery of the ABC," *Slavic Review* 56, no. 1 (Spring 1997), 62. Isaac Deutscher believed that "[t]he Bolshevik was therefore inclined to see the essential features of fully fledged communism embodied in the war economy of 1919–1920." Cited by Lih, "The Mystery of the ABC," 56. Stalin did not view War Communism as a development model. "All these measures [taken during War Communism], which were necessitated by the exceptionally difficult conditions of national defense, and bore a temporary character were in their entirety known as War Communism." See Commission of the Central Committee of the CPSU, *History of the Communist Party of the Soviet Union (Bolsheviks)* (New York: International Publishers, 1939), 228.

20. William Parsons, "Experiments in Social Change: A History of Soviet Society" (St. Petersburg, FL: Eckerd College, 1977), 5.

21. Michael Kort, *The Soviet Colossus: History and Aftermath* (Armonk, NY: M.E. Sharpe, 2001), 221.

22. The commonality between War Communism and the state socialism of Stalin is also revealed by the fact that, although he paid some lip service to the NEP, Stalin actually was very much against it. Once he was in power, he restored communist principles embodied in War Communism and put an end to the NEP. Stalin alleged at a Central Committee plenum that "speeches were heard which were incompatible with communism." This was a dangerous epidemic, he warned, and it was caused by the the NEP. Robert Himmer, "The Transition from War Communism to the New Economic Policy: An Analysis of Stalin's Views," *Russian Review* 53, no. 4 (October 1994), 515–29.

23. Kort, *Soviet Colossus,* 247.

24. Natalia Pliskevitch, "Russian Reforms: Utopianism and Pragmatism," *Social Sciences* 29, no. 3 (August 1998).

25. Commission of the Central Committee of the CPSU, *History of the Communist Party of the Soviet Union,* 228.

26. After the war, the War-Communism principle continued; for example, the Red Army was used for production purposes. Ruth Fischer, "Background of the New Economic Policy," *Russian Review* 7, no. 2 (Spring 1948), 15–33.

27. Vadim Medish, *The Soviet Union,* 2nd ed. (Englewood Cliffs, NJ: Prentice-Hall, 1984), 142–43.

28. See Khrushchev, "On Some Questions of the Further Organizational and Economic Strengthening of the Collective Farms," April 25, 1950, in Thomas P. Whiney, *Khrushchev Speaks: Selected Speeches, Articles, and Press Conferences, 1949–1961* (Ann Arbor: University of Michigan Press, 1963), 23–37. Toward 1953, there was more centralization. Donald W. Treadgold, *Twentieth Century Russia* (Chicago: Rand McNally, 1959), 460.

29. Khrushchev, *Khrushchev Remembers: The Last Testament,* 115.

30. War Communism had no comprehensive plans for development priorities because all of Russian industry was in ruins. For instance, by 1921, heavy industrial output had declined to only 20% of 1913 levels.

31. Kort, *Soviet Colossus,* 198; Treadgold, *Twentieth Century Russia,* 463.

32. Commission of the Central Committee of the CPSU, *History of the Communist Party of the Soviet Union,* 228.

33. Basil Dmytryshyn, *USSR: A Concise History,* 2nd ed. (New York: Charles Scribner's Sons, 1971), 107–108.

34. Nikolai Bukharin, *Buhalin wenxuan* (Bukharin: Selections), vol. 2, edited by Zhong Gong, et al. (Beijing: Dongfang chubanshe, 1988), 2.

35. Fischer, "Background of the New Economic Policy," 15–33; V.I. Lenin, *On Utopian and Scientific Socialism* (Moscow: Progress Publishers, 1965), 173–76.

36. Khrushchev, "For Close Ties," 272; Khrushchev, *Khrushchev Remembers: The Last Testament,* 114.

37. Khrushchev, "On Building and Improvements on the Collective Farms," CDSP 3, no. 7 (1951), 13–15.

38. In the Russian calendar, it was November 8.

39. Lenin, *On Utopian and Scientific Socialism,* 173–76.

40. Nikolai Bukharin, "The Russian Revolution and Its Significance," in *In Defense of the Russian Revolution,* ed. Al Richardson (London: Porcupine Press, 1995), 190.

41. Dmytryshyn, *USSR: A Concise History,* 107–108.

42. Ibid., 120–21.

43. Kort, *Soviet Colossus,* 193.

44. Charles Ziegler, *The History of Russia* (Westport, CT: Greenwood, 1999), 95.

45. Commission of the Central Committee of the CPSU, *History of the Communist Party of the Soviet Union,* 228.

46. Fischer, "Background of the New Economic Policy."

47. N.S. Khrushchev, "Speech by N.S. Khrushchev on the Stalin Cult Delivered February 25, 1956," at the closed session of the 20th Congress of the Soviet Communist Party, in *Khrushchev Speaks: Selected Speeches, Articles and Press Conferences (1949–1961),* ed. Thomas P. Whiney (Ann Arbor: University of Michigan Press, 1963), 220–21.

48. Treadgold, *Twentieth Century Russia,* 460–61.

49. Andrzej Walicki, *Marxism and the Leap to the Kingdom of Freedom: The Rise and Fall of the Communist Utopia* (Stanford, CA: Stanford University Press, 1995), 350.

50. Fischer, "Background of the New Economic Policy."

51. Nikolai Bukharin, "The New Economic Policy of Soviet Russia," in *In Defense of the Russian Revolution,* ed. Al Richardson (London: Porcupine Press, 1995), 190.

52. Fedor Burlatsky, *Khrushchev and the First Russian Spring: The Era of Khrushchev through the Eyes of His Adviser* (New York: Charles Scribner's Sons, 1988), 50.

53. Ibid., 44.

54. Volin, "Khrushchev's Neo-Economic Stalinism," 445–64. Compared to industry, agriculture lagged. From 1940 to 1952, agricultural output grew by only 10 percent, and industry, 250%. Khrushchev blamed the lag of agricultural growth on investments in heavy industry in terms of capital and quality cadres, as well as the lack of incentives for the peasants. N. Khrushchev, "On Measures for Further Development of USSR Agriculture," *CDSP* 5, no. 39 (1953), 11–12, 24–41.

55. John Bushnell, "The New Soviet Man Turns Pessimist," in *The Khrushchev and Brezhnev Years,* ed. Alexander Dallin (New York: Garland Publishing, 1992), 139.

56. Burlatsky, *Khrushchev and the First Russian Spring,* 30.

57. Bertrand M. Petenaude, "Peasants into Russians: The Utopian Essence in War Communism," *Russian Review* 54, no. 4 (October 1995), 553.

58. The workers resented the inequality that followed NEP. Bolshevik officials were jealous of the lifestyle enjoyed by NEP men, who often showed off their wealth and sometimes engaged in such dubious businesses as prostitution. Many did not feel comfortable with the sharp contrast between War Communism and the NEP in terms of atmosphere. Resistance to the NEP peaked in 1924 when about 300,000 private enterprises were shut down and NEP functionaries were harassed. The backlash occurred because there was a lack of laws and regulations to guarantee the normal functioning of private enterprises. Alan Ball, "NEP's Second Wind: The New Trade Practice," *Soviet Studies* 37, no. 3 (July 1985), 374.

59. Industrial production, which had been at about 18 percent of prewar output in 1920–1921, rose to 27 percent of prewar levels in 1921–1922, and to 35 percent in 1922–1923. Basil Dmytryshyn, *USSR: A Concise History,* 120–21. By 1925, the government enjoyed a revenue surplus. Jonathan J. Bean, "Nikolai Bukharin and the New Economic Policy," *Independent Review* 2, no. 1 (Summer 1997), 79–98.

60. F. Lee Benns, *Europe since 1914* (New York: F.S. Crofts and Co., 1944), 341–42.

61. Catherine Merridale, "The Reluctant Opposition: The Right Deviation in Moscow, 1928," *Soviet Studies* 41, no. 3 (July 1989), 385–86.

62. Dmytryshyn, *USSR: A Concise History,* 120–21.

63. In their view, "If in the process of competition in the marketplace, state industry and trade and the cooperatives gradually drive out the private entrepreneur—this is victory in the class struggle, not in a mechanical clash of forces, not with the help of armed combat, but a victory in a completely new form that did not exist earlier and which was completely unthinkable for the working class and peasantry under the capitalist regime." Ball, "NEP's Second Wind," 377.

64. Martin McCauley, "Khrushchev as Leader," in *Khrushchev and Khrushchevism,* ed. Martin McCauley (Bloomington: Indiana University Press, 1987), 14.

65. Robert C. Tucker, "The Politics of Soviet De-Stalinization," *World Politics* 9, no. 4 (July 1957), 574.

66. McCauley, "Khrushchev as Leader," 16.

67. Petroff, *The Red Eminence,* 111.

68. McCauley, "Khrushchev as Leader," 16.

69. Khrushchev, "For Close Ties between Literature and Art and the Life of the People," 271.

70. Commission of the Central Committee of the CPSU, *History of the Communist Party of the Soviet Union,* 260.

71. Benns, *Europe since 1914,* 341–42.

72. Lih, "The Mystery of the ABC," 248.

73. Ibid., 244.

74. Volin, "Khrushchev's Neo-Economic Stalinism," 445–64.

75. This is a measure adopted by Khrushchev in September 1953. Seigei Roy, "Yesteryear."

76. *Khrushchev Remembers: The Last Testament,* 120.

77. Bean, "Nikolai Bukharin and the New Economic Policy," 79–98.

78. Merridale, "The Reluctant Opposition," 382–400.

79. Nicolai I. Bukharin, *Economics of the Transformation Period: With Lenin's Critical Remarks* (New York: Bergman Publishers, 1971), 142.

80. Volin, "Khrushchev's Neo-Economic Stalinism," 445–64.

81. N.S. Khrushchev, "Report on the Program of the Communist Party of the Soviet Union," *Documents of the 22nd Congress of the CPSU,* vol. 2 (New York: Crosscurrents Press, 1961), 42. Also see Volin, "Khrushchev's Neo-Economic Stalinism," 445–64.

82. Burlatsky, "New Thinking about Socialism," 256–66.

83. A. Kemp-Welch, "'The New Economic Policy in Culture' and Its Enemies," *Journal of Contemporary History* 13, no. 3 (July 1978), 449–65.

84. Burlatsky, *Khrushchev and the First Russian Spring,* 65.

85. V. Zhuravlyov and A. Pyzhikov, "The Khrushchev Thaw," *Social Sciences,* June 30, 2004, 144–46.

86. Khrushchev, *Khrushchev Remembers: The Glasnost Tapes,* 40.

87. Roy Medvedev and Zhores Medvedev, *Khrushchev: The Years in Power* (New York: W.W. Norton and Company, 1978), 19–20.

88. Militia Major Yef. Popok, "The Collapse of Pavlov & Co.," *Sovetskaya kultura,* January 12, 1962, *CDSP* 12, no. 4 (1962), 31.

89. Peter Hauslohner, "Politics before Gorbachev: De-Stalinization and the Roots of Reform," in *The Khrushchev and Brezhnev Years,* ed. Alexander Dallin (New York: Garland Publishing, 1992), 101.

90. V.I. Lenin, *Selected Works, Theoretical Principles,* vol. 11 (New York: International Publishers, 1943), 180–94.

91. "At best, pre-Marxist 'sociology' and historiography brought forth an accumulation of raw facts, collected at random, and a description of individual aspects of the historical process." V.I. Lenin, *Certain Features of the Historical Development of Marxism* (Moscow: Progress Publishers, 1966), 31.

92. George W. Breslauer, "Khrushchev Reconsidered," in *The Khrushchev and Brezhnev Years,* ed. Alexander Dallin (New York: Garland Publishing, 1992), 35.

93. Dmytryshyn, *USSR: A Concise History,* 262–308.

94. Burlatsky, *Khrushchev and the First Russian Spring,* 76.

95. Ibid., 200.

96. Bukharin, "The New Economic Policy of Soviet Russia," 192.

97. Commission of the Central Committee of the CPSU, *History of the Communist Party of the Soviet Union,* 260.

98. Lars T. Lih, "Political Testament of Lenin and Bukharin and the Meaning of NEP," *Slavic Review* 50, no. 2 (Summer 1991), 241–52.

99. Khrushchev, *Khrushchev Speaks,* 142.

100. "Indoctrination Role Demanded for Culture Universities," *CDSP* 12, no. 46 (1960).

101. Khrushchev, "For Close Ties," 289–94.

102. "The materialist world view is the ideological and philosophical foundation of socialist humanism. The materialist concept of humanism is based on the fact that the flourishing of the spiritual life of mankind is impossible without the extensive development of material production on the basis of public ownership of the means of production. [Under socialism,] [f]ree labor is the basis of freedom of the individual." P. Fedoseyev, "Socialism and Humanism," *Pravda,* September 21, 1957, in *CDSP* 9, no. 37 (1957), 15–16.

103. Khrushchev, *Khrushchev Remembers: The Last Testament,* 77–79.

104. Zbigniew Bzrezinski, "The Nature of the Soviet System," in *The Khrushchev and Brezhnev Years,* ed. Alexander Dallin (New York: Garland Publishing, 1992), 1–2. Commenting on the War Communism that led to NEP, Russian scholar Natalia Pliskevitch wrote that "even at the dawn of the Soviet regime, the adopted model revealed its inability to ensure the people a more or less acceptable standard of existence. The leadership was forced to retreat: to introduce the New Economic Policy. But that was a strictly temporary departure from the original plans caused by the weakness of the state power which was failing, at that moment, to force the still unvanquished economic agents (peasants, first of all) to perform in conformity with its ideas. As soon as urban life became more or less tolerable and agriculture somewhat revived, all the efforts were concentrated on the priority tasks set by the earlier plans, and the concessions of the New Economic Policy were quickly forgotten." Pliskevitch, "Russian Reforms: Utopianism and Pragmatism," *Social Sciences* 29, no. 3 (August 1998), 21–38.

105. For Bzrezinski, "[o]ne of the most distinctive features of the Soviet system, and particularly of its ruling regime, is its conscious purposefulness. Everything it does—in fact, its very existence—is related to a conscious striving towards an announced but not exactly defined goal." Bzrezinski, "The Nature of the Soviet System," in *The Khrushchev and Brezhnev Years,* ed. Alexander Dallin (New York: Garland Publishing, 1992), 8–9.

106. Nikolai Ivanovich Bukharin, *Historical Materialism: A System of Sociology* (Ann Arbor: University of Michigan Press, 1969), 15.

107. Bukharin adds, "For, if the human will were entirely independent of everything,

it would be impossible to act at all, since there would be no possibility of reckoning or of predicting." Ibid., 33, 35.

108. Commission of the Central Committee of the CPSU, *History of the Communist Party of the Soviet Union.*

109. Chinese reformers during the Deng era divide the socialist stages into "primary" and "advanced."

110. Bukharin, *Economics of the Transformation Period,* 79.

111. Stephen F. Cohen, "Marxist Theory and Bolshevik Policy: The Case of Bukharin's Historical Materialism," *Political Science Quarterly* 85, no. 1 (March 1970), 40–60.

112. Bukharin made many indeterminist remarks, although his evolutionary political strategies are in accordance with a determinist understanding of historical materialism. See Cohen, "Marxist Theory and Bolshevik Policy," 40–60.

113. See Bertrand M. Petenaude, "Peasants into Russians: The Utopian Essence in War Communism," *Russian Review* 54, no. 4 (October 1995), 553.

114. Burlatsky, *Khrushchev and the First Russian Spring,* 2. Also see Nordlander, "Khrushchev's Image," 248–64.

115. Petroff, *The Red Eminence,* 115.

116. M.A. Suslov, "Suslov Speaks on Communist Theory and Ideology," *Pravda,* January 31, 1959, in *CDSP* 9, no. 8 (1959), 22–24.

117. Petroff, *The Red Eminence,* 111–12.

118. Ibid., 127.

119. In the view of orthodox Marxism, dialectics has two essential qualities: everything changes and things cannot be viewed in a static way; everything exists in contradiction with its opposite part, but at the same time, it cannot live without its opposite. See Commission of the Central Committee of the CPSU, *History of the Communist Party of the Soviet Union.*

120. "The division of the one and cognition of its contradictory parts is the essence of dialectics. And natural science shows us objective nature with the same qualities, the transformation of singular into the general, of the contingent into the necessary, transitions, modulations, and the reciprocal connection of opposites." Lenin, *Selected Works, Theoretical Principles,* 81.

121. "The idea of determinism, which establishes the necessity of human acts and rejects the absurd fable of freedom of will, in no way destroys man's reason or conscience, or the judgment of his actions. Quite the contrary, the determinist view alone makes a strict and correct judgment possible, instead of attributing everything one faces to freedom of will. Similarly, the idea of historical necessity in no way undermines the role of the individual in history; all history is made up of the actions of individuals, who are undoubtedly active figures. The real question that arises in judging the social activity of an individual is: what conditions ensure the success of this activity, what guarantee is there that this activity will not remain an isolated act lost in a welter of contrary acts." Ibid., 439.

122. Although Lenin made many determinist remarks, he is more flexible than Bukharin in interpreting historical materialism. Lenin called this being "dialectical." He said that "Bukharin is the most valuable and most important theoretician of the Party but . . . I believe he never completely understood dialectics." In Bukharin, *Economics of the Transformation Period,* 211.

123. For Bukharin, the basic understanding of Marx's methods in economics in-

cluded the following elements: (1) humans are social beings; (2) production rather than consumption is of primary importance; (3) the mode of economics is historically shaped, rather than following some general laws; and (4) the postulate of equilibrium. Ibid., 136.

124. Bukharin's equilibrium method explains that "[r]oughly speaking: society could not exist, unless the system of things [stores, harbors, etc.], the system of persons [who are divided into classes] and the system of ideas [values] were adapted each to the other." Bukharin, *Historical Materialism,* 134.

125. James D. White, "Chinese Studies of Bukharin," *Soviet Studies* 43, no. 4 (1991), 739–40.

126. John Salter, "On the Interpretation of Bukharin's Economic Ideas," *Soviet Studies* 44, no. 4 (1992), 563–78.

127. Ibid., 573.

128. Khrushchev, "For Close Ties," 279.

129. Ibid.

130. Petroff, *The Red Eminence,* 131.

131. Commission of the Central Committee of the CPSU, *History of the Communist Party of the Soviet Union.*

132. Petroff, *The Red Eminence,* 140–43. Khrushchev's political reforms also hurt the vested interest of the bureaucracy. These reformist policies include the bifurcation of the party apparatus adopted in 1958 and the systematic renewal of the cadres adopted at the Twenty-Second Congress in 1961, which undermined the security of tenure of sitting Central Party Committee members, whose prospects for reelection at the Twenty-Third Congress were no longer certain. The rules required minimum rates of turnover in party bodies and limits on the terms of officeholders. William J. Tompson, "The Fall of Nikita Khrushchev," *Soviet Studies* 43, no. 6 (1991), 1101–21.

133. Khrushchev, *Khrushchev Remembers: The Glasnost Tapes,* 198–99.

134. Burlatsky, *Khrushchev and the First Russian Spring:* 51–54.

135. George W. Breslauer, "Khrushchev Reconsidered," in *The Khrushchev and Brezhnev Years,* ed. Alexander Dallin (New York: Garland Publishing, 1992), 37. A Central Party Committee document noted in 1960 "that the molding of people with communist character traits is one of the chief practical tasks. The chief thing in ideological work is to strive for highly effective propaganda that has practical results. Ideological questions must be settled on a day-to-day basis, simultaneously with economic questions." "Bring the Ideas of Marxism-Leninism to the Masses in an Inspired Way," a Conference in the Central Party Committee Devoted to Questions of Ideological Work, *Pravda,* September 14, 1960, 3, in *CDSP* 12, no. 37 (1960), 11–15. Another Central Party Committee document noted in 1960 that the main problem of the USSR's propaganda work was that it was too abstract, did not serve the purpose of economic construction of the country, and relied too much on the *Short Course in the History of the Communist Party of the Soviet Union (Bolsheviks).* Also, the ideological work did not reach the masses. "The leading place in all ideological work must be given to the struggle for strict realization of the principle 'he who does not work does not eat,' against persons who shun participation in socially useful work, and for inculcating a communist attitude and developing moral incentives to work." "Resolution of the Party Central Committee: On the Task of Party Propaganda in Present-Day Conditions," *Pravda,* January 10, 1960, in *CDSP* 12, no. 2 (1960), 17–23.

136. Bukharin, *Economics of the Transformation Period,* 28–34.

137. Ibid., 25.

138. "Surplus value" is an important concept in Marx's works. It is created by the working class, but is taken away by the capitalists in an unjust way. This is the root of exploitation in a capitalist society. Bukharin, *Economics of the Transformation Period* (New York: Bergman Publishers, 1971), 74.

139. Ibid., 377.

140. "But for the main mass of small producers, an incorporation into the process of organization becomes possible chiefly through the sphere of circulation—that is, formally in the same way as in the system of state capitalism." Ibid., 93.

141. Ibid., 248.

142. Bukharin, *Economics of the Transformation Period,* 94.

143. Lenin's view on transition in 1919 was exactly the same as Bukharin's: "The basic forms of social economy are capitalism, petty commodity production, and communism. The basic forces are the bourgeoisie, the petty bourgeoisie (the peasantry in particular) and the proletariat." *On Utopian and Scientific Socialism,* 172.

144. Khrushchev, "Report on the Program of the Communist Party of the Soviet Union," *Documents of the 22nd Congress of the CPSU,* vol. 2 (New York: Crosscurrents Press, 1961), 104. "As for the Soviet Union, it has already passed the stage of social development that all the other peoples still have to pass. . . . They show that the theoretical conclusion of Marxist-Leninist science about the working class inevitably winning power is an objective law of social development." Fedor Burlatsky, *The State and Communism* (Moscow: Progress Publishers, 1964), 40–43. The Party's theoretical framework as late as 1961 was still orthodox Marxism: class struggle, contradiction between productive forces and relations of production, the objective laws of social development, and so forth. "The Draft of the Party Program," *CDSP* 13, no. 28 (1961).

145. Burlatsky, *The State and Communism,* 9.

146. Ibid., 96.

Notes to Chapter 5

1. Roderick MacFarquhar, "The Secret Speeches of Chairman Mao," in *The Secret Speeches of Chairman Mao: From the Hundred Flowers to the Great Leap Forward,* ed. Roderick MacFarquhar, Timothy Cheek, and Eugene Wu (Cambridge, MA: Harvard University Press, 1989), 3.

2. National Intelligence Council, "Tracking the Dragon: National Intelligence Estimates on China during the Era of Mao, 1948–1976," May 13, 1967, and "Economic Outlook for Communist China," May 25, 1967 (Washington, DC: National Intelligence Council, 2004), 494.

3. Although the Eighth Party Congress raised the issue of democracy, it was not guaranteed by law. China had a highly centralized political and economic power structure, and economic reform was limited to decentralization. Market mechanisms were not stressed and not included in Mao's "On the Ten Great Relationships." In fact, decentralization was the only thing that the Maoist reformers shared with the followers of Khrushchev insofar as the reformist strategies were concerned. In other words, there was no effective political and economic structural mechanism to check the incorrect policies of the Great Leap Forward. This interpretation is one-sided, because when Deng Xiaoping embarked on his reforms in 1978 that turned out to be successful, China's polit-

ical and economic structure was similar to that in 1956. Xie Chuntao, "Bada luxian weineng jianchi xiaqu de yuanyin" (Why the Line of the Eighth Congress Was Not Carried Out), *Dangdai zhongguoshi yanjiu,* no. 5 (1996), 21–22. Also see Huang Aijun, "Dayuejin yundong fasheng yuanyin yanjiu shuping" (Comments on Studies of the Origins of the Great Leap Forward), *Dangdai zhongguoshi yanjiu, no.* 1 (2005).

4. The Chinese people enthusiastically supported the regime because of the improved socioeconomic situation after 1949 and the party's success in the "anti-rightist movement" and collectivization. Huang Aijun, *Dangdai zhongguoshi yanjiu.* This interpretation cannot explain that the similar event of the Cultural Revolution was initiated even though the prestige of the party was seriously damaged as a result of Great Leap Foward.

5. Kenneth Lieberthal, "The Great Leap Forward and the Split in the Yenan Leadership," in *The Cambridge History of China,* vol. 14, ed. Denis Twitchett and John K. Fairbank (New York: Cambridge University Press, 1987), 293–359; Xie Chuntao, "Dayuejin yundong yanjiu shuping," 31–32.

6. Due to the isolationist policy imposed on China by the West, China had no choice but to rely on itself, and its greatest resource was an abundant labor supply. Huang Aijun, "Dayuejin yundong fasheng yuanyin yanjiu shuping."

7. It was rooted in China's hundred years of humiliation inflicted by foreign powers. Xie Chuntao, "Dayuejin yundong yanjiu shuping," 31–32. The limitation of this theory is that similar humiliations were inflicted on many other non-Western countries, not just China.

8. Lieberthal, "The Great Leap Forward."

9. The composition of the membership of the Central Party Committee of the Eighth Party Congress is important with regard to the departure from its policy orientation. In terms of knowledge base, most members were professional revolutionaries and few were technically oriented. In terms of their backgrounds, most were peasants. Among the total party members of 10.73 million, 14 percent were workers, 69 percent were peasants, and only 12 percent were intellectuals. In terms of their professions, most were military personnel, for whom obeying an order was more important than independent thinking. Li Jianchun, "Cong zhonggong di bajie zhongyang weiyuanhui de jiegou, kan bada luxian de zhongduan" (Looking at the Policies Results of the Eighth Congress by the Membership Composition of the CCP Central Committee), *Dangdai zhongguoshi yanjiu,* no. 2 (2001), 19–21. This situation was similar to the conflict between Joseph Stalin and Nikolai Bukharin in the late 1920s in the sense that most of the party members in the Soviet Union at that time were not intellectuals and did not understand Bukharin's sophisticated theories. Stalin's simple analysis had greater appeal for the majority of party members, who were mostly workers and soldiers. Fedor Burlatsky, *Khrushchev and the First Russian Spring: The Era of Khrushchev through the Eyes of His Adviser* (New York: Charles Scribner's Sons, 1988), 51–54. The limitation of this explanation is that the Cultural Revolution, which had similar orientations, occurred in spite of the different sociological situations of communist cadres ten years later.

10. Lieberthal, "The Great Leap Forward and the Split in the Yenan Leadership."

11. In December 1957, Mao saw that his guards brought to him the bad food that the peasants ate. Li Yinqiao, *Zai Mao Zedong shen bian shi wu nian* (At the Side of Mao Zedong for Fifteen Years) (Shijiazhuang, Hebei: Renmin chubanshe, 1992), 229. The limitation of this interpretation is that most Third World countries were also poor, but few, except North Korea, experienced something like the Great Leap Forward.

12. It had origins in the egalitarianism embodied in the Confucian datong concept and Zhang Lu's self-governing peasant society. Bo Yibo, *Ruo gan zhongda juece yu shijian de huigu* (Reflections on Some Important Decisions and Events) (Beijing: Zhonggong zhongyang dangxiao chubanshe, 1993), 775–76.

13. This is one of the roots of Chinese utopianism. Xie Chuntao, "Dayuejin yundong yanjiu shuping," 31–32; Huang Aijun, "Dayuejin yundong fasheng yuanyin yanjiu shuping."

14. Paul J. Hiniker, "The Cultural Revolution Revisited: Dissonance Reduction or Power Maximization," *The China Quarterly,* no. 94 (June 1983), 282–303.

15. Yan Jiaqi, *Wenhua dageming shinianshi* (Ten-Year History of the Cultural Revolution) (Taipei: Yuanliu chubanshe, 1990), 9–22. At an international conference held on July 29–31, 2005 in San Francisco, a prominent scholar from Renmin University of China, Li Jingzhi, also shared this view.

16. Liu Shaoqi, a former president of the People's Republic of China, had a good reputation in the early 1960s for his moderate policies after the failure of the Great Leap Forward. Hong Yong Lee, *The Politics of China's Cultural Revolution* (Berkeley: University of California Press, 1987). Also see Mao Mao, *Wo de fuqin Deng Xiaoping* (My Father Deng Xiaoping) (Beijing: Zhongyang wenxian chubanshe, 2000).

17. National Intelligence Council, "Tracking the Dragon," 471.

18. MacFarquhar, "The Secret Speeches of Chairman Mao," 3. The top leadership was split due to Mao's opposition to "anti-radicalism" advocated by Liu Shaoqi and Zhou Enlai. Mao's personality, his belief in altruism, and his self-confidence all played significant roles. Xie Chuntao, "Dayuejin yundong yanjiu shuping," 31–32.

19. Jin Chunming, "Liu shi nian dai zuo qing cuowu de fazhan yu wenhua dageming de baofa" (The Development of Mistakes in Leftist Thought in the 1960s and the Outbreak of the Cultural Revolution), *Zhonggong dangshi yanju,* no. 1 (1996), 47–53.

20. Stuart Schram, "To Utopia and Back: A Cycle in the History of the Chinese Communist Party," *The China Quarterly, no.* 87 (September 1981), 407–39. Also see Wolfgang Bauer, *China and the Search for Happiness* (New York: Seabury Press, 1976), 400.

21. Ye Yonglie, *Chen Boda Zhuan* (Biography of Chen Boda) (Beijing: Renmin ribao chubanshe, 1999), 294.

22. Deng Xiaoping, *Deng Xiaoping wenxuan* (Selections of Deng Xiaoping), vol. 2 (Beijing: Renmin chubanshe, 1994), 296.

23. Yang Shengqun and Tian Songnian, *Gongheguo zhongda juece de lailong qumai* (The PRC's Major Decisions) (Nanjing, China: Zhejiang renmin chuban she, 1995), 288. This is in spite of the fact that Liu was against "radicalism" (*fan mao jin*) in 1956. Xie Chuntao, "Dayuejin yundong yanjiu shuping," 31–32.

24. Xie Chuntao, "Dayuejin yundong yanjiu shuping," 66.

25. Li Jianchun, "Cong zhonggong di bajie zhongyang weiyuanhui de jiegou," 19–21.

26. Huang Aijun, "Dayuejin yundong fasheng yuanyin yanjiu shuping."

27. Empirically, the current study complements existing studies about Chen Boda in the sense that Chen's role in the Great Leap Forward and the entire period of the Cultural Revolution is covered. Currently, there are two major studies about Chen Boda. Raymond F. Wylie's *The Emergence of Maoism: Mao Tse-tung, Ch'en Po-ta [Chen Boda], and the Search for Chinese Theory, 1935–1945* (Stanford, CA: Stanford University Press, 1980), deals with Chen's career during the 1935–1945 period. Parris H. Chang's "The Role of Ch'en Po-ta in the Cultural Revolution," *Asia Quarterly,* no. 1

(1973), 17–58, deals with Chen's career in the early part of the Cultural Revolution, that is, before 1968.

28. As explained in Chapter 2, the "Let the Hundred Flowers Blossom, Let the Hundred of Schools of Thought Contend Movement" (Hundred Flowers) was limited to intellectuals.

29. Yu Guangyuan, "Chu shi Chen Boda" (First Impression of Chen Boda), *Dushu,* no. 6 (1998).

30. Yang Shengqun and Tian Songnian, *Gongheguo zhongda juece de lailong qumai,* 204. Also see Ye Yonglie, *Chen Boda Zhuan,* 287–88.

31. The idea was in his essay, "Brand New Society, Brand New Man," published on July 1, 1958, in *Hong qi,* a month earlier than when Mao said that a "people's commune" was a good idea when he visited the Qiliying Village.

32. Chen Boda, "Zai Mao Zedong tongzhi de qizhi xia" (Under the Banner of Comrade Mao Zedong), *Hongqi,* July 16, 1958, in Liu Cunshi, ed., *Chen Boda wenji* (Hong Kong: Lishi ziliao chubanshe, 1971), 113.

33. Mao Mao, *Wo de fuqin Deng Xiaoping,* 13. Also see Ye Yonglie, *Chen Boda Zhuan,* 17, 411–12, 457.

34. "Two lines of struggle" refer to the ideological orientation of the left represented by the radical Mao, and that of the right, represented by the moderate Liu Shaoqi and Deng Xiaoping. Chen Boda, *Chen Boda yi gao* (Leftover Manuscripts by Chen Boda) (Hohhot: Neimong renmin chubanshe, 1999), 65.

35. Ye Yonglie, *Chen Boda Zhuan,* 566.

36. Ibid., 535–40.

37. In spite of all these, Chen's impact on China's cultural scene can still be felt today, although in an indirect way. The New Enlightenment Movement (NEM) in 1936 and early 1937 led by Chen is viewed by current Chinese scholars as the most important cultural movement after the New Culture Movement (NCM) during the period of 1917–1923 led by Chen Duxiu. Current Chinese intellectuals try to avoid using Chen Boda's name. Instead, they say that the NEM was led by Lu Xun, Mao Dun (Shen Yanbing), and Feng Xuefeng. Significantly, the slogan that Chen raised during the NEM is still viewed as the direction in which Chinese culture should move: nationalist (*minzu de*), scientific (*kexue de*), democratic (*minzhu de*), and populist (*dazhong de*). Chen Duxiu's NCM lacked the elements of nationalist and populist. The NEM was nationalist because of the pending Japanese invasion, and populist because the NCM was appealing mostly to the elites. Fang Delin, "Cong jindai zhongxi wenhua lunzheng kan Zhongguo xinwenhua de fazhan luxiang" (A Look at China's New Culture Direction from the Cultural Debates about the Cultures of the East and West in Modern Chinese History), *Xinhua Wenzhai,* no. 12 (2003), 58–59.

38. Roderick MacFarquhar, "The Secret Speeches of Chairman Mao," 3.

39. Yang Shengqun and Tian Songnian, *Gongheguo zhongda juece de lailong qumai,* 131.

40. Li Qing, "1957 nian fanyoupai douzheng jiqi yanzhong kuodahua de qiyin he jiaoxun" (Origins and Lessons of the Anti-Rightist Movement in 1957 and Its Exaggeration), *Zhonggong dangshi yanju,* no. 6 (1995), 66.

41. For instance, the incident in Hungary made Renmin University students doubt their communist ideals. Believing that "expert is red," they wanted to become specialists without having to worry about politics. Lu Shichao, "Liangzhong shijieguan de douzheng" (The Conflict between Two World Outlooks), *Renmin ribao,* January 5, 1958, 7.

42. Compared with the USSR, the Chinese economy was less efficient. China was able to plan the first FYP only during the Maoist era. During 1957–1976, China's cost of producing one ton of steel was US $920, 37 percent higher than that of USSR during the same period. From 1949 through 1978 when the Dengist reform started, China's economy also had the following characteristics: (1) Although the government's power was great, its management skill was limited. (2) Planning was divided into the cities and the countryside. For the countryside, the government's plan was inaccurate because of lack of data. (3) The government's control switched back and forth like a pendulum between the center and the provinces. Wu Li, "Zhonguo jihua jingji de chongxin shenshi yu pingjia" (Reflections on and Evaluation of China's Planned Economy), *Xinhua wenzhai,* November 2003, 62.

43. Liu Guoguang, "Gaigekaifang qian de zhongguo de jingji fazhan he jingjitizhi" (China's Economic Development and Economic Structure before the Reform), *Zhonggong dangshi yanju,* no. 4 (2002),14–17.

44. Yang Shengqun and Tian Songnian, *Gongheguo zhongda juece de lailong qumai,* 111.

45. National Intelligence Council, "Tracking the Dragon," 122–31.

46. Zheng Yougui, "Chongdu Mao Zedong 'Lun shida guanxi' zhong guanyu gongnong guanxi de lunshu" (Reread Mao Zedong's Views on the Relationship between Industry and Agriculture in "On Ten Great Relationships"), *Dangdai zhongguoshi yanjiu,* no. 5 (1996), 22–25.

47. Deng Liqun, "Qiqianren dahui, dao xilou huiyi" (From the 7000 People Conference to Xilou Conference), *Dangdai zhongguoshi yanjiu, no.* 5 (1998), 15.

48. Two small islands occupied by the Kuomingtang after the communist takeover in 1949.

49. Lin Ke, *Wo suo zhidao de Mao Zedong* (My Knowledge of Mao Zedong) (Beijing: Zhongyang wenxian chubanshe, 2000), 60.

50. Ibid., 94.

51. *Hong qi* was the official maganize, while *Renmin ribao* is the official newspaper of the Chinese Communist Party.

52. Ye Yonglie, *Chen Boda Zhuan.*

53. Zhang Suhua, "'60 niandai de shehuizhuyi jiaoyu yundong" (Socialist Education Movement in the 1960s), *Dangdai zhongguoshi yanjiu,* 8, no. 1 (2001), 62. Chen Boda, "Ji nian Mao Zhuxi zai Yan'an wenyi zuotan hui yi shang de jianghua" (Talk at the Seminar about Issues of Literature in Yan'an), *Renmin ribao,* May 24, 1967.

54. Guo Fang Da Xue (National Defense University), *Zhonggong dangshi cankao ziliao* (Reference Materials for Party History) (Beijing: Guofang Daxue chubanshe, 1986), 205.

55. Wang Zhen, "50 niandai zhongqi woguo dui sulian jianshe moshi de tupo" (China's Departures from the Soviet Model in the Mid-1950s), *Dangdai zhongguoshi yanjiu,* no. 2 (1995), 15.

56. Shang Ying, "Stalin, Zhou Enlai huitan jiyao" (Record of Stalin and Zhou Enlai Conversation), *Dangdai zhongguoshi yanjiu,* no. 5 (1997), 104.

57. Gao Huamin, "Nongye hezuohua de chenggong jingyan" (The Successful Experience of Agricultural Collectivization), *Dangdai zhongguoshi yanjiu,* no. 4 (1995), 38.

58. Yang Shengqun and Tian Songnian, *Gongheguo zhongda juece de lailong qumai,* 107.

59. Wang Zhen, "50 niandai zhongqi woguo dui sulian jianshe moshi de tupo," 16–17.

60. Lieberthal, "The Great Leap Forward," 299.

61. These so-called "democracy parties" refer to the eight small parties established before the communist takeover in 1949. These parties were friendlier to the communists than to the Kuomintang. The Chinese communist government allowed the parties to exist on the condition that they agreed to be under the leadership of the Communist Party.

62. Wang Zhen, "50 niandai zhongqi woguo dui sulian jianshe moshi de tupo,"18–20.

63. The CCP's first important debate article with the Soviets after Stalin, "On the Historical Experiences of the Dictatorship of the Proletariat" (*Lun wuchan jieji zhuanzheng de lishi jingyan*), was drafted by Chen. So was the "Political Report" of the Eighth Party Congress, which departed from the Stalinist model. Mao Mao, *Wo de fuqin Deng Xiaoping,* 13.

64. Editorial Department, "Lun Wuchanjieji zhuanzheng de lishi jingyan" (On the Historical Experience of the Dictatorship of the Proletariat), *Renmin ribao,* April 5, 1956.

65. Ye Yonglie, *Chen Boda Zhuan,* 307.

66. Yang Shengqun and Tian Songnian, *Gongheguo zhongda juece de lailong qumai,* 199–201.

67. After the launching of the Hundred Flowers and the Great Leap Forward, Mao would have liked others to believe that he had always been against the resolution of the Eighth Party Congress, which was adopted in 1956. Mao Mao, *Wo de fuqin Deng Xiaoping,* 62. Mao was hypocritical, because, as mentioned earlier, the three documents, that is, the *Renmin ribao* editorial, the Political Report of the Eighth Party Congress, and Mao's own "On Ten Great Relationships," were consistent in orientation. In fact, Mao played an active part in the drafting of the Political Report. There were about eighty drafts of the Political Report of the Eighth Congress, and Mao made comments on twenty-one of them. Yang Shengqun, "Bu neng shuo bada hou dang de luxian ji fasheng genbenxing ni zhuan" (We Can't Say That the Party Line Changed Drastically Immediately after the Eighth Party Congress), *Dangdai zhongguoshi yanjiu,* no. 5 (1996), 11–13. Mao said earlier, "Widespread political struggle is already basically at an end. The Eighth Party Congress concluded it." Mao Zedong, "Talk at the Hangchow Conference of the Shanghai Bureau (April 1957)," in Joint Publications Research Service, *Miscellany of Mao Tse-tung Thought (1959–1968),* Part I (Washington, DC: Distributed by National Technical Information Service, U.S. Department of Commerce, 1974), 66.

68. Lieberthal, "The Great Leap Forward," 300.

69. Mao Zedong, *Mao Zedong Wenji* (Collected Works of Mao Zedong), vol. 7 (Beijing: Renmin chubanshe), 24–30.

70. Deng Xiaoping, *Deng Xiaoping wenxuan,* 333.

71. Because of Mao's change of position, he would not allow the publication of his book "On Ten Great Relationships." Other leaders who either disagreed with Mao from the beginning or changed their utopian mentality because of the disastrous policies of GLF and CR found it convenient to persuade Mao to switch back to the Eighth Party Congress line by reminding Mao that his "On Ten Great Relationships" was consistent with the line of the Eighth Party Congress. Liu Shaoqi wrote to Mao at the end of 1965 and suggested that "On Ten Great Relationships" be distributed at and above the levels of counties in provinces and regiments in the military. Mao rejected Liu's proposal. Li

Lian, "Yan zhe jianshe you zhongguo tese shehuizhuyi daolu qianjin" (March along the Road to Build Socialism According to Chinese Characteristics), *Dangdai zhongguoshi yanjiu,* no. 6 (1996), 5. Similarly, on July 13, 1975, Deng Xiaoping suggested that Mao publish it. Mao agreed but said it could only be circulated among Politburo members. CCP Central Committee, *Guanyu jianguo yilai dang de ruogan lishi wenti jueyi* (Resolution on Certain Historical Issues of the Party since the Founding of the People's Republic of China) (Beijing: Renmin chubanshe, 1986), 245.

72. In response to the call from the party, many intellectuals started to criticize the leaders in various ways. The severity and scale of the criticism were unexpected, and the CCP fought back, turning the Hundred Flowers into the so-called Anti-Rightists Movement. Those labeled "rightists" were expelled from the party. More than 50 percent of the half-million rightists lost their jobs. Between 1959 and 1963, over 300,000 of these individuals were rehabilitated. Li Qing, "1957 nian fanyoupai douzheng jiqi yanzhong kuodahua de qiyin he jiaoxun" (Origins and Lessons of the Anti-Rightist Movement in 1957 and Its Exaggeration), *Zhonggong dangshi yanju,* no. 6 (1995), 66. It was not until 1980 that 540,000 of the 550,000 "rightists," or 98 percent, were rehabilitated. Wang Suli and Liu Zhiguang, "Fan youpai douzheng yanjiu zongshu" (A Discussion of the Anti-Rightist Movement), *Dangdai zhongguoshi yanjiu,* no. 6 (1997), 115.

73. Lieberthal believed that the switch from moderate policies was due to simple "impatience" by the Chinese. See Lieberthal, "The Great Leap Forward," 313.

74. Wu Lengxi, "Tong Jiaying gongshi de rizi" (The Days When I Worked with Tian Jiaying), in *Mao Zedong he tade mishu Tian Jiaying* (Mao Zedong and His Secretary, Tian Jiaying), eds. Dong Bian and Tan Deshan (Beijing: Zhongyang wenxian chubanshe, 1996), 142.

75. Zhang Suhua, "60 niandai de shehuizhuyi jiaoyu yundong" (The Socialist Education Movement in the 1960s), *Dangdai zhongguoshi yanjiu,* 8, no. 1 (2001), 68.

76. Pei Run, "San ci tong Jiaying tongzhi dao nong cun tiaocha" (Three Investigations I Performed with Comrade Jiaying), in *Mao Zedong he tade mishu Tian Jiaying,* 273.

77. Wu Lengxi, "Tong Jiaying gongshi de rizi," in *Mao Zedong he tade mishu Tian Jiaying,* 145.

78. Feng Xianzhi, "Mao Zedong he tade minshu Tian Jiaying" (Mao Zedong and His Secretary Tian Jiaying), in *Mao Zedong he tade minshu Tian Jiaying,* 92.

79. The movement got its name because Mao said, "in the field of arts, 'Let a hundred flowers bloom,' and in the literary field, 'Let a hundred schools of thought contend.'" Mao Zedong, "Speech at the Extended Meeting of the CCP Political Bureau (April 1956)," in Joint Publications Research Service, *Miscellany of Mao Tse-tung Thought (1949–1968),* Part I (Washington, DC: Distributed by NTIS, U.S. Department of Commerce, 1974), 33.

80. Land reform started in the base areas before 1949 and continued after the communist takeover. The party seized land from big landlords, and distributed it among the poor peasants.

81. Zhang Suhua, "60 niandai de shehuizhuyi jiaoyu yundong," 61.

82. Ibid., 60.

83. Yang Mingsheng, "Woguo jingji tizhi gaige licheng, jiqi lishi jingyan" (Paths and Historical Experiences of China's Economic Structural Reform), *Dangdai zhongguoshi yanjiu,* no. 2 (1999), 34.

84. Ibid., 67.

85. Zhang Suhua, "60 niandai de shehuizhuyi jiaoyu yundong," 62.

86. "Work team": Members were often cadres at various government levels, a method used by the CCP to implement certain policies. For instance, this method was used before the communist takeover for land reforms in the base areas. Ibid., 66.

87. Liu Jinfeng, *Chen Boda yu Xiaozhan Siqing* (Chen Boda and the Four Cleanings of Xiao Zhan, 1995–2004) (Tsinghua Tonfang Optical Disc Co., Ltd.).

88. Mao Mao, *Wo de fuqin Deng Xiaoping,* 32.

89. Wu Lengxi, *Yi Mao Zuxi* (In Memory of Mao Zedong) (Beijing: Xinhua chubanshe, 1995), 47.

90. Xie Chuntao, "Dayuejin yundong yanjiu shuping," 25–33.

91. During the 1958–1962 period, agricultural output annually decreased by 5.9 percent, light industry decreased by 2 percent, and heavy industry increased by 3 percent annually. Workers' salaries decreased by 20 percent annually during this period. For three consecutive years, the government suffered deficits. Yang Mingsheng, "Woguo jingji tizhi gaige licheng, jiqi lishi jingyan," 34.

92. Mao Zedong, "Speech to the Albanian Military Delegation (1 May 1967)," in Joint Publications Research Service, *Miscellany of Mao Tse-tung Thought (1949–1968),* Part II (Washington, DC: Distributed by NTIS, U.S. Department of Commerce, 1974), 456. Yao Wenyuan, from Shanghai, was another important left-wing theoretician during the Cultural Revolution.

93. Marshall Lin Biao, the second person in command during the early period of the Cultural Revolution, later tried to assassinate Mao, largely because of power struggle motives.

94. The Cultural Revolution was bad for China's economy, although it was less serious than the Great Leap Forward. During the Cultural Revolution, in terms of industrial and agricultural growth, 1967 and 1968 showed negative growth. In 1967, industry decreased by 14 percent and government revenue dropped by 25 percent. The trend continued through 1968. Yu Qiuli, "Qi yi renmin de zong guan jia" (General Manager of 700 Million People), in *Zhou Enlai de zuihou Suiyue* (The Last Years of Zhou Enlai), ed. An Jianshe (Beijing: Zhongyang wenxian chubanshe, 1995), 88–93. In 1968, 1972, 1976, and 1977, growth was negative. From 1952 to 1995, China's average annual growth rate in agriculture was 4.3 percent, while during the 1966–1976 period, it was 2 percent. In 1966–1976, average annual population growth was 2.2 percent. Thus, food production lagged behind population growth. Zheng Yougui, "Wenhua dageming shiqi nongye shengchan bodong ji dongyin tanxi" (An Analysis of the Fluctuation of Agricultural Production during the Cultural Revolution), *Zhonggong dangshi yanjiu,* no. 3 (1998), 71–72.

95. Mao Zedong, "Talks with Directors of Various Cooperative Areas (November–December 1958)," in Joint Publications Research Service, *Miscellany of Mao Tse-tung Thought (1949–1968),* Part I (Washington, DC: Distributed by NTIS, U.S. Department of Commerce, 1974), 136.

96. Chen Boda, "Zai Mao Zedong tongzhi de qizhi xia" (Under the Banner of Comrade Mao Zedong), *Hong qi,* July 16, 1958, in Liu Cunshi, ed., *Chen Boda wenji* (Hong Kong: Lishi ziliao chubanshe, 1971), 116–17.

97. Mao Zedong, "Speech at the Extended Meeting of the CCP Political Bureau (April 1956)," 32.

98. Dong Zhikai, "Mao Zedong zai bada qianhou gaige jingji guanli tizhi de shexiang (Mao's Thought about Economic Management Structure around the Eighth Party

Congress), *Dangdai zhongguoshi yanjiu*, no. 1 (1996), 22. Also see Zhao Shigang, "Mao Zedong fadong dayuejin de yuanwang yu maojin chengyin bianxi" (The Motivation for Mao to Launch the Great Leap Forward and the Factors That Led to the Leap), *Dangdai zhongguoshi yanjiu*, no. 2 (1995), 39.

99. Yang Shengqun and Tian Songnian, *Gongheguo zhongda juece de lailong qumai*, 380.

100. Jin Shan, "Beijing daxue wu bai duo ganbu xiafang" (More than 500 Cadres Went to Grassroots Units), *Renmin ribao*, January 4, 1958, 7. Also see "Dao liandui, dao bianjiang qu duanlian ziji: dapi junguan jianjue yaoqiu xiafang" (Massive Numbers of Military Officers Want to Go to Grassroots Units in Frontier Areas), *Renmin ribao*, January 11, 1958.

101. Chen Donglin, "Wenge shiqi Mao Zedong de jingji sixiang tanxi" (An Analysis of Mao's Economic Thought during the Cultural Revolution), *Dangdai zhongguoshi yanjiu*, no. 1 (1996), 27–37.

102. Liu Guoguang, "Gaige kaifang qian de zhongguo de jingji fazhan he jingji tizhi" (Economic Development and Economic Structure before the Deng Reforms), *Zhonggong dangshi yanju*, no. 4 (2002).

103. Mao Zedong, "Talks at the Beidaihe Conference," August 21, 1958, in *The Secret Speeches of Chairman Mao*, eds. MacFarquhar, et al., 428.

104. Mao Zedong, "Speech at the Hankow Conference (6 April 1958)," in Joint Publications Research Service, *Miscellany of Mao Tse-tung Thought (1949–1968)*, Part I (Washington, DC: Distributed by NTIS, U.S. Department of Commerce, 1974), 87.

105. According to Mao, Khrushchev criticized the Hundred Flowers policy. Zhu Di, "Yelun dayuejin de yuanqi" (Comment on the Origins of the Great Leap Forward), *Zhonggong dangshi yanju*, no. 1 (2001), 60–65.

106. Ni Heyi, "Tunliu xian jinnian yao biancheng siwu xian" (Tunliu County Is Determined to Kill All Sparrows and Rats within Its Territory This Year), *Renmin ribao*, January 8, 1958, 7.

107. *Renmin ribao*, January 13, 1958, 7.

108. Mao Zedong, "Speech at the Sixth Plenum of the Eighth Central Committee (19 December 1958)," in *The Secret Speeches of Chairman Mao*, eds. MacFarquhar, et al., 140.

109. Mao Zedong, "Critique of Stalin's 'Economic Problems of Socialism in the Soviet Union (1959),'" in Joint Publications Research Service, *Miscellany of Mao Tse-tung Thought (1949–1968)*, Part I (Washington, DC: Distributed by NTIS, U.S. Department of Commerce, 1974), 191.

110. Ibid., 76. It means that ideas originated from the masses. These ideas will then be discussed among the leaders who select the good ones. These good ideas will become policies to be implemented by the masses.

111. Chen Po-ta, *Mao Tse-tung on the Chinese Revolution: Written in the Commemoration of the 30th Anniversary of the Communist Party of China* (Beijing: Foreign Languages Press, 1953), 3.

112. The first People's Commune was founded in Suiping County, Henan Province. Qi Yuan, "Yi Jiaying dui nongcun gongshe he bianshi gongzuo de yixie tanhua" (In Memory of Tian Jiaying's Talks on People's Communes and Compiling of Histories), in *Mao Zedong he tade mishu Tian Jiaying*, 234. Qi Li Ying, in Henan Province, was another famous People's Commune. The commune was quasi-communistic at a very low level of the productive forces. It was responsible for members' clothing, food, housing,

electricity, transportation, births, funerals, health care, elder care, education, preschool, and weddings, among other things. But this is low-level egalitarianism. The total cost for one person was only 78 RMB a year. See Wu Lengxi, *Yi Mao Zuxi*, 99.

113. Yang Shengqun and Tian Songnian, *Gongheguo zhongda juece de lailong qumai*, 287. Mao added, "I think in the future a few large cities will be dispersed; residential areas of 20,000 to 30,000 people will have everything; villages will become small cities where the majority of philosophers and scientists will be assigned. The characteristics of the People's Communes are one, big, and two, public." Mao Zedong, "Talks at the Beidaihe Conference, August 21, 1958," in *The Secret Speeches of Chairman Mao*, eds. MacFarquhar, et al., 430–31.

114. Yang Shengqun and Tian Songnian, *Gongheguo zhongda juece de lailong qumai*, 289.

115. Chen's essay, "Under the Banner of Mao Zedong," was published in *Hong qi*, the official party organ on July 16, 1958. Ye Yonglie, *Chen Boda Zhuan*, 320.

116. As a political strategy, mass mobilization was a conventional method for the Chinese communists even before the two movements. Chen wrote in 1949, "In order to turn policies into concrete results, we must mobilize the masses. We must learn constantly from the experiences of the campaigns. In New China, the reconstruction of the economy is a campaign by the masses on a grand and spectacular scale. Think about it. How can we develop agricultural production and raise the level of industrial production without mobilizing the masses? It has been proved beyond doubt that the policies of the New China have been correct, the policy of relying on the masses, relying on those masses who were engaged in production, has been correct." Chen Boda, Preface, "Buyao daluan yuanlai de qiye jigou" (Don't Abolish the Structure of the Old Enterprises), in Chen Boda, *Zhongguo jingji de gaizao* (The Transformation of China's Economy) (Hong Kong: Xinminzhu chubanshe, 1949).

117. Chen Boda, "Wuchan jieji wenhuadageming zhong de liangtiao luxian" (The Two Lines in the Great Proletarian Cultural Revolution), in Tianjinshi geming weiyuanhui zhengzhibu, *Wuchanjieji wenhuadageming zhongyao wenxian xuanbian* (Selections of the Important Documents of the Great Proletarian Cultural Revolution) (Tianjin: N.p., May 1969), 350–85.

118. Editorial, *Hong qi*, no. 3 (1967), 17. Mao Zedong, "Interjection at Enlarged Meeting of the CCPCC, Standing Committee (4 August 1966)," in Joint Publications Research Service, *Miscellany of Mao Tse-tung Thought (1949–1968)*, Part II, 449.

119. Mao did not approve this idea. Instead, he instructed the rebels to establish "revolutionary committees." *Wehhui bao*, February 6, 1967.

120. Liu Huiming, "Bali gongshe de quanmian xuanju zhi" (The Electoral System of the Paris Commune), *Hong qi*, no. 11 (1966), 36–37.

121. Mao Mao, *Wo de fuqin Deng Xiaoping*, 41.

122. CCP Central Party Committee, "Zhonggong zhongyang guanyu wuchanjieji wenhuadageming de jueding" (CCP Central Committee's Resolution on the Proletarian Cultural Revolution), *Renmin ribao*, August 9, 1966.

123. State Statistical Bureau, *Ten Great Years* (Beijing: Foreign Languages Press, 1960), 35.

124. Yang Shengqun and Tian Songnian, *Gongheguo zhongda juece de lailong qumai*, 274.

125. Liu Ya, "Mubiao, shouduan, zizhu xuyao" (Goals, Means, and the Needs for Independence), *Dangdai zhongguoshi yanjiu* 10, no. 1 (2003), 51. Also see Wang Jun-

wei, "Dui chengshi renmin gongshe de chubu kaocha" (A Preliminary Investigation about People's Communes in the Cities), *Dangdai zhongguo shi yanjiu* 2 (1997), 23.

126. Liang Shuzhen, "Daban nongcun gonggong shitang de lishi jiaoxun" (Historical Lessons of Public Dining Halls in the Countryside), *Zhonggong dangshi yanju*, no. 3 (2000), 92–93.

127. Liu Guoguang, "Gaigekaifang qian de zhongguo de jingji fazhan he jingjitizhi" (China's Economic Development and Economic Structure before the Reform), *Zhonggong dangshi yanju*, no. 4 (2002), 14–17.

128. Zhonghua renmin gongheguo guojia nongye weiyuanhui bangongting, *Nongye jiti hua zhongyao wenjian huibian 1958–1981* (Important Documents about Agricultural Collectivization, 1958–1981) (Beijing: Zhonggong zhongyang dangxiao chubanshe, 1981) 2, 765.

129. Chen Boda, "Quanxin de shehui, quanxin de ren" (Brand New Society, Brand New People), *Hong qi* (Beijing), no. 3 (1958), 9–11. Chen said that workers, peasants, businessmen, students, and soldiers should abolish their division of labor to form a large commune. Chen Boda, "Zai Mao Zedong tongzhi de qizhi xia" (Under the Banner of Comrade Mao Zedong), *Hong qi*, July 16, 1958, in *Chen Boda wenji*, ed. Liu Cunshi (Hong Kong: Lishi ziliao chubanshe, 1971), 116–17.

130. Yang Shengqun and Tian Songnian, *Gongheguo zhongda juece de lailong qumai*, 293.

131. Mao Zedong, "Talks with Directors of Various Cooperative Areas (November–December 1958)," Joint Publications Research Service, *Miscellany of Mao Tsetung Thought (1949–1968)*, Part I (Washington, DC: Distributed by NTIS, U.S. Department of Commerce, 1974), 134.

132. Zhang Guangnian, "Zai tan gerenzhuyi yu ai" (Another Comment on Individualism and Cancer), *Renmin ribao*, January 21, 1958.

133. With the People's Commune system, Chinese peasants were organized into "production brigades," usually part of a village; "big brigades," which usually coincided with a village, and "communes," which consisted of a number of villages.

134. Zheng Yougui, "Wenhua degeming shiqi nongye shengchan bodong ji dongyin tanxi" (An Analysis of the Fluctuation of Agricultural Production during the Cultural Revolution), *Zhongong dangshi yanju*, no. 3 (1998), 71–72.

135. Ibid.

136. He Yuqing, "San zi yi bao jiu shi fubi zibenzhuyi" (The Responsibility System Is Restoring Capitalism), *Renmin ribao*, September 5, 1967.

137. Da Lianwei, Commerce Ministry, "Ziyou shichang zai sulian de da fanlan" (Too Many Private Markets in the USSR), *Renmin ribao*, January 11, 1969.

138. *Renmin ribao*, May 5, 1967, 5.

139. Chen Boda (in the name of Editorial Board of *Renmin ribao*) "Hengsao yiqie niu, gui, she, shen" (Sweep Away All Cows, Ghosts, Snakes, and Gods), *Renmin ribao*, June 1, 1966, 1.

140. Lin Ke, *Wo suo zhidao de Mao Zedong*, 43–44. Also see Yan Jiaqi and Gao Gao, *Wenhua dageming shinianshi* (Ten-Year History of the Cultural Revolution) (Tianjin: Renmin chubanshe, 1988), 306–7.

141. Chen Boda, *Zai wenhua zhanxian shang* (On the Culture Front) (Chongqing: Shenghuo shudian, 1939), 31.

142. Ibid., 174–81.

143. Chen Boda (Chen Po-Ta), *Mao Tse-tung on the Chinese Revolution* (Peking: Foreign Languages Press, 1953), 52.

144. Mao Zedong, *Mao Zedong xuanji,* 1031.

145. Mao Zedong, *Renmin ribao,* June 17, 1963.

146. Mao Zedong, "Critique of Stalin's *Economic Problems of Socialism in the Soviet Union (1959),*" in Joint Publications Research Service, *Miscellany of Mao Tse-tung Thought (1949–1968),* Part I, 192.

147. See Lucian Pye, *Mao Tse-tung: The Man in the Leader* (New York: Basic Books, 1976), 24.

148. Chen Boda, *Zai wenhua zhanxian shang,* 166–67.

149. Chen Boda, "Zai Mao Zedong tongzhi de qizhi xia," *Hong qi,* July 16, 1958, in *Chen Boda wenji,* ed. Liu Cunshi (Hong Kong: Lishi ziliao chubanshe, 1971), 117.

150. Mao Zedong, "Speech at the Conference of Delegation Heads to the Second Session of the Eighth Party Congress (18 May 1958)," in Joint Publications Research Service, *Miscellany of Mao Tse-tung Thought (1949–1968),* Part I, 123.

151. Yang Shengqun and Tian Songnian, *Gongheguo zhongda juece de lailong qumai,* 281.

152. *Renmin ribao,* August 3, 1958.

153. Mao Zedong, "Talks at the Beidaihe Conference," August 21, 1958, in *The Secret Speeches of Chairman Mao,* 419.

154. Ibid., 433.

155. During the New Enlightenment Movement, a cultural movement promoting modernization in the late 1930s, Chen promoted datong. Chen Boda, *Zai wenhua zhanxian shang,* 7–9, 25, 75, 79.

156. Li Sizhen, "Kang Youwei yu Datongshu," 23–24.

157. "Xuesheng zhi gongzuo" (Work of the Students), *Hunan Jiaoyu Yuekan,* no. 12, cited in Ling Zhijun, *Chen Fu: Zhongguo jingji gaige beiwanglu* (Ups and Downs: A Memorandum of China's Economic Reform, 1989–1997) (Shanghai: Dongfang chubanzhongxin, 1998), 143.

158. Chen Boda, *Zai wenhua zhanxian shang,* 42.

159. Yang Shengqun and Tian Songnian, *Gongheguo zhongda juece de lailong qumai,* 292.

160. Ling Zhijun, *Chen Fu: Zhongguo jingji gaige beiwanglu,* 142.

161. Mao Zedong, "Talks at the Beidaihe Conference," 424.

162. Jerome Chen and Michael Bullock, *Mao and the Chinese Revolution* (London: Oxford University Press, 1965), 338–39.

163. Yang Shengqun and Tian Songnian, *Gongheguo zhongda juece de lailong qumai,* 291–92. According to Bo Yibo, Mao interpreted Zhang Lu's *zhi yi mi rou* (free rice and meat) and *zhi yi cang* (free grain storage) as free meals, and thus as the dining halls; *shen dao zhi bing* (treating patients with divine means), as free medical care, *bu she zhang* li as running the commune not only as an economic organization, but as a government as well. Also see Bo Yibo, *Ruo gan zhongda juece yu shijian de huigu* (Reflections on Some Important Decisions and Events) (Beijing: Zhonggong zhongyang dangxiao chubanshe, 1993), 775–76.

164. Lin Ke, *Wo suo zhidao de Mao Zedong,* 45.

165. Ibid., 46.

166. Ibid., 104.

167. Mao Zedong, "Critique of Stalin's 'Economic Problems of Socialism in the Soviet Union (1959)," in Joint Publications Research Service, *Miscellany of Mao Tse-tung Thought (1949–1968)*, Part I, 191.

168. Editorial Board, Red Guards of the Capital, in *Renmin ribao*, September 3, 1967, 4.

169. Fan Xiubing, "Pi chou 'zhongguo He lu xiao fu' de jingji zhuyi" (Criticize Thoroughly the Economism of China's Khrushchev), *Renmin ribao*, September 14, 1967.

170. Yan Jiaqi and Gao Gao, *Wenhua dageming shinian shi*, 313.

171. For the Chinese difficulty in understanding the modern scientific method, see Shiping Hua, "Scientism and Humanism," *Encyclopedia of Chinese Philosophy*, ed. Anthonio S. Cua (London: Routledge, 2003), 663–69.

172. Lao Tzu, *Tao Teching*, translated by Stephen Addiss and Stanley Lombardo (Indianapolis: Hackett Publishing Company, 1993), 22.

173. Ibid., 39.

174. Ibid., 43.

175. Ibid., 58.

176. Zhao Shigang, "Mao Zedong fadong dayuejin de yuanwang yu maojin chengyin bianxi," 36.

177. Chen Boda, "Zai Mao Zedong tongzhi de qizhi xia," 113; Chen Boda, *Chen Boda yi gao*, 326–27.

178. Mao Zedong, "Interjections at Conference of Provincial and Municipal Committee Secretaries" (January 1957), Joint Publications Research Service, *Miscellany of Mao Tse-tung Thought (1949–1968)*, Part I, 49.

179. Mao Zedong, *Mao Zedong Wenji*, vol. 7, 195.

180. Mao Zedong, "Speech at the Conference of Heads of Delegations to the Second Session of the Eighth Party Congress (18 May 1958)," in Joint Publications Research Service, *Miscellany of Mao Tse-tung Thought (1949–1968)*, Part I, 121.

181. Wang Xifeng is one of the leading characters in the Chinese classic. See Mao Zedong, "Examples of Dialectics (1959)," Joint Publications Research Service, *Miscellany of Mao Tse-tung Thought (1949–1968)*, Part I, 203.

182. Ding Xuelei, "Wuchanjieji da minzhu jiushi hao" (The Big Democracy by the Proletariat Is Good), *Renmin ribao*, September 12, 1967, 5.

183. Mao Mao, *Wo de fuqin Deng Xiaoping*, 352–56.

184. Mao Zedong, "Talks at the Beidaihe Conference," August 21, 1958, in *The Secret Speeches of Chairman Mao*, 428.

185. Chen Boda, "Ji nian Mao Zhuxi zai Yan'an wenyi zuotan hui yi shang de jianghua" (Talk at the Seminar about Issues of Literature in Yan'an), *Renmin ribao*, May 24, 1967.

186. Mao Zedong, "Speech at the Hankow Conference (6 April 1958)," Joint Publications Research Service, *Miscellany of Mao Tse-tung Thought (1949–1968)*, Part I, 87.

187. CCP Central Party Committee, "Zhonggong zhongyang guanyu wuchanjieji wenhuadageming de jueding" (CCP Central Committee's Resolution on the Proletarian Cultural Revolution), *Renmin ribao*, August 9, 1966.

188. Chen Boda, "Ji nian Mao Zhuxi zai Yan'an wenyi zuotan hui yi shang de jianghua," *Renmin ribao*, May 24, 1967, 168.

189. Ye Yonglie, *Chen Boda Zhuan*.

Notes to Chapter 6

1. Thomas A. Metzger, *Escape from Predicament: Neo-Confucianism and China's Evolving Political Culture* (New York: Columbia University Press, 1977), 214–15.

2. Donald W. Treadgold, *The West in Russia and China,* vol. 2, *China, 1582–1949* (New York: Cambridge University Press, 1973), 174–75.

3. Steven Lee Solnick, "The Breakdown of Hierarchies in the Soviet Union and China," *World Politics* 48, no. 2 (January 1996), 209–38.

4. Barry R. Weingast, "Federalism, Chinese Style: The Political Basis for Economic Success in China," *World Politics* 48, no. 1 (October 1995), 50–81.

5. Frederick Barghoon, cited in R. Judson Mitchel and Randal Arrington, "Gorbachev, Ideology and the Fate of Soviet Communism," *Communist and Post-Communist Studies* 33 (2000), 457–74.

6. Yan Sun, "The Chinese and Soviet Reassessment of Socialism: The Theoretical Bases of Reform and Revolution in Communist Reforms," *Communist and Post-Communist Studies* 27, no. 1 (1994), 39–58.

7. Nancy B. Tucker, "China as a Factor in the Collapse of the Soviet Empire," *Political Science Quarterly* 110, no. 4 (Winter 1995–1996), 501–18.

8. See Hu Qiaomu, "Dang qian sixiang zhan xian shang de ruogang wenti," (On Some Issues in the Current Ideological Front), *Hong qi* 23 (1981), 10; and "Lun rendao zhui he yi hua wenti" (On Humanism and the Issue of Alienation) *Renmin Ribao,* January, 27, 1984, 5.

9. However, he said that his appointment was not confirmed for political reasons. Thomas F. Remington, "Alexander Yakovlev and the Limits of Reform," in Alexander Yakovlev, *The Fate of Marxism in Russia* (New Haven, CT, and London: Yale University Press, 1993), x.

10. Paul Hollander comments on flap page, in Alexander Yakovlev, *A Century of Violence in Soviet Russia* (New Haven, CT, and London: Yale University Press, 2003).

11. Paul Hollander, foreword, in Yakovlev, *A Century of Violence in Soviet Russia,* ix.

12. Archie Brown, *The Gorbachev Factor* (New York: Oxford University Press, 1996), 76.

13. A.N. Yakovlev, *Gai ge xin si wei yu Sulian zhi ming yun* (New Thinking on Gorbachev's Reform and the Fate of the USSR), eds. Gao Hongshan, et al. (Changchun, China: Jilin ren min chubanshe, 1992), 6. This is a translation from the Russian book by A.N. Yakovlev, *Muki Prochteniia Bytiia: Perestroika—nadezhdy i real'nosti* (Moscow: Moskva Novosti, 1991).

14. Yu Junxiao, "Dui woguo geti jingji zhuangkuang de fenxi" (An Analysis of the State of China's Individually Owned Enterprises), *Dangdai zhongguoshi yanjiu,* no. 2 (1997), 35.

15. G. Smirnov, "Creating Socialist Consciousness in Youth," *Pravda,* August 24, 1984, in *Current Digest of the Soviet Press (CDSP)* 36, no. 34 (1984), 9.

16. Y. Lukin, "Ideology, Politics and Culture: In the Struggle for the Future of Mankind," *Literaturnaya gazeta,* November 2, 1984, 2, in *CDSP* 35, no. 52 (1984), 18.

17. K. Chernenko, "Toward the 27th Party Congress: At the Level of the Requirements of Developed Socialism," December 18, 1984, in *CDSP* 37, no. 4 (1984), 1–5.

18. "On the Reform of the Economic System in China," *Pravda,* October 25, 1984, in *CDSP* 36, no. 43 (1984), 9.

19. Yang Mingsheng, "Woguo jingji tizhi gaige licheng, jiqi lishi jingyan" (Paths and Historical Experiences of China's Economic Structural Reform), *Dangdai zhongguoshi yanjiu,* no. 2 (1999), 34.

20. *Hu Qiaomu wenji* (Hu Qiaomu's Collected Works), vol. 2 (Beijing: Renmin Chubanshe, 1993), 415.

21. Ibid., 427.

22. Ibid., 428.

23. Hu Qiaomu, *Zhongguo gongchandang zenyang fazhanle makesizhuyi—wei jinian jiandang qishi zhounian zuo* (How Has the CCP Developed Marxism—In Celebration of the 70th Anniversary of the Party) (Beijing: Renmin chubanshe, 1991), 26.

24. Mikhail Gorbachev and Zdenek Mlynar, *Conversations with Gorbachev: On Perestroika, the Prague Spring, and the Crossroads of Socialism,* trans. George Shriver (New York: Columbia University Press, 2002), 67.

25. "Communiqué on the Plenary Session of the Central Committee of the Communist Party of the Soviet Union," *Pravda* and *Izvestia,* June 17, 1986, in *CDSP* 38, no. 24 (1986), 5.

26. M. Gorbachev, "Initiative, Organization and Efficiency," *Pravda,* April 12, 1985, 1–2, in *CDSP* 37, no. 15 (1985), 1–2.

27. "Brushstrokes in the Portrait of the Working Man," *Izvestia,* May 3, 1985, in *CDSP* 37, no. 18 (1985), 1–4.

28. Tatyana Zaslavskaya, "Viewpoint: Restructuring as a Social Revolution," *Izvestia,* December 24, 1989, in *CDSP* 40, no. 51 (1989), 1–4.

29. M. Gorbachev, "Initiative, Organization and Efficiency," *Pravda,* April 12, 1985, 1–2, in *CDSP* 37, no. 15 (1985), 1–2.

30. Yakovlev, *Gai ge xin si wei yu Sulian zhi ming yun,* 8.

31. "Learn Democracy," *Pravda,* July 18, 1987, in *CDSP* 39, no. 29 (1987).

32. That is, Jiang Qing, Mao's wife; Zhang Chunqiao, the party boss in Shanghai; Wang Hongwen, the rebel leader, also from Shanghai; and Yao Wenyuan, a major party theoretician of the Cultural Revolution.

33. M. Gorbachev, "Restructuring Is an Urgent Matter That Affects Everyone and Everything," *Pravda,* August 2, 1986, in *CDSP* 38, no. 31 (1986), 1–4.

34. "Restructuring and the Economic Mechanism: The Reality of Hopes," *Izvestia,* May 5, 1987, in *CDSP* 39, no. 18 (1987), 5.

35. "Ligachev Keynotes November 7 Celebration," *Pravda* and *Izvestia,* November 7, 1986, in *CDSP* 38, no. 45 (1986), 1–5.

36. Gao Xuejun, "Nongcun gaige de lishi xing tupo" (Historic Breakthrough in Agricultural Reform), *Xuexi shibao,* June 18, 2001, 1.

37. June Teufel Dreyer, *China's Political System: Modernization and Tradition,* 2nd ed. (Boston: Allyn and Bacon, 1996), 151.

38. *Hu Qiaomu wenji,* vol. 2, 162–86.

39. "Be in the Vanguard, Work in the New Way," *Pravda,* November 21, 1987, in *CDSP* 39, no. 47 (1987), .

40. M. Gorbachev, "Initiative, Organization and Efficiency," 1–2.

41. "October and Restructuring: The Revolution Continues," *Pravda* and *Izvestia,* November 3, 1987, in *CDSP* 39, no. 44 (1987), 9.

42. Edward Friedman believes that "the political arena is a largely autonomous one" and China's economic boom has not advanced the cause of democracy. Edward Fried-

man, "Immanuel Kant's Relevance to an Enduring Asia-Pacific Peace," in *What If China Doesn't Democratize?*, ed. Edward Friedman and Barrett L. McCormick (Armonk, NY: M.E. Sharpe, 2000), 224–58. Minxin Pei, however, believes that political changes took place in China after the late 1970s, and China's political system can be described as "soft authoritarianism." Pei, "China's Evolution toward Soft Authoritarianism," in *What If China Doesn't Democratize?*, 74–98.

43. Yakovlev, *"Gai ge xin si wei," yu Sulian zhi ming yun,* 13.

44. Merle Goldman and Roderick MacFarquhar, "Dynamic Economy, Declining Party-State," in Merle Goldman and Roderick MacFarquhar, *The Paradox of China's Post-Mao Reforms* (Cambridge, MA: Harvard University Press, 1999), 3–29.

45. Richard Baum gives credit to Deng Xiaoping's attempts toward limited political liberalization in the 1980s. The efforts were sabotaged by the conservatives. See Baum, "The Road to Tiananmen: Chinese Politics in the 1980s," in *The Politics of China*, 2nd ed., ed. Roderick MacFarquhar (Cambridge: Cambridge University Press, 1997), 340–50.

46. Hu Qiaomu, "Guanyu rendaozhuyi he yihua wenti" (On Humanism and the Issue of Alienation), *Renmin ribao,* January 27, 1984.

47. Hu was largely referring to the Democracy Wall Movement, which started in December 1978. Beijing citizens posted "big character posters" to expose the wrongdoings of the Cultural Revolution. Some of the posters showed sympathy with the Western democratic system. Later, at the order of the Deng regime, the Democracy Wall was shut down.

48. Hu Qiaomu, "Dang qian sixiang zhanxian de ruogan wenti" (Certain Issues on the Ideological Front), in *Hu Qiaomu wenji* (Collections of Hu Qiaomu), vol. 2 (Beijing: Renmin Chubanshe, 1993), 458.

49. *Hu Qiaomu wenji,* vol. 3 (Beijing: Renmin Chubanshe, 1994), 151–52.

50. Suzanne Ogden, *Inklings of Democracy in China* (Cambridge, MA: Harvard University Asia Center, 2002), 99–113.

51. Chih-yu Shih, "Political Culture of Election in Taiwanese and Chinese Minority Areas," in Shiping Hua, ed., *Chinese Political Culture: 1989–2000* (Armonk, NY: M.E. Sharpe, 2001), 246–75.

52. Gorbachev and Mlynar, *Conversations with Gorbachev,* 9.

53. "Ulyanovsk: Some Lax Officials Ousted, But It's Only the Beginning," *Pravda,* April 3, 1985, in *CDSP* 37, no. 14 (1985), 10. "Perm: Naming of Unqualified Managers Leads to High Replacement Rate," March 28, 1985, *Pravda,* in *CDSP* 37, no. 13 (1985), 7. "Leaders Must Set High Moral Example: Those Whose Performance Doesn't Measure Up Should Be Ousted," *Pravda,* March 18, 1985, in *CDSP* 37, no. 11 (1985), 1.

54. Yakovlev, *Gai ge xin si wei yu Sulian zhi ming yun,* 173.

55. Ibid., 123.

56. Gorbachev and Mlynar, *Conversations with Gorbachev,* 112.

57. Ibid., 69–73.

58. Alexander N. Yakovlev, "The Future of Democracy in Russia: The Lessons of Perestroika and the Question of the Communist Party," Sanford S. Elberg Lecture in International Studies, February 22, 1993 (http://globetrotter.berkeley.edu/Elberg/Yakovlev/).

59. Gorbachev and Mlynar, *Conversations with Gorbachev,* 101.

60. Ibid, 67.

61. Yakovlev, *Gai ge xin si wei yu Sulian zhi ming yun,* 105.

62. Yakovlev, "The Future of Democracy in Russia."

63. "*Time* Interviews Gorbachev," *Pravda* and *Izvestia*, September 2, 1985, in *CDSP* 37, no. 35 (1985), 17.

64. "Communiqué on the Plenary Session of the Central Committee . . ." 3, 4.

65. Fedor Burlastsky, *Khrushchev and the First Russian Spring: The Era of Khrushchev through the Eyes of His Adviser* (New York: Charles Scribner's Sons, 1988), 13.

66. David Nordlander, "Khrushchev's Image in the Light of Glasnost and Perestroika," *The Russian Review* 52 (April 1993), 248–64.

67. B.P. Kuraturing, "A Proposal for Restructuring the Economy," *Ekonomika I organizatsia promyshlennovo proizvodstva*, no. 5 (May 1984), in *CDSP* 37, no. 41 (1984), 1–5.

68. Hu Qiaomu, "Zhongguo wei shenmo fan 20 nian de zuoqing cuowu" (Why Did China Commit the Mistake of Leftism for 20 Years?) in Hu Qiaomu, *Hu Qiaomu wenji*, vol. 2, 261–69.

69. Ibid., 447.

70. David Kelly, "The Emergence of Humanism: Wang Ruoshui and the Critique of Socialist Alienation," in *China's Intellectuals and the State: In Search of a New Relationship*, eds. Merle Goldman, Timothy Cheek, and Carol L. Hamrin (Cambridge, MA: Council on East Asian Studies, 1987), 159–82.

71. *Hu Qiaomu wenji*, vol. 2, 589.

72. Su Shaozhi, *Democratization and Reform* (Nottingham, England: Spokesman, 1983), 162–63.

73. Chen Boda, "Buyao daluan yuanlai de qiye jigou" (Don't Abolish the Structure of the Old Enterprises), in Chen Boda, *Zhongguo jingji de gaizao* (The Transformation of China's Economy) (Hong Kong: Xinminzhu chubanshe, 1949), 63.

74. Hu Qiaomu, "Guanyu rendaozhuyi he yihua wenti."

75. *Hu Qiaomu wenji*, vol. 2, 180.

76. Hu Qiaomu, "Zhongguo gongchandang zenyang fanzhan le Makesizhuyi," in *Hu Qiaomu wenji*, vol. 2, 293–320.

77. Yakovlev, *The Fate of Marxism in Russia*, 30.

78. With the belief that productive forces are the primary engine for social change, historical materialism is a kind of economic determinism. Ibid., 37–39.

79. Ibid., 46–47.

80. Ibid., 15.

81. Ibid., 48.

82. Metzger, *Escape from Predicament*, 214–15.

83. *Hu Qiaomu wenji*, vol. 3 (Beijing: Renmin Chubanshe, 1994), 151–52.

84. Yakovlev, *The Fate of Marxism in Russia*, 193.

85. Ibid., 15.

86. Ibid., 52.

87. Ibid., 14.

88. Thomas F. Remington, "Alexander Yakovlev and the Limits of Reform," in Yakovlev, *The Fate of Marxism in Russia*, vii, 6.

89. A. Tsipko, "The Roots of Stalinism," *Nauka I zhizn*, no. 1 (January 1989), in *CDSP* 41, no. 12 (1989), 21–22.

90. However, the parallel between empiricism and liberals was unclear during the post-Mao period, because intellectual debates during the period were too politicized. For

instance, such liberal intellectuals as Su Shaozhi and Wang Ruoshui did not take a stand on the issue of empiricism and positivism. Shiping Hua, "Scientism and Humanism," in *Encyclopedia of Chinese Philosophy,* ed. Anthonio S. Cua (London: Routledge, 2003), 663–69.

91. Su Xiaokang, "River Elegy," *Chinese Sociology and Anthropology* 24, no. 2 (Winter 1991–1992).

92. Hu Qiaomu, "Xiwang renren dou kan Hua Huan," in *Hu Qiaomu Wenji,* vol. 3, 374–76.

93. Geremie R. Barme, *In the Red: On Contemporary Chinese Culture* (New York: Columbia University Press, 1999), 103.

94. Shiping Hua, "Literature as Civic Discourse in the Reform Era: Utopianism and Cynicism in Chinese Political Consciousness," in *Civic Discourse, Civil Society, and Chinese Communities,* eds. John Powers, et al. (Stamford, CT: Ablex Press, 1999).

95. Geremie R. Barme, *In the Red: On Contemporary Chinese Culture,* 103.

96. The May Fourth Movement occurred in 1919 when Beijing college students took to the street to demonstrate against the weak Chinese government in the face of Western aggression. It was turned into a movement against Chinese cultural tradition.

97. Joseph Fewsmith, *China Since Tiananmen: The Politics of Transition* (New York: Cambridge University Press, 2001), 101–32.

98. Yakovlev, *A Century of Violence in Soviet Russia,* 24.

99. Ibid., 235.

100. Yakovlev, *The Fate of Marxism in Russia,* 199.

101. A. Tsipko, "The Roots of Stalinism," *Nauka Izhizn,* no. 1 (January 1989), in *CDSP* 41, no. 12 (1989), 21–22.

102. S.L. Tikhvinskii, *Dvizhenie za reformy v Kitae v kontse XIX veka I Kan Iu-vei* (Moscow, 1959), cited in Donald W. Treadgold, *The West in Russia and China,* vol. 2, *China, 1582–1949* (New York: Cambridge University Press 1973), 109.

103. Thomas Metzger, "Modern Chinese Utopianism and the Western Concept of the Civil Society," in *KuoT'ing-I hsien sheng 9 chih tan ch'en chi nien lun wen chi: hsia ts'e* (Taipei: Chung Yang yen chiu yuan chin tai shih yen chiu so fa hsing, 1995).

104. Yakovlev, *Gai ge xin si wei yu Sulian zhi ming yun,* 321.

105. Wang said that history progresses not because man is "benevolent," but because man is "greedy." He made the remark at a seminar in 1984 at the Journalism Institute, Chinese Academy of Social Sciences. Wang was never able to put such "outrageous" remarks in writing.

106. Yakovlev, *Gai ge xin si wei yu Sulian zhi ming yun,* 102.

107. Yakovlev, *The Fate of Marxism in Russia,* 15.

108. Ibid., 178.

109. Ibid., 69, 85.

Notes to the Conclusion

1. Frederick Barghoon, cited in R. Judson Mitchel and Randal Arrington, "Gorbachev, Ideology and the Fate of Soviet Communism," *Communist and Post-Communist Studies* 33 (2000), 457–74.

2. Alexander Yakovlev, *The Fate of Marxism in Russia* (New Haven, CT, and London: Yale University Press, 1993), 102, 164.

3. Alexander Yakovlev, *Gai ge xin si wei yu Sulian zhi ming yun* (New Thinking of Gorbachev's Reform and the Fate of the USSR), edited by Gao Hongshan, et al. (Changchun, China: Jilin ren min chubanshe, 1992), 17.

4. Alexis de Tocqueville believed that "aristocratic nations are by nature liable to restrict too much the bounds of human perfectibility while democratic nations stretch them sometimes to excess." Alexis de Tocqueville, *Democracy in America and Two Essays on America* (New York: Penguin Books, 2003), 523.

5. Derek Sayer, *Marx's Method* (Atlantic Highlands, NJ: Humanities Press, 1979).

6. Carl J. Friedrich and Zbigniew K. Brzezinsky, *Totalitarian Dictatorship and Autocracy* (Cambridge, MA: Harvard University Press, 1965), 106.

7. In the 1980s, Sergei Khrushchev said, "On many issues we are about where we were twenty years ago. . . . [Khrushchev] pondered the very many issues that we are debating now." David Nordlander, "Khrushchev's Image in the Light of Glasnost and Perestroika," *The Russian Review* 52 (April 1993), 250. In fact, the Khrushchev era laid the foundation for Gorbachev's reforms. Ibid., 264–65.

8. Fedor Burlatsky, *Khrushchev and the First Russian Spring: The Era of Khrushchev through the Eyes of His Advisor* (New York: Charles Scribner's Sons, 1988).

9. Suzanne Ogden, *Inklings of Democracy in China* (Cambridge, MA: Harvard University Asia Center, 2002), 1–10.

10. Thomas A. Metzger, "Modern Chinese Utopianism and the Western Concept of the Civil Society," in *Kuo T'ing-I hsien sheng 9 chih tan ch'en chi nien lun wen chi: hsia ts'e* (Taipei: Chung Yang yen chiu yuan chin tai shih yen chiu so fa hsing, 1995).

11. Xu Jilin, "In Search of a Third Way," in Introduction by Gloria Davies to *Voicing Concerns: Contemporary Chinese Critical Inquiry,* ed. Davies (Lanham, MD: Roman and Littlefield Publishers, 2001), 199.

12. Philip C.C. Huang, "Biculturality in Modern China and in Chinese Studies," *Modern China* 26, no. 1 (January 2000), 3–31.

13. See David Kelly, "Freedom—an Eurasia Mosaic," in *Asian Freedoms: The Idea of Freedom in the East and Southeast Asia,* eds. David Kelly and Anthony Reid (Cambridge: Cambridge University Press, 1998), 1–5.

14. Xu Jilin, "In Search of a Third Way," 210.

15. Although both datong and xiaokang are Confucian concepts, most monarchs in premodern times seemed to be satisfied with xiaokang, and they did not strive for the utopian goal of datong. Wolfgang Bauer, *China and the Search for Happiness: Recurring Themes in Four Thousand Years of Chinese Cultural History* (New York: Seabury Press, 1976), 132. Also see Maurice J. Meisner, *Marxism, Maoism and Utopianism: Eight Essays* (Madison: University of Wisconsin Press, 1982), 4, 8. However, the peasant rebellions wanted to have datong immediately by demanding total egalitarianism.

16. Pye was referring to the authoritarian political culture reflected in Dengism and the rebellion's political culture reflected in Maoism. Lucian W. Pye, *The Mandarin and the Cadre: China's Political Cultures* (Ann Arbor: Center for Chinese Studies, University of Michigan, 1988), 73.

17. Brantly Womack, "The Phases of Chinese Modernization," *Collected Papers of History Studies,* no. 4 (1999), 1–15.

18. Shiping Hua, "Testimony at the US–China Economic and Security Commission," February 1–2, 2007. The theory was based on Jin Guantao and Liu Qing Feng, *Xingsheng yu weiji: Zhongguo fengjian shehui de chaowending jiegou* (Prosperity and Crisis: The Ultrastable System of China's Feudal Society) (Changsha, China: Hunan Renmin Chubanshe, 1984).

19. Edwin O. Reischauer and Marius B. Jansen, *The Japanese Today: Change and Continuity* (Cambridge, MA: Harvard University Press, 1995).

20. Akira Iriye and Warren I. Cohen, *The United States and Japan in the Postwar World* (Lexington: University Press of Kentucky, 1989).

21. Marius B. Jansen, "The Meiji Restoration," in *The Cambridge History of Japan,* ed. Jansen, vol. 5, *The Nineteenth Century* (New York: Cambridge University Press, 1989), 308–13.

22. Fukuzawa Yukichi, *An Outline of a Theory of Civilization,* translated by David A. Dilworth and G. Cameron Hurst (Tokyo: Sophia University, 1973), 143–44.

23. Theodore von Laue, "A Perspective on History: The Soviet System Reconsidered," *The Historian* 61, no. 2 (Winter 1999) 383.

24. Donald W. Treadgold, *The West in Russia and China,* vol. 1, *Russia 1472–1917* (New York: Cambridge University Press, 1973), 250.

25. Attributing Russia's authoritarian tradition to geography, Yakovlev pointed out that Russia is too large, and the distance between the center and the provinces too far. Russia could be kept in check only from the center, "since the level of exchange relations was obviously insufficient for the economic integration of such a large and sparsely populated territory" and educational level. Western Europe was different in the sense that each of the countries were considerably smaller, a situation that made it easier for the countries to endorse freedom. Yakovlev, *The Fate of Marxism in Russia,* 96.

26. Richard Pipes, *The Formation of the Soviet Union* (Cambridge, MA: Harvard University Press, 1964), 1–10.

27. Theodore H. von Laue, *Why Lenin? Why Stalin? A Reappraisal of the Russian Revolution, 1900–1930* (New York: J.B. Lippincott Company, 1964), 39.

28. Richard Pipes, *The Formation of the Soviet Union,* 1–10.

29. Richard Pipes, "Flight from Freedom," *Foreign Affairs* 83, no. 3 (May/June 2004), 9–15.

30. Jin Guantao and Liu Qingfeng, *Xingsheng Yu Weiji,* 17–59.

31. Legalism and Confucianism were the most important schools of thought during this time period. The most important difference between the legalists and Confucianists is that while the former believed in the rule of law, the latter believed in the rule by virtue.

32. Xu Zhenzhou, "Zhongguo chuantong zhong de fei ziyouzhuyi qingxiang" (Antiliberalism Tendency in China's Tradition), *Zhongguo dalu yanju jiangxue tongxun,* no.54 (December 2002), 10–14.

33. Ibid.

34. Thomas M. Magstadt and Peter M. Schotten, *Understanding Politics: Ideas, Institutions, and Issues,* 5th ed. (New York: Worth Publishers, 1999), 151.

35. These massive projects were often paid for with enormous human sacrifice. At Shan-hai-guan Pass, the eastern end of the Great Wall, there is a temple called Jiangniu Miao, or the Temple of Meng Jiangniu, a woman in Qin (221–205 BCE). The Qin Dynasty started the construction of the Great Wall. According to the story, Meng's husband was one of the hundreds of thousands of peasants who were forced to build the Great

Wall. He died performing hard labor, like thousands of others, and was buried under the Great Wall. Upon learning of her husband's death, Meng went to the site of the Great Wall. The woman was so heartbroken that her tears started to possess magical powers that brought down several hundred miles of the Great Wall. She was then able to recover her husband's body from where he was buried under the Great Wall. In modern times, this pragmatic spirit that emphasizes unlimited achievements has contributed to China's environmental problems, because traditionally the Chinese have believed that the resources of the Earth are unlimited and subject to human exploitation. Elizabeth C. Economy, *The River Runs Black* (Ithaca, NY: Cornell University Press, 2004).

36. Reischaruer and Jansen, *The Japanese Today.*

37. Boris N. Mironov, "Peasant Popular Culture and the Origins of Soviet Authoritarianism," in *Cultures in Flux: Lower-Class Values, Practices and Resistance in Late Imperial Russia,* eds. Stephen P. Frank and Mark D. Steinberg (Princeton, NJ: Princeton University Press, 1994), 54–73; A.A. Zimin, "On the Political Preconditions for the Emergence of Russian Absolutism," in *Major Problems in Early Modern Russian History,* ed. Nancy S. Kollmann (New York: Garland Publishing, 1992), 79–108.

38. Jin Guantao, "Zhongguo wenhua de u-tuo-bang jingshen" (The Utopian Spirit in Chinese Culture), *Er shi yi shi ji* (Twenty-First Century) (December 1990), 16–33.

39. Liu Guoguang, "Zhongguo xiandaihua zhongjiang chengzhen" (Chinese Modernization Will Finally Be Realized), in *Jiedu shi wu da: Zhongguo gaoceng quanwei fangtanlu* (Explaining the Fifteenth Party Congress: Interviews of High-Level Leaders) (Beijing: Xinhua chubanshe, 2001), 3–4.

40. This has universal validity. John Stuart Mill observed that the maximization of liberty was appropriate only for a civilized society without serious national security problems. Thomas Metzger, *Escape from Predicament: Neo-Confucianism and China's Evolving Political Culture* (New York: Columbia University Press, 1986), 288, 305, 310.

41. Elkins and Simeon, "A Cause in Search of Its Effect," 125–45.

42. The article was later developed into a book with the same title. Francis Fukuyama, *The End of History and the Last Man* (New York: Avon Books, 1993).

43. This article was also developed into a book. Samuel P. Huntington, *The Clash of Civilizations and the Remaking of World Order* (New York: Simon and Schuster, 1998), chapter 4.

44. Kathryn Wallace, "America's Brain Drain Crisis: Why Our Best Scientists Are Disappearing, and What's Really at Stake," *Reader's Digest,* December 2005, 109–15.

45. Benjamin R. Barber, *Jihad vs. McWorld* (New York: Times Books, 1995).

46. Arnold Toynbee and Daisaku Ikeda, *Choose Life: A Dialogue* (New York: Oxford University Press, 1976).

47. More visible changes took place in Chinese political culture in the 1990s. Xudong Zhang, *Whither China: Intellectual Politics of Contemporary China,* edited and introduction by Xudong Zhang (Durham, NC: Duke University Press, 2002); Joseph Fewsmith, *China since Tiananmen: The Politics of Transition* (New York: Cambridge University Press, 2001), 101–31; Merle Goldman, "The Emergence of Politically Independent Intellectuals," in *The Paradox of China's Post-Mao Reforms,* eds. Merle Goldman and Roderick MacFarquhar (Cambridge, MA: Harvard University Press, 1999). As in the case of China, post-Soviet political culture has also been in flux. See Alexander N. Domrin, "Ten Years Later: Society, 'Civil Society,' and the Russian State," *The Russian Review* 62 (April 2003), 193–211. In the words of Richard Pipes, at the turn of the twenty-first century, "Russians . . . do not know in which direction to proceed. A verita-

ble battle for Russia's soul is in progress. . . . Countries like Russia . . . are capable of swinging wildly from one extreme to another often in response to a demagogue who promises quick and easy solutions." Pipes, "Is Russia Still an Enemy?" *Foreign Affairs* 76, no. 5 (September/October 1997), 66–70.

48. Wang Hui, *China's New Order: Society, Politics and Economy in Transition,* translated by Theodore Huters and edited by Wang Hui (Cambridge, MA: Harvard University Press, 2003), 78–115.

49. Jiwei Ci, *Dialectic of the Chinese Revolution: From Utopianism to Hedonism* (Stanford, CA: Stanford University Press, 1994), 6.

Bibliography

Almond, Gabriel A. "The Study of Political Culture." In Lane Crothers and Charles Lockhart, *Culture and Politics: A Reader.* New York: St. Martin's Press, 2000.

Ames, Roger. "New Confucianism: A Native Response to Western Philosophy." *China Studies* (Zhonguo yanjiu), no. 5 (1999).

———. "New Confucianism: A Native Response to Western Philosophy." In Shiping Hua, *Chinese Political Culture.* Armonk, NY: M.E. Sharpe, 2001.

An, Jianshe. "Zhou Enlai yu wenhuadageming qianqi de guomin jingji" (Zhou Enlai and China's Economy on the Eve of the Cultural Revolution). *Dangdai zhongguoshi yanjiu,* no. 1 (1998).

Augustine, St., *The City of God.* Garden City, NY: Image Books, 1958.

Ball, Alan. "NEP's Second Wind: 'The New Trade Practice.'" *Soviet Studies* 37, no. 3 (July 1985).

Barber, Benjamin R. *Jihad vs. McWorld.* New York: Times Books, 1995.

Barme, Geremie R. *In the Red: On Contemporary Chinese Culture.* New York: Columbia University Press, 1999.

Bauer, Wolfgang. *China and the Search for Happiness: Recurring Themes in Four Thousand Years of Chinese Cultural History.* New York: Seabury Press, 1976.

Baum, Richard. "The Road to Tiananmen: Chinese Politics in the 1980s." In *The Politics of China,* 2nd ed., edited by Roderick MacFarquhar. Cambridge: Cambridge University Press, 1997.

Bean, Jonathan J. "Nikolai Bukharin and the New Economic Policy." *Independent Review* 2, no. 1 (Summer 1997).

Beasley, W.G. *The Rise of Modern Japan.* New York: St. Martin's Press, 1995.

Benns, F. Lee. *Europe since 1914.* New York: F.S. Crofts and Co, 1944.

Bo, Yibo. *Ruo gan zhongda juece yu shijian de huigu* (Reflections on Some Important Decisions and Events). Beijing: Zhonggong zhongyang dangxiao chubanshe, 1993.

Brown, Archie. *The Gorbachev Factor.* New York: Oxford University Press, 1996.

Brown, Delmer M. "The Early Evolution of Historical Consciousness." In *The Cambridge History of Japan,* edited by John Whitney Hall, et al. Vol. 1, *Ancient Japan.* New York: Cambridge University Press, 1993.

Bukharin, Nicolai I. *Historical Materialism: A System of Sociology.* Ann Arbor: University of Michigan Press, 1969.

157

———. *Economics of the Transformation Period: With Lenin's Critical Remarks.* New York: Bergman Publishers, 1971.

———. *Buhalin wenxuan* (Bukharin: Selections), edited by Zhong Gong, et al. Beijing: Dongfang chubanshe, 1988.

———. "The Russian Revolution and Its Significance." In *In Defense of the Russian Revolution,* edited by Al Richardson. London: Porcupine Press, 1995.

Burlatsky, Fyodor M. *The State and Communism.* Moscow: Progress Publishers, 1964.

———. "New Thinking About Socialism." In *Breakthrough: Emerging New Thinking: Soviet and Western Scholars Issue a Challenge to Build a World Beyond War,* edited by Anatoly Gromyko and Martin Hellman. New York: Walker and Company, 1988.

———. *Khrushchev and the First Russian Spring: The Era of Khrushchev through the Eyes of His Adviser.* New York: Charles Scribner's Sons, 1988.

Bushnell, John. "'The New Soviet Man' Turns Pessimist." In *The Khrushchev and Brezhnev Years,* edited by Alexander Dallin. New York: Garland Publishing, Inc., 1992.

Bzrezinski, Zbigniew. "The Nature of the Soviet System." In *The Khrushchev and Brezhnev Years,* edited by Alexander Dallin. New York: Garland Publishing, 1992.

Carr, E.H. "The Bolshevik Utopia." *October Revolution: Before and After.* New York: Knopf, 1969.

CCP Central Committee. "Zhongguo gongchandang zhongyang weiyuanhui tongzhi" (CCP Central Committee Announcement). *Renmin ribao,* May 17, 1966.

———. "Zhonggong zhongyang guanyu wuchanjieji wenhuadageming de jueding" (CCP Central Committee Resolution on the Proletarian Cultural Revolution). *Renmin ribao,* August 9, 1966.

———. *Guanyu jianguo yilai dang de ruogan lishi wenti jueyi* (Resolution on Certain Historical Issues of the Party since the Founding of the People's Republic of China). Beijing: Renmin chubanshe, 1986.

Chang, Hao. *Liang Chi-Chao and Intellectual Transition in China, 1890–1907.* Cambridge, MA: Harvard University Press, 1971.

———. "Intellectual Change and the Reform Movement, 1890–1898." In *The Cambridge History of China,* edited by Denis Twitchett and John K. Fairbank. Vol. 11, *Late Ch'ing, 1800–1911.* New York: Cambridge University Press, 1989.

Chang, Parris H. "The Role of Ch'en Po-ta in the Cultural Revolution." *Asia Quarterly,* no. 1 (1973).

Cheek, Timothy, and Anthony Saich. *New Perspectives on State Socialism in China.* Armonk, NY: M.E. Sharpe, 1997.

Chen, Boda. *Zai wenhua zhanxian shang* (On the Front of Culture). Chongqing: Shenghuo shudian, 1939.

———. "Buyao daluan yuanlai de qiye jigou" (Don't Abolish the Structure of the Old Enterprises). In Chen Boda, *Zhongguo jingji de gaizao* (The Transformation of China's Economy). Hong Kong: Xinminzhu chubanshe, 1949.

———. *Zai zhongguo kexueyuan yanjiu renyuan xuexihui shang de jianghua* (Talk at the Study Meeting of the Researchers of the Chinese Academy of Sciences). Beijing: Renmin chubanshe, 1952.

———. *Mao Tse-tung on the Chinese Revolution: Written in Commemoration of the 30th Anniversary of the Communist Party of China.* Beijing: Foreign Languages Press, 1953.

———. *Zhongguo nongye de shehuizhuyi gaizao* (Socialist Transformation of China's Agriculture). Beijing: Renmin chubanshe, 1956.

———. "Quanxin de shehui, quanxin de ren" (Brand New Society, Brand New People). *Hong qi,* no. 3, July 1, 1958.

———. "Zai Mao Zedong tongzhi de qizhi xia" (Under the Banner of Comrade Mao Zedong). *Hong qi,* July 16, 1958.

———, for the Editorial Board of *Renmin ribao.* "Hengsao yiqie niu, gui, she, shen" (Wipe Out All Enemies). *Renmin ribao,* June 1, 1966.

———. "Ji nian Mao Zhuxi zai Yan'an wenyi zuotan hui yi shang de jianghua" (Talk at the Seminar about Issues of Literature in Yan'an). *Renmin ribao,* May 24, 1967.

———. "Wuchan jieji wenhuadageming zhong de liangtiao luxian" (The Two Lines in the Great Proletarian Cultural Revolution). In Tianjinshi geming weiyuanhui zhengzhibu, *Wuchanjieji wenhuadageming zhongyao wenxian xuanbian* (Selections of the Important Documents of the Great Proletarian Cultural Revolution). Tianjin: N.p., May 1969.

———. *Chen Boda yi gao* (Leftover Manuscripts by Chen Boda). Hohhot, China: Neimong renmin chubanshe, 1999.

Chen, Donglin. "Wenge shiqi Mao Zedong de jingji sixiang tanxi" (An Analysis of Mao's Economic Thought during the Cultural Revolution). *Dangdai zhongguoshi yanjiu,* no. 1 (1996).

Chen, Jerome, and Michael Bullock. *Mao and the Chinese Revolution.* London: Oxford University Press, 1965.

Chen, Ji. "Mao Zedong yu wenhua de shehuizhuyi zhuanbian" (Mao Zedong and Socialist Cultural Transformation). *Zhonggong dangshi yanju* 2 (2002).

Chen, Zhengyan, and Lin Qiyan. *Zhonguo Guodai Datong Sixiang* (Utopian Thought in Pre-Modern China). Shanghai: Shanghai renmin chubanshe, 1986.

Chernenko, Konstantin. "Toward the 27th Party Congress: At the Level of the Requirements of Developed Socialism." *Current Digest of the Soviet Press* 37, no. 4 (December 1984).

Chilcote, Ronald H. *Theories of Comparative Politics: The Search for a Paradigm.* Boulder, CO: Westview Press, 1981.

Chong, W.L. "Su Xiaokang on his film 'River Elegy.'" *China Information* 4, no. 3 (Winter 1989–1990).

———. ed. *China's Great Proletarian Cultural Revolution: Master Narratives and Post-Mao Counternarratives.* Lanham, MD: Roman and Littlefield, 2002.

Chuang, Tzu. *Basic Writings.* Translated by Burton Watson. New York: Columbia University Press, 1996.

Ci, Jiwei. *Dialectic of the Chinese Revolution: From Utopianism to Hedonism.* Stanford: Stanford University Press, 1994.

Cohen, Paul, and Merle Goldman. *Ideas across Cultures: Essays on Chinese Thought in Honor of Benjamin I. Schwartz.* Cambridge, MA: Harvard East Asian Monographs, 1990.

Cohen, Steven. "Marxist Theory, and Bolshevik Policy: The Case of Bukharin's Historical Materialism." *Political Science Quarterly* 85, no. 1 (March 1970).

———. "The Friends and Foes of Change: Reformism and Conservatism in the Soviet Union." *Slavic Review* 38, no. 2 (June 1979).

———. *Bukharin and the Bolshevik Revolution: A Political Biography, 1888–1938.* Oxford: Oxford University Press, 1985.

"Communiqué on the Plenary Session of the Central Committee of the Communist Party of the Soviet Union." *Pravda* and *Izvestia,* June 17, 1986. *Current Digest of the Soviet Press* 38, no. 24 (1986).

Confucius. *The Analects.* Translated with an introduction and notes by D.C. Lau. London: Penguin Classics, 1979.

Da, Lianwei. "Ziyou shichang zai sulian de da fanlan" (Too Many Private Markets in the USSR). *Renmin ribao,* January 11, 1969.

Dallin, Alexander, ed. *The Khrushchev and Brezhnev Years.* New York: Garland Publishing, Inc., 1992.

Davies, Gloria, ed. *Voicing Concerns: Contemporary Chinese Critical Inquiry.* Lanham, MD: Roman and Littlefield, 2001.

de Bary, William T., ed. *Sources of Chinese Tradition,* vol. 1. New York: Columbia University Press, 1960.

Deng, Liqun. "Qiqianren dahui, dao xilou huiyi" (From 7,000 People Conference to Xilou Conference). *Dangdai zhongguoshi yanjiu,* no. 5 (1998).

Deng, Xiaoping. *Deng Xiaoping wenxuan* (Selections of Deng Xiaoping), vol. 2. Beijing: Renmin chubanshe, 1994.

Dickson, Bruce J. "What Explains Chinese Political Behavior? The Debate over Structure and Culture." *Comparative Politics,* no. 1 (October 1992).

Ding, Xuelei. "Wuchanjieji da minzhu jiushi hao" (Big Democracy by the Proletariat Is Good). *Renmin ribao,* September 12, 1967.

Dmytryshyn, Basil. *USSR: A Concise History,* 2nd ed. New York: Charles Scribner's Sons, 1971.

Domrin, Alexander N. "Ten Years Later: Society, 'Civil Society,' and the Russian State." *The Russian Review,* no. 62 (April 2003).

Dong, Bian, and Tan Deshan, eds. *Mao Zedong He Tade Mishu Tian Jiaying* (Mao Zedong and His Secretary Tian Jiaying). Beijing: Zhongyang wenxian chubanshe, 1996.

Dong, Zhikai. "Mao Zedong zai bada qianhou gaige jingji guanli tizhi de shexiang" (Mao's Thoughts about the Economic Management Structure around the Eighth Party Congress). *Dangdai zhongguoshi yanjiu,* no. 1 (1996).

Dreyer, June Teufel. *China's Political System: Modernization and Tradition,* 2nd ed. Boston: Allyn and Bacon, 1996.

Economy, Elizabeth C. *The River Runs Black: The Environmental Challenge to China's Future.* Ithaca, NY: Cornell University Press, 2004.

Editorial Department, *Renmin ribao.* "Lun Wuchanjieji zhuanzheng de lishi jingyan" (On the Historical Experience of the Dictatorship of the Proletariat). *Renmin ribao,* April 5, 1956.

Elkins, David, and Richard E.B. Simeon. "A Cause in Search of Its Effect, or What Does Political Culture Explain?" *Comparative Politics* 11 (January 1979).

Engels, Frederick. *Socialism: Utopian and Scientific.* New York: International Publishers, 1972.

Fan, Xiubing. "Pi chou 'zhongguo He lu xiao fu' de jingji zhuyi" (Criticize Thoroughly the Economism of China's Khrushchev). *Renmin ribao,* September 14, 1967.

Fang, Delin. "Cong jindai zhongxi wenhua lunzheng kan Zhongguo xinwenhua de fazhan luxiang" (A Look at China's New Culture Direction from the Cultural Debates about the Cultures of the East and West in Modern Chinese History). *Xinhua Wenzhai,* no. 12 (2003).

Fedoseyev, P. "Socialism and Humanism." *Pravda,* September 21, 1957. *Current Digest of the Soviet Press* 9, no. 37 (1957).

Feng, Xianzhi. "Mao Zedong he tade minshu Tian Jiaying" (Mao Zedong and His Secretary Tian Jiaying). In *Mao Zedong he tade mishu Tian Jiaying,* edited by Dong Bian and Tan Deshan (Mao Zedong and His Secretary Tian Jiaying). Beijing: Zhongyang wenxian chubanshe, 1996.

Fewsmith, Joseph. *China since Tiananmen: The Politics of Transition.* New York: Cambridge University Press, 2001.

Fischer, Ruth. "Background of the New Economic Policy." *Russian Review* 7, no. 2 (Spring 1948).

Friedman, Edward. "Immanuel Kant's Relevance to an Enduring Asia-Pacific Peace." In *What If China Doesn't Democratize?,* edited by Edward Friedman and Barrett L. McCormick Armonk, NY: M.E. Sharpe, 2000.

Friedrich, Carl J., and Zbigniew K. Brzezinsky. *Totalitarian Dictatorship and Autocracy.* Cambridge, MA: Harvard University Press, 1965.

Fukuyama, Francis. *The End of History and the Last Man.* New York: Avon Books, 1993.

Gao, Huamin. "Nongye hezuohua de chenggong jingyan" (The Successful Experience of Agricultural Collectivization). *Dangdai zhongguoshi yanjiu,* no. 4 (1995).

Gao, Min. *Qin-han shi lun ji* (Historical Works about Qin-Han). Zhengzhou: Zhongzhou shuhua she, 1982.

Gao, Xuejun. "Nongcun gaige de lishi xing tupo" (Historical Breakthrough in Agricultural Reform). *Xuexi shibao,* June 18, 2001.

Ge, Zhaoguang. *Zhongguo Sixiang Shi* (History of Chinese Thought), vol. 1. Shanghai: Fudan daxue chubanshe, 1997.

Gee, James Paul. *An Introduction to Discourse Analysis: Theory and Method.* London and New York: Routledge, 1999.

Geertz, Clifford. *Islam Observed: Religious Development in Morocco and Indonesia.* Chicago: University of Chicago Press, 1971.

Gluck, Carol. *Japan's Modern Myths: Ideology in the Late Meiji Period.* Princeton, NJ: Princeton University Press, 1985.

Goldman, Merle. "The Emergence of Politically Independent Intellectuals." In *The Paradox of China's Post-Mao Reforms,* edited by Merle Goldman and Roderick MacFarquhar. Cambridge, MA: Harvard University Press, 1999.

———, and Leo Ou-fan Lee. *An Intellectual History of Modern China.* Cambridge: Harvard University Press, 2002.

Goodwin, Barbara. "Utopianism." In *The Blackwell Encyclopedia of Political Thought,* edited by David Miller. New York: Basil Blackwell, 1987.

Gorbachev, Mikhail. "Initiative, Organization and Efficiency." *Pravda,* April 12, 1985. *Current Digest of the Soviet Press* 37, no. 15 (1985).

———. "Restructuring Is an Urgent Matter That Affects Everyone and Everything." *Pravda,* August 2, 1986. *Current Digest of the Soviet Press* 38, no. 31 (1986).

———, and Zdenek Mlynar. *Conversations with Gorbachev: On Perestroika, the Prague Spring, and the Crossroads of Socialism.* Translated by George Shriver. New York: Columbia University Press, 2002.

Gu, Edward X. "Who Was Mr. Democracy? The May Fourth Discourse of Populist

Democracy and the Radicalization of Chinese Intellectuals (1915–1922)." *Modern Asian Studies* 35, no. 3 (2001).

Guan, Haiting. "Wenhua dageming zhong zhishiqingnian shangshan xiaxiang yuntong shulun" (Comments on the Movement of Educated Youths Being Sent down to the Countryside during the Cultural Revolution). *Dangdai zhongguoshi yanjiu,* no. 5 (1995).

Guo, Moro. *Guo Moro Quanji* (Works of Guo Moro). Vol. 10, *Literature.* Beijing: Renmin wenxue chubanshe, 1985.

Guo Fang Da Xue (National Defense University). *Zhonggong dangshi cankao ziliao* (Reference Materials for the Party's History). Beijing: Guofang Daxue Chubanshe, 1986.

Han, Suyin. "Cong bajie shi er zhong quanhui dao jiuda." In An Jianshe, *Zhou Enlai de zuihou Suiyue* (Zhou Enlai's Last Years). Beijing: Zhongyang wenxian chubanshe, 1995.

Harding, Harry. "The Study of Chinese Politics: Toward a Third Generation of Scholarship." *World Politics* 36 (January 1984).

Harootunian, Harry D. "The Function of China in Tokugawa Thought." In *The Chinese and the Japanese: Essays in Political and Cultural Interactions,* edited by Akira Iriye. Princeton, NJ: Princeton University Press, 1980.

He, Ping. *China's Search for Modernity: Cultural Discourse in the Late 20th Century.* Houndmill, Basingstoke, Hampshire; New York: Palgrave MacMillan in association with St. Anthony's College, Oxford, 2002.

He, Yuqing. "San zi yi bao jiu shi fubi zibenzhuyi" (The Responsibility System Is Restoring Capitalism). *Renmin ribao,* September 5, 1967.

Himmer, Robert. "The Transition from War Communism to the New Economic Policy: An Analysis of Stalin's Views." *Russian Review* 53, no. 4 (October 1994).

Hiniker, Paul J. "The Cultural Revolution Revisited: Dissonance Reduction or Power Maximization." *The China Quarterly,* no. 94 (June 1983).

Hobsbawm, Eric. *The Age of Extremes: A History of the World, 1914–1991.* New York: Vintage Books, 1996.

Horn, David G. "Reading History: Toward Comparative Cultural Studies: A Review Article." *Comparative Studies in Society and History* 39, no. 4 (1997).

Howell, David L. "Visions of the Future in Meiji Japan." In *Historical Perspectives on Contemporary East Asia,* edited by Merle Goldman and Andrew Gordon. Cambridge, MA: Harvard University Press, 2000.

Howland, Douglas. "Society Reified: Herbert Spencer and Political Theory in Early Meiji Japan." *Comparative Studies in Society and History,* no. 42 (2000).

Hsiao, Kung-Chuan. *A Modern China and a New World: K'ang Yu-wei, Reformer and Utopian, 1858–1927.* Seattle and London: University of Washington Press, 1975.

Hu, Qiaomu. "Guanyu rendaozhuyi he yihua wenti" (On Humanism and the Issue of Alienation). *Renmin ribao,* January 27, 1984.

———. *Zhongguo gongchandang zenyang fazhanle makesizhuyi—wei jinian jiandang qishi zhounian zuo* (How the CCP Developed Marxism—In Celebration of the 70th Anniversary of the Party). Beijing: Renmin chubanshe, 1991.

———. "Dang qian sixiang zhanxian de ruogan wenti" (Certain Issues on the Ideological Front). In *Hu Qiaomu wenji* (Collections of Hu Qiaomu), vol. 2. Beijing: Renmin chubanshe, 1993.

———. *Hu Qiaomu wenji* (Collections of Hu Qiaomu), vol. 2. Beijing: Renmin chubanshe, 1993.

————. "Zhongguo wei shenmo fan 20 nian de zuoqing cuowu" (Why Did China Commit the Mistake of Leftism for Twenty Years?). In Hu Qiaomu, *Hu Qiaomu wenji* (Collections of Hu Qiaomu), vol. 2. Beijing: Renmin chubanshe, 1993.

————. "Xiwang renren dou kan Hua Huan" (We Hope Everybody Goes to See the Garland at the Foot of the Mountain). In *Hu Qiaomu wenji* (Collections of Hu Qiaomu), vol. 3. Beijing: Renmin chubanshe, 1994.

Hu, Xiwei, and Tian Wei. "Er shi shi ji zhongguo wenhua jijin zhuyi sichao fu yi" (On Cultural Radicalism of Twentieth-Century China). *Tianjin shehui kexue,* no. 1 (2002).

Hua, Shiping. *Scientism and Humanism: Two Cultures in Post-Mao China, 1978–1989.* Albany, NY: State University of New York Press, 1995.

————. "Literature as Civic Discourse in the Reform Era: Utopianism and Cynicism in Chinese Political Consciousness." In *Civic Discourse, Civil Society, and Chinese Communities,* edited by John Powers, et al. Stamford, CT: Ablex Press, 1999.

————. "Political Cultures." In *Encyclopedia of Government and Politics,* 2nd ed., edited by Mary Hawkesworth and Maurice Koga. London: Routledge, 2004.

Hua, Shiping and Ming Xia, eds. "Falungong: Qigong, Code of Ethics and Religion." *Chinese Law and Government* 32, nos. 6 and 7 (September–October and November–December 1999).

Huang, Aijun. "Dayuejin yundong fasheng yuanyin yanjiu shuping" (Comments on Studies of the Origins of the Great Leap Forward). *Dangdai zhongguoshi yanjiu,* no. 1 (2005).

Huang, Philip. "Biculturality in Modern China and in Chinese Studies." *Modern China* 26, no. 1 (January 2000).

Huang, Yasheng. "Information, Bureaucracy, and Economic Reforms in China and the Soviet Union." *World Politics* 47, no. 1 (October 1994).

Huntington, Samuel P. *The Clash of Civilizations and the Remaking of World Order.* New York: Simon and Schuster, 1998.

Inglehart, Ronald. "The Renaissance of Political Culture." *American Political Science Review* 82, no. 4 (December 1988).

Iriye, Akira, and Warren I. Cohen. *The United States and Japan in the Postwar World.* Lexington: University Press of Kentucky, 1989.

Janita, Tuetuo. *The Intellectual Foundations of Modern Japanese Politics.* Chicago: University of Chicago Press, 1974.

Jansen, Marius B. "The Meiji Restoration." In *The Cambridge History of Japan,* edited by Marius B. Jansen. Vol. 5, *The Nineteenth Century.* New York: Cambridge University Press, 1989.

Jiang, Jianshe. *Zhou qin shidai lixiangguo tansuo* (Exploring Utopias in the Zhou and Qin Periods). Zhengzhou, Henan: Zhong zhou guji chubanshe, 1998.

Jin, Chunming. "Liu shi nian dai zuo qing cuowu de fazhan yu wenhua dageming de baofa" (Development of Mistakes in Leftist Thought in the 1960s and the Outbreak of the Cultural Revolution). *Zhonggong dangshi yanju,* no. 1 (1996).

Jin, Shan. "Beijing daxue wu bai duo ganbu xiafang" (More than 500 Cadres Went to Grassroots Units). *Renmin ribao,* January 4, 1958.

Jin Guantao. "Zhongguo wenhua de utuobang jingshen" (The Utopian Spirit of Chinese Culture). In *Ershiyi shiji* (Twenty-First Century), (December 1990).

Johnson, Chalmers. "What's Wrong with Chinese Political Studies." *Asian Survey* 22, no. 10 (October 1992).

Kane, Anthony J. "The Humanities in Contemporary China Studies: An Uncomfortable Tradition." In David Shambaugh, ed., *American Studies of Contemporary China.* Washington, DC: Woodrow Wilson Center Press, 1993.

K'ang, Yu-wei. *Ta T'ung Shu: The One-World Philosophy of K'ang Yu-wei.* London: George Allen and Unwin Ltd., 1958.

———. "Chunqiu Dong Shi Xue" (Dong Zhongshu on Chunqiu Period). In *Kang Youwei Quanji* (Works of Kang Youwei), vol. 2, edited by Jiang Yihua and Wu Genliang. Shanghai: Guji chubanshe, 1990.

———. "Kongzi gaizhi" (Confucius's Reform). In *Kang Youwei Quanji* (Works of Kang Youwei), vol. 2, edited by Jiang Yihua and Wu Genliang. Shanghai: Guji chubanshe, 1990.

———. "Shanghai Qiangxuehui hou xu" (Shanghai Strengthening China Society Constitution). In *Kang Youwei Quanji* (Works of Kang Youwei), vol. 2, edited by Jiang Yihua and Wu Genliang. Shanghai: Guji chubanshe, 1990.

———. "Shang qingdi di er shu" (Second Letter of Appeal to the Emperor). In *Kang Youwei Quanji* (Works of Kang Youwei), vol. 2, edited by Jiang Yihua and Wu Genliang. Shanghai: Guji chubanshe, 1990.

———. *Da Tong Shu* (Da Tong Shu with Comments by Li Sizhen). Zhengzhou, China: Zhongzhou guji chubanshe, 1998.

Kautsky, John H. "Centralization in the Marxist and Leninist Tradition." *Communist and Post-Communist Studies* 30, no. 4 (1997).

Kelley, Robert. "Comparing the Incomparable: Politics and Ideas in the United States and the Soviet Union." *Comparative Studies in Society and History* 26, no. 4 (1984).

Kelly, David. "The Emergence of Humanism: Wang Ruoshui and the Critique of Socialist Alienation." In *China's Intellectuals and the State: In Search of a New Relationship,* edited by Merle Goldman, Timothy Cheek and Carol L. Hamrin. Cambridge, MA: Council on East Asian Studies, 1987.

———. "Freedom—An Eurasia Mosaic." In *Asian Freedoms: The Idea of Freedom in the East and Southeast Asia,* edited by David Kelly and Anthony Reid. Cambridge: Cambridge University Press, 1998.

Kemp-Welch, A. "The New Economic Policy in Culture and Its Enemies." *Journal of Contemporary History* 13, no. 3 (July 1978).

Khrushchev, Nikita. "On Building and Improvements on the Collective Farms." *Current Digest of the Soviet Press* 3, no. 7 (1951).

———. "On Measures for Further Development of USSR Agriculture." *Current Digest of the Soviet Press* 5, no. 39 (1953).

———. "On Wide-Scale Introduction of Industrial Methods, Improving the Quality and Reducing the Cost of Construction." *Current Digest of the Soviet Press* 6, no. 52 (1954).

———. "Report of the Central Committee of the Communist Party of the Soviet Union to the 20th Party Congress." *Current Digest of the Soviet Press* 8, no. 6 (1956).

———. "For Close Ties between Literature and Art and the Life of the People." *Current Digest of the Soviet Press* 9, no. 35 (1957).

———. "Three Interviews with N. S. Khrushchev." *Current Digest of the Soviet Press* 9, no. 46 (1957).

———. "Report on the Program of the Communist Party of the Soviet Union." *Documents of the 22nd Congress of the CPSU,* vol. 2. New York: Crosscurrents Press, 1961.

———. "Speech by N.S. Khrushchev on the Stalin Cult Delivered February 25, 1956" (at the Closed Session of the 20th Congress of the Soviet Communist Party). In *Khrushchev Speaks: Selected Speeches, Articles and Press Conferences (1949–1961)*, edited by Thomas P. Whiney. Ann Arbor: University of Michigan Press, 1963.

———. "On Some Questions of the Further Organizational and Economic Strengthening of the Collective Farms," April 25, 1950. In *Khrushchev Speaks: Selected Speeches, Articles and Press Conferences (1949–1961)*, edited by Thomas P. Whitney. Ann Arbor: University of Michigan Press, 1963.

———. *Khrushchev Remembers: The Last Testament.* Translated and edited by Strobe Talbott. Boston: Little Brown and Company, 1974.

———. *Khrushchev Remembers: The Glasnost Tapes.* Translated and edited by Jerrod L. Schecter with Vyacheslav V. Luchkov. Boston: Little, Brown and Company, 1990.

Koizumi, Tokashi. "Fukuzawa Yukichi and Religion." *Asian Philosophy* 4, no. 2 (1994).

Kornai, Janos. *The Socialist System.* Princeton, NJ: Princeton University Press, 1992.

Kuhn, Thomas S. *The Structure of Scientific Revolutions.* Chicago: University of Chicago Press, 1962.

Kuraturing, B.P. "A Proposal for Restructuring the Economy." *Ekonomika I organizatsia promyshlennovo proizvodstva,* no. 5 (May 1984). *Current Digest of the Soviet Press* 37, no. 41 (1984).

Kwong, Luke S.K. "The Ti-Yung Dichotomy and the Search for Talent in Late-Ch'ing China." *Modern Asian Studies* 27, no. 2 (1993).

———. "Chinese Politics at the Crossroads: Reflections on the Hundred Days Reform of 1898." *Modern Asian Studies* 34, no. 3 (2000).

Lao-Tzu. *Tao Te Ching.* Translated by Stephen Addiss and Stanley Lombardo. Indianapolis: Hackett Publishing Company, 1993.

Laue, Theodore H. von. *Why Lenin? Why Stalin? A Reappraisal of the Russian Revolution 1900–1930.* New York: J.B. Lippincott Company, 1964.

———. "A Perspective on History: The Soviet System Reconsidered." *The Historian* 61, no. 2 (Winter 1999).

Le Nong. *Li xiang guo de tan qiu: zhongguo datong shihua* (Looking for Utopia: China's Datong Tradition). Zhengzhou: Henan reminchubanshe, 1981.

Lee, Hong Yung. *The Politics of China's Cultural Revolution.* Berkeley: University of California Press, 1987.

Lenin, V. I. *The State and Revolution.* New York: International Publishers, 1932.

———. *On Utopian and Scientific Socialism.* Moscow: Progress Publishers, 1965.

———. *Certain Features of the Historical Development of Marxism.* Moscow: Progress Publishers, 1966.

———. *On the Material and Technical Basis of Communism.* Moscow: Novosti Press Agency Publishing House, 1969.

———. "Two Utopias." In *Lenin, Collected Works,* vol. 18. Moscow: Progress Publishers, 1975.

Levenson, Joseph, R. *Confucian China and Its Modern Fate: The Problem of Intellectual Continuity.* Berkeley, CA: University of California Press, 1958.

Lewin, Moshe. *Political Undercurrents in Soviet Economic Debates.* Princeton, NJ: Princeton University Press, 1974.

Li Chengrui. "Dayuejin yinqi de renkou biandong" (Population Change Due to the Great Leap Forward). *Zhonggong dangshi yanju,* no. 2 (1997).

Li Dao, ed. *Gaobie utobang* (Farewell, Utopia). Lanzhou, China: Gansu renmin chubanshe, 1998.

Li Jianchun. "Cong zhonggong di bajie zhongyang weiyuanhui de jiegou, kan bada lux-ian de zhongduan" (A Look at the Ending of the Policies of the 8th Congress by the Membership Composition of the CCP Central Committee). *Dangdai zhongguoshi yanjiu*, no. 2 (2001).

Li Lian. "Yan zhe jianshe you zhongguo tese shehuizhuyi daolu qianjin" (March along the Road to Build Socialism According to Chinese Characteristics). *Dangdai zhong-guoshi yanjiu*, no. 6 (1996).

Li Qing. "1957 nian fanyoupai douzheng jiqi yanzhong kuodahua de qiyin he jiaoxun" (Origins and Lessons of the Anti-Rightist Movement in 1957 and Its Exaggeration). *Zhonggong dangshi yanju*, no. 6 (1995).

Li Qingting. "Mingzhiweixin yu Wuxubianfa chengyin youzhi beijiao" (Why Did the Meiji Restoration Succeed and the Late Qing Reform Fail?). *Journal of the Teacher's College, Qingdao University* 12, no. 2 (June 1995).

Li Sizhen. "Kang Youwei yu Datongshu" (Kang Youwei and Datongshu [Introduction]). In Kang Youwei, *Datongshu: Chuantong waiyi xia de jinshi lixiang guo* (Datongshu: Modern Utopia Wrapped Up in Traditions), edited by Li Sizhen. Zhengzhou: Zhongzhou guji chubanshe, 1998.

Li Yinqiao. *Zai Mao Zedong shen bian shi wu nian* (At the Side of Mao Zedong for 15 Years). Shijiazhuang, Hebei: Renmin chubanshe, 1992.

Li Zehou. "Lun Kang Youwei de Da Tong Shu" (On Kang Youwei's *Datongshu*). *Wen, Shi, Zhe* no. 2 (1955).

———, with Liu Zaifu. *Gaobie Geming: Huiwang ershi shiji zhongguo* (Farewell, Rev-olution: Retrospective of Twentieth-Century China). Hong Kong: Tiandi Tushu youxian gongsi, 1995.

Li Zhenzhong. *Taiping tianguo de xingwang* (The Rise and Fall of the Kingdom of Heav-enly Peace). Taipei: Cheng Chun Book Co., Ltd., 1999.

Liang Shuming. *Dontxi wenhua jiqi zhexue* (The Cultures and Philosophies of the East and West). Beijing: Shangwu yinshuguan, 2003.

Liang Shuzhen. "Daban nongcun gonggong shitang de lishi jiaoxun" (Historical Lessons of Public Dining Halls in the Countryside). *Zhonggong dangshi yanju*, no. 3 (2000).

Liao Yuren. "Ruhe jiasu sanminzhuyi quanmian dengshang dalu" (How to Quicken the Process during Which the Three Principles of the People Conquer Mainland China). In *Heping Yanbian zhanlue de chanseng jiqi fazhan* (The Origin and Development of the Strategy of Peaceful Restoration of Capitalism), edited by Qi Fang. Beijing: Dengfang chubanshe, 1990.

Lieberthal, Kenneth. "The Great Leap Forward and the Split in the Yenan Leadership." In *The Cambridge History of China*, vol. 14, edited by Denis Twitchett and John K. Fairbank. New York: Cambridge University Press, 1987.

Lih, Lars T. "Political Testament of Lenin and Bukharin and the Meaning of NEP." *Slavic Review* 50, no. 2 (Summer 1991).

———. "The Mystery of the ABC." *Slavic Review* 56, no. 1 (Spring 1997).

Lin, Daizhao, et al. *Zhongguo Jindai Zhengzhi Zhidushi* (A History of Modern China's Political System). Chongqing, China: Chongqing chubanshe, 1988.

Lin, Ke. *Wo suo zhidao de Mao Zedong* (My Knowledge of Mao Zedong). Beijing: Zhongyang wenxian chubanshe, 2000.

Lin, Keguang. *Lun Da Tong Shu* (On Da Tong Shu). Beijing: Sanlian shudian, 1957.

Lin, Yusheng. *The Crisis of Chinese Consciousness: Radical Anti-Traditionalism in the May Fourth Era.* Madison: University of Wisconsin Press, 1979.

Ling, Zhijun. *Chen Fu: Zhongguo jingji gaige beiwanglu* (Ups and Downs: A Memorandum of China's Economic Reform 1989–1997). Shanghai: Dongfang chubanzhongxin, 1998.

Liu, Cunshi, ed. *Chen Boda wenji.* Hong Kong: Lishi ziliao chubanshe, 1971.

Liu, Guoguang. "Zhongguo xiandaihua zhongjiang chengzhen" (Chinese Modernization Will Be Realized Finally). In *Jiedu shi wu da: Zhongguo gaoceng quanwei fangtanlu* (Explanation of the 15th Party Congress: Interviews of High-Level Leaders), edited by He Ping. Beijing: Xinhua chubanshe, 2001.

———. "Gaige kaifang qian de zhongguo de jingji fazhan he jingji tizhi" (Economic Structure before the Deng Reforms). *Zhonggong dangshi yanju,* no. 4 (2002).

Liu, Huiming. "Bali gongshe de quanmian xuanju zhi" (The Election System of the Paris Commune). *Hong qi,* no. 11 (1966).

Liu, Jinfeng. *Chen Boda yu Xiaozhan Siqing.* Beijing: Tsinghua Tonfang Optical Disc Co., Ltd., 1995–2004.

Liu, Qingfeng. *Rang kexue de guangmang zhaoliang ziji* (Let the Light of Science Shine on Us). Chengdu, China: Sichuan renmin chubanshe, 1984.

Liu, Ya. "Mubiao, shouduan, zizhu xuyao" (Goals, Means, and the Need for Independence). *Dangdai zhongguoshi yanjiu* 10, no. 1 (2003).

Liu, Zehua, eds. *Zhongguo gudai zhengzhi sixiang shi* (A History of Chinese Political Thought in Pre-Modern Times). Tianjin: Nankai daxue chubanshe, 1994.

Lu, Shichao. "Liangzhong shijieguan de douzheng" (The Conflict between Two World Outlooks). *Renmin ribao,* January 5, 1958.

Lukin, Y. "Ideology, Politics and Culture: In the Struggle for the Future of Mankind." *Literaturnaya gazeta. Current Digest of the Soviet Press* 35, no. 52 (1984).

Ma, Shu-Yun. "Chinese Discourse on Civil Society." *The China Quarterly,* no. 137 (March 1994).

MacFarquhar, Roderick, Timothy Cheek, and Eugene Wu, eds. *The Secret Speeches of Chairman Mao,* with contributions by Merle Goldman and Benjamin I. Schwartz. Cambridge: Harvard University Press, 1989.

———, and Merle Goldman. "Dynamic Economy, Declining Party-State." In Merle Goldman and Roderick MacFarquhar, *The Paradox of China's Post-Mao Reforms.* Cambridge: Harvard University Press, 1999.

Macridis, Roy C. *Contemporary Political Ideologies: Movements and Regimes.* New York: HarperCollins Publishers, 1992.

Magstadt, Thomas M., and Peter M. Schotten. *Understanding Politics: Ideas, Institutions and Issues,* 5th ed. New York: Worth Publishers, 1999.

Mannheim, Karl. *Ideology and Utopia.* New York: Harcourt, Brace and World, Inc., 1936.

Manuel, Frank E., and Fritzie P. Manuel. *Utopian Thought in the Western World.* Cambridge: The Belknap Press of Harvard University Press, 1979.

Mao, Mao. *Wo de fuqin Deng Xiaoping* (My Father Deng Xiaoping). Beijing: Zhongyang wenxian chubanshe, 2000.

Mao Tse-tung. *Selected Works of Mao Tsetung,* vol. 5. Beijing: Foreign Languages Press, 1977.

Mao Zedong. *Mao Zedong xuanji* (Selected Works of Mao Zedong). Beijing: Renmin chubanshe, 1953.

———. "Speech at the Extended Meeting of the CCP Political Bureau (April 1956)." In Joint Publications Research Service, *Miscellany of Mao Tse-tung Thought (1949–1968)*, Part I. Washington, DC: Distributed by National Technical Information Service, U.S. Department of Commerce, 1974.

———. "Speech at the Hankow Conference (6 April 1958)." In Joint Publications Research Service, *Miscellany of Mao Tse-tung Thought (1949–1968)*, Part I. Washington, DC: Distributed by National Technical Information Service, U.S. Department of Commerce, 1974.

———. "Speech at the Conference of Head Delegations to the Second Session of the Eighth Party Congress (18 May 1958)." In Joint Publications Research Service, *Miscellany of Mao Tse-tung Thought (1949–1968)*, Part I. Washington, DC: Distributed by National Technical Information Service, U.S. Department of Commerce, 1974.

———. "Talks at the Beidaihe Conference, August 21, 1958." In *The Secret Speeches of Chairman Mao,* edited by Roderick MacFarquhar, Timothy Cheek and Eugene Wu, with contributions by Merle Goldman and Benjamin I. Schwartz. Cambridge: Harvard University Press, 1989.

———. "Talks with the Directors of Various Cooperative Areas (November–December 1958)." In Joint Publications Research Service, *Miscellany of Mao Tse-tung Thought (1949–1968)*, Part I. Washington, DC: Distributed by National Technical Information Service, U.S. Department of Commerce, 1974.

———. "Speech at the Sixth Plenum of the Eighth Central Committee (December 1958)." In Joint Publications Research Service, *Miscellany of Mao Tse-tung Thought (1949–1968)*, Part I. Washington, DC: Distributed by National Technical Information Service, U.S. Department of Commerce, 1974.

———. "Examples of Dialectics (1959)." In Joint Publications Research Service, *Miscellany of Mao Tse-tung Thought (1949–1968)*, Part I. Washington, DC: Distributed by National Technical Information Service, U.S. Department of Commerce, 1974.

———. "Speech at the Conference of Provincial and Municipal Committee Secretaries" (2 February 1959). In Joint Publications Research Service, *Miscellany of Mao Tse-tung Thought (1949–1968)*, Part I. Washington, DC: Distributed by National Technical Information Service, U.S. Department of Commerce, 1974.

———. "Critique of Stalin's *Economic Problems of Socialism in the Soviet Union (1959).*" In Joint Publications Research Service, *Miscellany of Mao Tse-tung Thought (1949–1968)*, Part I. Washington, DC: Distributed by National Technical Information Service, U.S. Department of Commerce, 1974.

———. "Interjection at the Enlarged Meeting of the CCPCC Standing Committee (4 August 1966)." In Joint Publications Research Service, *Miscellany of Mao Tse-tung Thought (1949–1968)*, Part II. Washington, DC: Distributed by National Technical Information Service, U.S. Department of Commerce, 1974.

———. "Speech to the Albanian Military Delegation (1 May 1967)." In Joint Publications Research Service, *Miscellany of Mao Tse-tung Thought (1949–1968)*, Part II. Washington, DC: Distributed by National Technical Information Service, U.S. Department of Commerce, 1974.

———. "Dialogue during the Inspection of North, Central-South and East China (July–Sept. 1967)." In Joint Publications Research Service, *Miscellany of Mao Tse-tung Thought (1949–1968)*, Part II. Washington, DC: Distributed by National Technical Information Service, U.S. Department of Commerce, 1974.

———. "Dialogue with Responsible Persons of the Capital Red Guards Congress (28

July 1968)." In Joint Publications Research Service, *Miscellany of Mao Tse-tung Thought (1949–1968), Part II.* Washington, DC: Distributed by National Technical Information Service, U.S. Department of Commerce, 1974.

McCauley, Martin, ed. *Khrushchev and Khrushchevism.* Bloomington and Indianapolis: Indiana University Press, 1987.

Medvedev, Roy, and Zhores Medvedev. *Khrushchev: The Years in Power.* New York: W.W. Norton and Company, 1978.

Meisner, Maurice J. *Marxism, Maoism and Utopianism: Eight Essays.* Madison: University of Wisconsin Press, 1982.

Mencius. *Mencius.* Translated with an introduction by D.C. Lau. New York: Penguin Books, 1970.

Merridale, Catherine. "The Reluctant Opposition: The Right Deviation in Moscow, 1928." *Soviet Studies* 41, no. 3 (July 1989).

Metzger, Thomas. *Escape from Predicament: Neo-Confucianism and China's Evolving Political Culture.* New York: Columbia University Press, 1986.

————. "Modern Chinese Utopianism and the Western Concept of the Civil Society." In *KuoT'ing-I hsien sheng 9 chih tan ch'en chi nien lun wen chi: hsia ts'e* (An Anthology in Memory of the 90th Birthday of KuoT'ing-I), vol. 1. Taipei: Chung Yang yen chiu yuan chin tai shih yen chiu so fa hsing, 1995.

————. "The Western Concept of the Civil Society in the Context of Chinese History." *Hoover Institution Essays,* [1997]. http://www.hoover.org/publications/he/2896546 .html.

Mironov, Boris N. "Peasant Popular Culture and the Origins of Soviet Authoritarianism." In *Cultures in Flux: Lower-Class Values, Practices and Resistance in Late Imperial Russia,* edited by Stephen P. Frank and Mark D. Steinberg. Princeton, NJ: Princeton University Press, 1994.

Mitchel, R. Judson, and Randal Arrington. "Gorbachev, Ideology and the Fate of Soviet Communism." *Communist and Post-Communist Studies* 33, no. 4 (2000).

Moore, Barrington. *Social Origins of Dictatorship and Democracy: Lord and Peasant in the Making of the Modern World.* Boston: Beacon Press, 1966.

More, Sir Thomas. *Utopia.* Translated and edited by Robert M. Adams. New York: W.W. Norton and Company, 1975.

Mote, Frederick. *Intellectual Foundations of China.* New York: Alfred A. Knopf, 1971.

Mu, Xin. "Tong 'zhongyang wenge xiaozu de jici douzheng" (Several Conflicts with the Cultural Revolution Leadership Group). In *Zhou Enlai de zuihou Suiyue* (The Last Years of Zhou Enlai), edited by An Jianshe. Beijing: Zhongyang wenxian chubanshe, 1995.

Mumford, Lewis. *The Story of Utopias.* New York: The Viking Press, 1962.

National Intelligence Council. "Tracking the Dragon: National Intelligence Estimates on China during the Era of Mao, 1948–1976," and "The Chinese Cultural Revolution," May 25, 1967. Washington, DC: National Intelligence Council, 2004.

Ni, Heyi. "Tunliu xian jinnian yao biancheng siwu xian" (Tunliu County is Determined to Kill All Sparrows and Rats within Its Territory This Year), *Renmin ribao,* January 8, 1958.

Nordlander, David. "Khrushchev's Image in the Light of Glasnost and Perestroika." *The Russian Review* 52 (April 1993).

Nove, Alec. *An Economic History of the USSR.* East Rutherford, NJ: Penguin Books, 1969.

Ogden, Suzanne. *Inklings of Democracy in China.* Cambridge, MA: Harvard University Asia Center, 2002.

Oksenberg, Michel C. "The American Study of Modern China: Toward the Twenty-first Century." In *American Studies of Contemporary China,* edited by David Shambaugh. Washington, DC: Woodrow Wilson Center Press, 1993.

Parsons, William. "Experiments in Social Change: A History of Soviet Society." St. Petersburg, FL: Eckerd College, 1977.

Pei, Minxin. *From Reform to Revolution: The Demise of Communism in China and the Soviet Union.* Cambridge, MA: Harvard University Press, 1994.

———. "China's Evolution toward Soft Authoritarianism." In *What If China Doesn't Democratize?,* edited by Edward Friedman, et al. Armonk, NY: M.E. Sharpe, 2000.

Pei, Run. "San ci tong Jiaying tongzhi dao nong cun tiaocha" (Three Investigations I Performed with Comrade Jiaying). In *Mao Zedong he tade mishu Tian Jiaying* (Mao Zedong and His Secretary Tian Jiaying), edited by Dong Bian and Tan Deshan. Beijing: Zhongyang wenxian chubanshe, 1996.

Peng, Ming, ed. *Cong kongxiang dao kexue: zhongguo shehui zhuyi sixiang fazhan de lish kaocha* (From Utopia to Science: Historical Overview of the Development of China's Socialist Thought). Beijing: Zhongguo renmin daxue chubanshe, 1986.

Perry, Elizabeth J. *Challenging the Mandate of Heaven: Social Protest and State Power in China.* Armonk, NY: M.E. Sharpe, 2002.

Petenaude, Bertrand M. "Peasants into Russians: The Utopian Essence in War Communism." *Russian Review* 54, no. 4 (October 1995).

Petroff, Serge. *The Red Eminence: A Biography of Mikhail A. Suslov.* Clifton, NJ: Kingston Press, Inc., 1988.

Philing, David. "Two Giants of Asia Must Find a New Way of Co-Existing," *Financial Times,* April 5, 2004.

Pipes, Richard. *The Formation of the Soviet Union.* Cambridge, MA: Harvard University Press, 1964.

———. *A Concise History of the Russian Revolution.* New York: Alfred A. Knopf, 1995.

———. "Is Russia Still an Enemy?" *Foreign Affairs* 76, no. 5 (September–October 1997).

———. "Flight from Freedom." *Foreign Affairs* 83, no. 3, May–June 2004.

Plato. *Euthyphro, Apology, Crito.* Translated by F.J. Church. Upper Saddle River, NJ: Prentice Hall, 1948.

———. *The Republic.* New York: W.W. Norton and Company, 1985.

Pliskevitch, Natalia. "Russian Reforms: Utopianism and Pragmatism." *Social Sciences* 29, no. 3 (August 1998).

Popok, Militia Major Yef. "The Collapse of Pavlov and Co." *Sovetskaya kultura,* January 12, 1960. *Current Digest of the Soviet Press* 12, no. 4 (1960).

Pusey, James Reeve. *China and Charles Darwin.* Cambridge, MA: Harvard University Press.

Putnam, Robert D. "Studying Elite Political Culture: The Case of 'Ideology.'" *The American Political Science Review* 65, no. 3 (September 1971).

Pye, Lucian W. *The Mandarin and the Cadre: China's Political Cultures.* Ann Arbor, MI: Center for Chinese Studies, University of Michigan, 1988.

———. *The Spirit of Chinese Politics.* Cambridge, MA: Harvard University Press, 1992.

Qi, Yuan. "Yi Jiaying dui nongcun gongshe he bianshi gongzuo de yixie tanhua" (In

Memory of Tian Jiaying's Talks on People's Communes and the Compiling of Histories). In *Mao Zedong he tade mishu Tian Jiaying* (Mao Zedong and His Secretary Tian Jiaying), edited by Dong Bian and Tan Deshan. Beijing: Zhongyang wenxian chubanshe, 1996.

Ragin, Charles C. *The Comparative Method: Moving beyond Qualitative and Quantitative Strategies.* Berkeley: CA: University of California Press, 1987.

Reischaruer, Edwin O. *Japan: The Story of a Nation.* New York: Alfred A. Knopf, 1970.

———, and Marius B. Jansen. *The Japanese Today: Change and Continuity.* Cambridge, MA: Harvard University Press, 1995.

Remington, Thomas F. Introduction, "Alexander Yakovlev and the Limits of Reform." In Alexander Yakovlev, *The Fate of Marxism in Russia.* New Haven, CT, and London: Yale University Press, 1993.

Renwick, Neil, and Qing Cao. "China's Political Discourse towards the 21st Century: Victimhood, Identity and Political Power." *East Asia: An International Quarterly* 17, no. 4 (Winter 1999).

Rosenberg, William G., and Marilyn Young. *Transforming Russia and China: Revolutionary Struggle in the Twentieth Century.* New York: Oxford University Press, 1982.

Roy, Seigei. "Yesteryear," *Moscow News,* February 23, 2000.

Saich, Anthony. "Negotiating the State: The Development of Socialist Organizations in China." *The China Quarterly,* no. 161 (March 2000).

Salter, John. "On the Interpretation of Bukharin's Economic Ideas." *Soviet Studies* 44, no. 4, 1992.

Sartori, Giovanni. "Politics, Ideology, and Belief Systems." *American Political Science Review,* no. 63 (1969).

Sayer, Derek. *Marx's Method.* Atlantic Highlands, NJ: Humanities Press, 1979.

Scarrow, H. *Comparative Political Analysis.* New York: Harper and Row, 1969.

Schmidt, Vivien A. "Does Discourse Matter in the Politics of Welfare State Adjustment?" *Comparative Political Studies* 35, no. 2 (March 2002).

Schram, Stuart. "To Utopia and Back: A Cycle in the History of the Chinese Communist Party." *The China Quarterly,* no. 87 (September 1981).

Schrecker, John. "The Reform Movement of 1898 and the Meiji Restoration as Ch'ing-I Movement." In Akira Iriye, *The Chinese and the Japanese: Essays in Political and Cultural Interactions.* Princeton, NJ: Princeton University Press, 1980.

Shambaugh, David. *American Studies of Contemporary China.* Washington, DC: Woodrow Wilson Center Press, 1993.

Shang, Huipeng. *Zhongguo ren yu ribenren* (The Chinese and the Japanese). Beijing: Beijing daxue chubanshe, 2000.

Shang, Ying. "Stalin, Zhou Enlai huitan jiyao" (Record of Conversation between Stalin and Zhou Enlai). *Dangdai zhongguoshi yanjiu,* no. 5 (1997).

Shih, Chih-yu. "Political Culture of the Election in Taiwanese and Chinese Minority Areas." In *Chinese Political Culture: 1989–2000,* edited by Shiping Hua. Armonk, NY: M.E. Sharpe, 2001.

Skinner, B.F. *Walden Two.* New York: Macmillan, 1962.

Skocpol, Theda, and Margaret Sommers. "The Uses of Comparative History in Macrosocial Inquiry." *Comparative Studies in Society and History,* no. 22 (1980).

Smirnov, G. "Creating Socialist Consciousness in Youth," *Pravda,* August 24, 1984. *Current Digest of Soviet Press* 36, no. 34 (1984).

Snow, Edgar. *Red Star over China.* New York: Random House, 1938.

Solnick, Steven Lee. "The Breakdown of Hierarchies in the Soviet Union and China." *World Politics* 48, no. 2 (January 1996).

State Statistical Bureau. *Ten Great Years.* Beijing: Foreign Languages Press, 1960.

Su, Shaozhi. *Democratization and Reform.* Nottingham, England: Spokesman, 1983.

Su, Xiaokang. "River Elegy." *Chinese Sociology and Anthropology* 24, no. 2 (Winter 1991–1992).

Sun, Yan. "The Chinese and Soviet Reassessment of Socialism: The Theoretical Bases of Reform and Revolution in Communist Reforms." *Communist and Post-Communist Studies,* no. 27, 1994.

———. "Reform, State and Corruption: Is Corruption Less Destructive in China Than in Russia?" *Comparative Politics* 32, no. 1 (October 1999).

Sun, Zhongshan. "Zhi Quan Yang Yi" (To Quan Yang Yi). In *Sun Zhongshan quan ji* (Works of Sun Zhongshan), vol. 8. Shanghai: Zhonghua Shujiu, 1986.

Suslov, M.A. "Suslov Speaks on Communist Theory and Ideology," *Pravda,* January 31, 1959. *Current Digest of the Soviet Press* 11, no. 8 (1959).

———. *Selected Speeches and Writings.* Oxford: Pergamon Press, 1980.

Tang, Zhijun. *Wuxu zhengbian shi* (A History of the Hundred Day Reform in 1898). Beijing: Renmin chubanshe, 1984.

Tao, Yuanming. Translated by James Robert Hightower, *The Poetry of T'ao Ch'ien.* Oxford: Clarendon Press, 1970.

Thompson, Laurence G. *Ta T'ung Shu: The One-World Philosophy of K'ang Yu-wei.* London: George Allen and Unwin, Ltd., 1958.

Tocqueville, Alexis de. *Democracy in America and Two Essays on America.* Translated by Gerald E. Bevan. New York: Penguin Books, 2003.

Tompson, William J. "The Fall of Nikita Khrushchev." *Soviet Studies* 43, no. 6 (1991).

Tong, Yanqi. *Transition from State Socialism: Political and Economic Changes in Hungary and China.* Lanham, MD: Roman and Littlefield, 1997.

Totman, Conrad. *The Collapse of the Tokugawa Bakufu, 1862–1868.* Honolulu: University of Hawaii Press, 1980.

Toynbee, Arnold, and Daisaku Ikeda. *Choose Life: A Dialogue.* London and New York: Oxford University Press, 1976.

Treadgold, Donald W. *The West in Russia and China.* Vol. 2, *China, 1582–1949.* New York: Cambridge University Press, 1973.

Tsipko, A. "The Roots of Stalinism." *Nauka I zhizn,* no.1, January 1989. *Current Digest of the Soviet Press* 41, no. 12 (1989).

Tucker, Nancy B. "China as a Factor in the Collapse of the Soviet Empire." *Political Science Quarterly* 110, no. 4 (Winter 1995–1996).

Tucker, Robert C. "The Politics of Soviet De-Stalinization." *World Politics* 9, no. 4 (July 1957).

———. *Marx and Engels Reader,* 2nd ed. New York, W.W. Norton and Company, 1978.

Volin, Lazar. "Khrushchev's Neo-Economic Stalinism." *American Slavic and East European Review* 14, no. 4 (December 1955).

Walicki, Andrzej. *Marxism and the Leap to the Kingdom of Freedom: The Rise and Fall of the Communist Utopia.* Stanford, CA: Stanford University Press, 1995.

Wallace, Kathryn. "America's Brain Drain Crisis: Why Our Best Scientists Are Disappearing, and What's Really at Stake." *Reader's Digest,* December 2005.

Wang, Hui. "Contemporary Chinese Thought and the Question of Modernity." In *China's New Order: Society, Politics and Economy in Transition,* translated by Theodore Huters and edited by Wang Hui. Cambridge, MA: Harvard University Press, 2003.

Wang, Junwei. "Dui chengshi renmin gongshe de chubu kaocha" (A Preliminary Investigation of People's Communes in the Cities). *Dangdai zhongguo shi yanjiu* 2 (1997).

Wang, Suli, and Liu Zhiguang. "Fan youpai douzheng yanjiu zongshu" (A Discussion of the Anti-Rightist Movement). *Dangdai zhongguoshi yanjiu,* no. 6, 1997.

Wang, Zhen. "50 niandai zhongqi woguo dui sulian jianshe moshi de tupo" (China's Departures from the Soviet Model in the mid-1950s). *Dangdai zhongguoshi yanjiu,* no. 2 (1995).

Weeks, Theodore R. *Nation and State in Late Imperial Russia: Nationalism and Russification on the Western Frontier 1863–1914.* DeKalb: Northern Illinios University Press, 1996.

Weingast, Barry R. "Federalism, Chinese Style: The Political Basis for Economic Success in China." *World Politics* 48, no. 1 (October 1995).

White, Howard. *Peace among the Willows: The Political Philosophy of Francis Bacon.* The Hague: Martinus Nijhoff, 1968.

White, James D. "Chinese Studies of Bukharin." *Soviet Studies* 43, no. 4 (1991).

Willcock, Hiroko. "Traditional Learning, Western Thought, and the Sapporo Agricultural College: A Case Study of Acculturation in Early Meiji Japan." *Modern Asian Studies,* no. 34 (2000).

Wilson, George M. "Plots and Motives in Japan's Meiji Restoration." *Comparative Studies in Society and History* 25, no. 2 (1983).

Wilson, Richard W. *Compliance Ideologies: Rethinking Political Culture.* Cambridge: Cambridge University Press, 1992.

Womack, Brantly. "The Phases of Chinese Modernization." *Collected Papers of History Studies,* no. 4 (1999).

Wu, Chun. *Zhongguo Siwei Xingtai* (Ways of Thinking among the Chinese). Shanghai: Shanghai renmin chubanshe, 1998.

Wu, Lengxi. *Yi Mao Zuxi* (In Memory of Mao Zedong). Beijing: Xinhua chubanshe, 1995.

———. "Tong Jiaying gongshi de rizi" (The Days When I Worked with Tian Jiaying). In *Mao Zedong he tade mishu Tian Jiaying* (Mao Zedong and His Secretary Tian Jiaying), edited by Dong Bian and Tan Deshan. Beijing: Zhongyang wenxian chubanshe, 1996.

Wu, Li. "Zhonguo jihua jingji de chongxin shenshi yu pingjia" (Reflections on and Evaluation of China's Planned Economy). *Xinhua wenzhai,* November 2003.

Wu, Yannan, et al., eds. *Gudai wu-tuo-bang yu jindai shehui zhuyi sichao* (Utopia in Ancient Times and Socialist Trends in Modern Times). Chengdu: Chengdu chubanshe, 1995.

Wuthnow, Robert. *Communities of Discourse: Ideology and Social Structure in the Reformation, the Enlightenment, and European Socialism.* Cambridge, MA: Harvard University Press, 1989.

Wylie, Raymond F. *The Emergence of Maoism: Mao Tse-tung, Ch'en Po-ta, and the Search for Chinese Theory, 1935–1945.* Stanford, CA: Stanford University Press, 1980.

Xiao, Tangyan. *Gudai u-tuo-bang yu jindai shehuizhuyi sichao* (Ancient Utopia and Socialist Trends in Modern Times). Chengdu, China: Sichuan chubanshe, 1994.

Xie, Chuntao. "Dayuejin yundong yanjiu shuping" (A Survey of the Studies on the Great Leap Forward). *Dangdai zhongguoshi yanjiu,* no. 2, 1995.

Xu, Jilin. "In Search of a Third Way." In *Voicing Concerns: Contemporary Chinese Critical Inquiry,* edited by Gloria Davies. Lanham, MD: Roman and Littlefield, 2001.

Xu, Zhenzhou. "Zhongguo chuantong zhong de fei ziyouzhuyi qingxiang" (The Anti-Liberalism Tendency in China's Tradition). *Zhongguo dalu yanju jiangxue tongxun,* no. 54 (December 2002).

Yakovlev, A.N. *Gai ge xin si wei yu Sulian zhi ming yun* (New Thinking of Gorbachev's Reform and the Fate of the USSR), edited by Gao Hongshan, et al. Changchun, China: Jilin ren min chubanshe, 1992. Translation from *Muki Prochteniia Bytiia: Perestroika—nadezhdy I real'nosti.* Moscow: Moskva Novosti, 1991.

———. *The Fate of Marxism in Russia.* New Haven, CT, and London: Yale University Press, 1993.

———. "The Future of Democracy in Russia: The Lessons of Perestroika and the Question of the Communist Party." Sanford S. Elberg Lecture in International Studies, February 22, 1993. http://globetrotter.berkeley.edu/Elberg/Yakovlev/

———. *A Century of Violence in Soviet Russia.* New Haven, CT, and London: Yale University Press, 2003.

Yan, Jiaqi and Gao Gao. *Wenhua dageming shinianshi* (Ten-Year History of the Cultural Revolution). Taipei: Yuanliu chubanshe, 1990.

Yang, Mingsheng. "Woguo jingji tizhi gaige licheng, jiqi lishi jingyan" (Paths and Historical Experiences of China's Economic Structural Reform). *Dangdai zhongguoshi yanjiu,* no. 2 (1999).

Yang, Shengqun. "Bu neng shuo bada hou dang de luxian ji fasheng genbenxing ni zhuan" (We Can't Say That the Party Line Changed Drastically Immediately after the Eighty Party Congress). *Dangdai zhongguoshi yanjiu,* no. 5 (1996).

———, and Tian Songnian, for Office of Documents, Museum of Archives, CCP Central Committee. *Gongheguo zhongda juece de lailong qumai* (The PRC's Major Decisions). Nanjing, China: Zhejiang renmin chubanshe, 1995.

Yao, Fenglian, and Zheng Yushuo, eds. *Jian ming zhongguo jindai zhengzhi sixiang shi* (A Concise History of Modern Chinese Political Thought). Lanzhou, China: Gansu renmin chubanshe, 1986.

Ye, Yonglie. *Chen Boda Zhuan* (Biography of Chen Boda). Beijing: Renmin ribao chubanshe, 1999.

Yu, Guangyuan. "Chu shi Chen Boda" (First Impression of Chen Boda). *Dushu,* no. 6 (1998).

Yu, Junxiao. "Dui woguo geti jingji zhuangkuang de fenxi" (An Analysis of the State of China's Individually Owned Enterprises). *Dangdai zhongguoshi yanjiu,* no. 2 (1997).

Yu, Qiuli. "Qi yi renmin de zong guan jia" (General Manager of 700 Million People). In An Jianshe, *Zhou Enlai de zuihou Suiyue* (The Last Years of Zhou Enlai). Beijing: Zhongyang wenxian chubanshe, 1995.

Yukichi, Fukuzawa. *An Encouragement of Learning.* Translated with an introduction by David A. Dilworth and Umeyo Hirano. Tokyo: Sophia University, 1969.

———. *An Outline of a Theory of Civilization.* Translated by David A. Dilworth and G. Cameron Hurst. Tokyo: Sophia University, 1973.

———. *The Autobiography of Fukuzawa Yukichi.* New York: Madison Books, 1992.

Zaslavskaya, Tatyana. "Viewpoint: Restructuring as a Social Revolution," *Izvestia,* December 24, 1989. In *Current Digest of the Soviet Press* 40, no. 51 (1989).

Zhang, Guangnian. "Zai tan gerenzhuyi yu ai" (On Individualism and Cancer Again). *Renmin ribao,* January 21, 1958.

Zhang, Letian. *Gao Bie Lixiang: Renmin gongshe zhidu Yanjiu* (Farewell, Idealism: A Study of People's Communes). Beijing: Dongfang chubanzhongxin, 1998.

Zhang, Longxi. "Utopian Vision, East and West." *Utopian Studies* 13 (2002).

Zhang, Suhua. "60 niandai de shehuizhuyi jiaoyu yundong" (The Socialist Education Movement in the 1960s). *Dangdai zhongguoshi yanjiu* 8, no. 1 (2001).

Zhang, Xudong, ed. *Whither China: Intellectual Politics in Contemporary China.* Durham, NC: Duke University Press, 2002.

Zhang, Yanru, and Zou Xiaoxiang. "Lun Riben Mingzhi Chuqi de Qimengsixiang" (On the Enlightenment Thought of the Early Japanese Meiji Period). *Riben Wenti Yanjiu* (Japan Studies), no. 122 (2002).

Zhao, Shigang. "Mao Zedong fadong dayuejin de yuanwang yu maojin chengyin bianxi." (The Motivation for Mao to Launch the Great Leap Forward and the Factors That Led to the Leap). *Dangdai zhongguoshi yanjiu,* no. 2 (1995).

Zheng, Yougui. "Chongdu Mao Zedong 'Lun shida guanxi' zhong guanyu gongnong guanxi de lunshu" (Re-read Mao Zedong's Views on the Relationship between Industry and Agriculture in "On Ten Great Relationships"). *Dangdai zhongguoshi yanjiu,* no. 5 (1996).

———. "Wenhua dageming shiqi nongye shengchan bodong ji dongyin tanxi" (An Analysis of the Fluctuation of Agricultural Production during the Cultural Revolution). *Zhonggong dangshi yanju,* no. 3 (1998).

Zhonghua renmin gongheguo guojia nongye weiyuanhui bangongting (Staff Office of PRC National Committee of Agriculture). *Nongye jiti hua zhongyao wenjian huibian 1958–1981* (Important Documents on Agricultural Collectivization, 1958–1981), vol. 2. Beijing: Zhonggong zhongyang dangxiao chubanshe, 1981.

Zhou, Ning. *Kong Jiao U-tuo-Bang* (Confucian Utopia). Beijing: Xueyuan chubanshe, 2004.

Zhu, Di. "Yelun dayuejin de yuanqi" (Comments on the Origins of the Great Leap Forward). *Zhonggong dangshi yanju,* no. 1 (2001).

Zhuravlyov, V., and A. Pyzhikov. "The Khrushchev Thaw." *Social Sciences,* June 30, 2004.

Zimin, A.A. "On the Political Preconditions for the Emergence of Russian Absolutism." In *Major Problems in Early Modern Russian History,* edited by Nancy S. Kollmann. New York: Garland Publishing, 1992.

Index

adjustment period (1961–65), 63–64, 66, 67–68
African societies, 29
agriculture: decentralization during Thaw, 49; Great Leap Forward, 73; incentives, 50; Khrushchev on, 48, 129n54; mechanization, 49, 55, 66; tax policies, 50
alienation, theory of, 91
Anti-Rightist Movement, 91, 135n4, 140n72
art and literature, 51, 54, 84
St. Augustine, 15, 116n40
authoritarianism, 91, 92, 94; collective good and, 107; compared, 103; datong worldview, 94; human nature and, 95; Russian, origins of, 95; Western views, 98

Bacon, Francis, 11
bafuku role, 28
Barber, Benjamin, 105
Beriya, Lavrentij, 52
Bismarck, Otto von, 32
bourgeois liberalization, 88
bourgeois right, 79–80
"boxers," 30, 122n25
Brezhnev, Leonid, on Khrushchev, 112n38
Buddhism, 115n16

Bukharin, Nikolai Ivanovich: background, 44; on capitalism, 58; as determinist, 55, 56, 132nn112, 121; on dialectics, 56, 132n121, 132–33n123; equilibrium method, 56, 133n124; on historical materialism, 54–55; on historical stages, 55; on incentives, 50; Khrushchev opposition to, 57; as NEP advocate, 43, 58–59; on peasants, 58–59; as reformer, 2–3, 42, 127n10; Right faction priorities, 51; role of state, 58. *See also* stage theory
bureaucracy: alienation, 91; bureaucratism problem (China), 64, 68, 70; compared, 82; coordination during reforms, 3; Deng Reform, 34; downsizing during decentralization, 49; Gorbachev on, 89; Khrushchev reforms, 52, 133n132
Burlatsky, Fyodor M.: Khrushchev's ideas, 42–43, 112n38; NEP, 51; on political pendulum, 48; political reform, 52–53; on state of the whole people, 59; on Thaw, 90; on War Communism, 127n19
Byzantine tradition, 15, 16, 95

capitalism, Bukharin on, 58
case studies, 4–7, 112n32